The Impossible Garden

The Impossible Garden

Rosa Steppanova

The Shetland Times Ltd.,
Lerwick
2004

The Impossible Garden

ISBN 1 898852 92 8

First published by The Shetland Times Ltd., 2004.

British Library Cataloguing-in-Publication Data
A catalogue record for this book is available from the British Library.

Front cover photograph © Derek Fell.
Back cover photograph © Magnie Robertson.

Published and printed by
The Shetland Times Ltd.,
Gremista, Lerwick,
Shetland ZE1 0PX.

Contents

Preface

Rosa's garden, one of the most northerly in the UK, is a revelation, filled with horticultural treasures. Most of the paths are arched over by branches or hemmed in by windbreak hedges and stone walls. It is hidden from the road by a shelter belt of bushy shrubs and small trees, but exposed to ferocious winds and salt spray from a sea loch that snakes in front of the property.

I enjoyed photographing her Eden more than any other private garden I have visited, exploring it at first light, and returning intermittently as the light and weather conditions changed.

Exposed to raw sea winds, yet intimate at the same time, Lea Gardens is a reflection of Rosa's boundless optimism and energy. Not only richly planted but also full of tactile textures — from weathered barn sidings, ancient algae-coated stones, rusty buoys used as decorative accents, to driftwood pieces polished by sand and salt spray. A garden to be savoured slowly, from dawn to dusk, in all seasons.

Thank you Rosa, for the opportunity to experience such a dramatic garden, and to contribute to such an inspirational book — a rare combination of absorbing bedtime reading and useful reference work for coastal gardeners around the temperate world.

Derek Fell

Acknowledgements

I am indebted to the following individuals, in no particular order, and would like to thank them for the help and encouragement they have given me:

Jane Bradish-Ellames and Kenneth Cox, Tony Schilling, Derek Fell, Vaila Wishart, Charlotte Black, Melvyn Leask, Magnie Robertson, and Rachel Eunson.

I'd also like to say a very special thank you to my husband James for his endless patience and many hours of late-night indexing and proofreading

Finally a big thank you to my daughter Anna for sticking (almost always and at times under the most trying of circumstances) to the "do not disturb" rule.

Foreword

On many occasions one needs to be an optimist, possibly a masochist, in order to survive as a gardener, but to create a garden on latitude 60°N amidst the bleak wind-swept landscape of Shetland one has to be someone special; such a person is Rosa Steppanova.

By studying the climatic conditions of Shetland she has skilfully manipulated them in order to grow as wide a range of plants as possible. Over the last twenty years or more she has created shelter belts in order to cut out wind damage and salt spray and, by composing a variety of habitats and microclimates, has achieved what some may well feel to be close to the inconceivable. In this case that well known maxim "The difficult we do immediately, the impossible takes a little longer" seems particularly apt.

The authoress admits that she enjoys pushing back the boundaries, and seeing what she can get away with in this most challenging of climates, whilst ever mindful of the need to follow the basic rules for success – choosing the right plant for the right site and creating as much shelter as possible.

This fascinating and easy to read book will surely serve as a reference book for all northern coastal gardeners. Her battles with storm force winds and sodden peat bogs will impress all those who recognise fortitude, imagination and dedication. Visitors to her garden often assume that her success with over 1,500 species and cultivars is made possible through some freak of nature or because her soil is very fertile; neither are true. What IS true is the fact that such a garden takes time, hard work, artistic flair, and above all else a passionate love of plants coupled to enthusiasm and commonsense by the bucketful; there are no shortcuts on the road to experience.

I particularly praise her writing for its open honesty. Rosa freely admits to being "climatically challenged" and she also confesses to moments of flat depression stating "… it has rained without reprieve for three days and the sky has closed in as heavy as lead … there are times when I feel this winter is never going to end." She also records that the hibernal sun stays glued to the southern horizon for three very long months; winter in Shetland must really push a gardener's resolve to near breaking point. The island in May can just as readily test one to the limits with frightening hurricane force winds battering and tearing all one is attempting to create. She sums up such moments by quoting "Wherever human beings garden magnificently there will be magnificent heartbreaks", but defeatism is not a word she really seems to understand.

If only others in positions of authority would heed her advice and catch on to her enthusiasm in order to learn from her hard won experience. Shetland is an almost entirely treeless landscape open to all the winds that nature can throw at it, but need not be so.

Anyone who sings "I'll sleep when I'm dead" whilst weeding, or takes a sick lamb into her bed for the night in order to save its life has to be admired. She writes "How lucky I am to have a garden – and a husband …"; how lucky Shetland and the gardening world is to have Rosa Steppanova. Such is her enthusiasm I can imagine her creating a garden in Spitzbergen if she had to.

Tony Schilling M.Arb., V.M.H.

Tony Schilling M. Arb. V.M.H., Joint President of the Tree Register of the British Isles, Curator of Wakehurst Place (Kew in the Countryside) from 1967 to 1991.

Introduction

In the summer of 1976 I spent a short holiday in the Shetland Islands, a group of over one hundred islands, windswept and salt-drenched by both the Atlantic Ocean and the North Sea. At sixty degrees north the nearest landfall to the east is Norway, and due west, the coast of Newfoundland. The journey by boat from Aberdeen covers 200 miles, takes 12 hours and can put even the sturdiest of sea legs to the test. Twelve of the islands are inhabited, with most of the population concentrated on the largest, called Mainland. The islands have more than 5000km of rugged, changing coastline; dramatic sea cliffs, long white beaches, and small, sheltered coves fringe the velvet-green pastures and heather-clad hills.

I fell head over heels in love with the Shetland landscape, so very different from my homeland, northern Bavaria, with its gently-rolling hills, tiny vineyards and ancient oak and beech forests. The natives were friendly, North Sea oil had been discovered, jobs were plentiful and wages high. I decided to live and work here for six months. Over a quarter of a century later, I am still here.

Shetland (only visitors from "abroad" call it The Shetlands) is one of the windiest places on earth. My first winter here was made memorable by storm force gales and a phenomenon called the wind chill factor, where temperatures just a few degrees below zero feel decidedly Arctic. My accommodation didn't help either. I shared a small house

Before it all began, The Lea in 1978.

on the west coast of the Shetland Mainland with James, my future husband, and some friends. The house was colloquially known as the "Tin Tabernacle", made of wood-lined corrugated iron, with no insulation in-between and highly susceptible to the dreaded wind chill factor. Nothing could keep out the icy draughts which chilled the inhabitants to the marrow and froze the milk into white blocks in the cartons. Despite multiple layers of quilts and blankets at night and multiple layers of clothing, which made me look like Michelin Man, in the daytime, I never once felt warm.

At the end of January 1977 James and I moved into The Lea, Tresta, a few miles further west, a small, traditional dry-stone cottage, two up two down, with a leaking roof and several dilapidated outhouses. Its mod. cons. were confined to a sink and cold tap in the porch and a rickety, draughty outdoor earth closet. For many years to come, whenever we ventured to the sunny south of England to visit James' parents, we were introduced at social gatherings thus: "These two live in great discomfort in the Shetland Islands."

Our house sits almost exactly in the centre of a nine-acre (three hectare) croft, about 200 metres from the sea, on a gentle, south-facing slope. Built snug against the hillside, it enjoys a good degree of shelter from the north. The soil, where it had been worked by our predecessors, is a black, acidic, peaty loam, which sticks together into rock-hard lumps, if not immediately broken up after digging. Land which had not been cultivated before, consists mostly of raw peat. The sub-soil is a sticky, stony, yellow clay, separated from the top soil by an impenetrable iron pan, which means much of the land is badly drained, and gets water-logged during the winter.

The stark beauty of Shetland's treeless landscape, which had attracted me in the first place, soon made me feel intensely homesick. I pined for the vineyards and forests, the chanterelles and blackberries in the autumn, sweet violets and apple blossom in spring. But most of all I longed for my mother's garden, the blowsy roses and peonies, her little crocus lawn, strawberries and greengages, and arbours dripping with clematis and wisteria.

I decided to make a garden of my own. It started modestly with a small piece of ground outside the kitchen window, planted with annuals and gifts from my gardening friends and neighbours Linda Tait and the late Joan Nicolson. They brought rooted honeysuckle cuttings, mossy saxifrages, Peruvian lilies (*Alstromeria aurantiaca*), sweet rocket (*Hesperis matronalis*), double white wood anemones, primroses and Australian daisies (*Senecio smithii*). All grew.

My gentle cure for homesickness soon became an all-consuming passion. Gardening had become an obsession, the small patch rapidly turned into several large ones, and my frequent bouts of horticultural retail therapy brought us to the brink of bankruptcy more than once. James, my husband by then, fed on duck eggs (we kept a small flock of khaki campbells) and any edible greenery I could find, was growing a little thin, and said to me casually one day: "I suppose starving in a beautiful garden is quite a pleasant way to go …"

Gardening in those early years was largely a matter of trial and error, plant losses were commonplace and replacing them became prohibitively expensive. There was a small nucleus of plants which did well in a harsh, windy climate, and could be found in every Shetland garden: *Fuchsia magellanica*, *Ribes sanguineum*, *Rosa rugosa*, a few gnarled elders, ancient, wind-pruned sycamores and the occasional rowan and whitebeam. Not far from Tresta, in a sheltered valley, about five miles from the open sea (about as far as one can get from it in Shetland), the walled garden of Kergord House, surrounded by shelterbelts of mature trees, and long past its heyday, still contained, among the couch grass and ground elder, treasures which filled me with envy. The hellebores, cushions of blue hepaticas and luxurious ferns seemed like the visitors from a distant, enchanted planet, a planet barred to me and my exposed garden.

In the north of Shetland Mainland, John Copland, a skilled gardener and plantsman, had established a small nursery for alpine plants and low-growing herbaceous perennials in the early 1980s. I was a frequent customer, but many of the plants, which not only survived, but thrived in his well-drained, neutral soil, rarely made it through their first winter on my wet, acid peat.

There had to be plants which could live in such extreme conditions. I started reading and soon found myself the owner of an extensive horticultural library, another step on the road to imminent financial ruin. Visits to Scottish nurseries, armed with lists of suitable candidates for the Shetland climate brought the same, predictable results: A mixture of veiled amusement and pity, and the same comment time and time again: "I think you are wasting your time and your money." A remark echoed by friends, neighbours and fellow Shetland gardeners who told me that I had to come to terms with the fact that very little grows in this extreme climate. An Aberdeenshire grower, after he had read my extensive list of desirable plants, scratched his head, looked me straight in the eye and put it bluntly: "I think you want the impossible, Rosa." I now have the

impossible, and that's how the title for this book, *The Impossible Garden*, came about.

I am told that the stubborn streak in our family comes from my father's side and that I am blessed with more than my fair share. In 1980 I decided to start a plant nursery and small landscaping business with the help of casual and seasonal staff. Most of the plants were propagated and grown on the premises, supplemented by bought-in trees, shrubs and hedging. All imported plants were wintered here and thoroughly hardened off, which meant losses occurred in the nursery, rather than in customers' and clients' gardens. It was a great success and not only paid off our ever-mounting debts, but financed a new roof, extensive renovations and a much-needed extension to the house, just in time for the adoption of our Romanian daughter Anna.

The garden now occupies one acre, is open to the public and attracts visitors from all over the world. It demonstrates that a wide variety of plants can be grown in one of the world's most inhospitable climates. It is home to a collection of about 1500 plant species and cultivars, representing 400 genera. A variety of different habitats has been created over the years: a large shelter belt, a wild flower meadow, shaded woodland plantings, traditional herbaceous borders, raised beds and sandy, well-drained banks for alpines and dwarf shrubs, a small peat garden, a sheltered rhododendron valley, beds for moisture lovers and a productive vegetable garden. Plans for a one-acre extension, more shelter, and a large pond are well underway.

In this book I want to share my garden, as well as my skills, experience and knowledge with you. I want to dispel the myth and clichés which surround coastal gardening, and above all show you that gardening in a wet and windy climate can be immensely rewarding and enjoyable.

Soil Preparation and Drainage

Soil and aspect are inextricably linked but don't in my case, create a conducive combination. Much has been written about coastal gardening in recent years. In all the classic literature on the subject, coasts with their inevitable wind and salt spray are invariably linked to well-drained, shingly or sandy soil and the plants which thrive on them. Heavy or peaty and often waterlogged soils never feature. These are not exclusive to the Shetland Islands, they are a problem in many coastal regions of the temperate world. Soil preparation is undoubtedly the most important element for successful gardening in a wet and windy climate. Breaking up compacted soil and digging to at least one spit deep, to allow for good root penetration, is sufficient where drainage is not a problem.

Apart from the obvious moisture lovers, few plants survive, let alone thrive, on ill-drained or water-logged soils. On a large scale, open ditches or a system of buried field drains are essential, especially for the establishment of shelter belts or large numbers of trees. On a smaller scale, raised beds are very effective. They don't have to be very high, a foot (30cm) is usually sufficient, provided the underlying soil has been dug to improve drainage and the infill consists of a free-draining mix. I use one part grit or coarse sand, one part soil or peat and one part leaf mould or well-rotted garden compost.

Where there is an iron pan between top and sub soil it is essential to at least break this up in part to improve drainage. On a large scale this can be done with machinery (sub-soiling); in a small garden, holes made with a pinch bar or pick are usually sufficient.

Ill-drained and heavy soil can be improved by incorporating large amounts of bulky organic matter. Garden compost, leaf mould, seaweed and well rotted farm yard manure are excellent for improving soil texture and drainage. These also add body to light and sandy soils and improve their moisture-holding capacity.

Mulching

High winter rainfalls compact soil and leach nutrients. Mulches go a long way in ameliorating or even preventing this. They also stop the soil from drying out and suppress the growth of weeds. I use well-rotted garden compost, leaf mould or chipped, composted bark to give a smart finish. Underneath trees and shrubs, where looks don't matter, straw or grass cuttings are a cheap option. Both take nitrogen from the soil during their process of decomposition. This is easily balanced by first applying a little general fertiliser (I use dried, concentrated farm yard manure). For mulches to remain effective, annual topping up is necessary.

For alpines and other plants which insist on good drainage, I use small stone chips (6mm and down) from a local quarry. During weeding and planting they eventually get worked into the soil, and need replacing every three or four years.

Sample carpet squares make durable mulching mats for young trees and are usually available free of charge from flooring retailers.

For field-grown vegetables such as leeks and cabbages I sometimes use landscaping membrane, secured with plastic pegs. Small holes can be burned into the membrane with a blow torch for the transplants. This makes the planting process more time-consuming, but eliminates all hoeing, and muddy boots. The membrane can be re-used for several seasons.

Feeding and liming

Apart from the organic mulches mentioned above, which eventually break down and provide nutrition, I don't feed my ornamental plantings. In analysis, this process only replaces what I have taken from beds and borders during annual cleaning operations. The remains of herbaceous plants, small prunings and leaves are simply returned in a more "digestible" and attractive form. Seaweed, farm yard manure and the bulk of our home-made compost are reserved for the vegetable garden, which also gets a top dressing of garden lime in late autumn.

On my acid, peaty soil, I also apply top dressings of ground limestone on an ad hoc basis to those plants which prefer a neutral or alkaline growing medium, such as peonies, pinks, pulsatillas, cyclamen and hellebores.

Trees and shrubs need a good start in life. I dig their planting holes to twice the necessary depth and replace the soil beneath their roots with a bucketful of garden compost. A handful of high phosphate fertiliser incorporated at planting time helps to establish a vigorous, wide-reaching root system (essential in a windy climate), and a top-dressing of sulphate of potash, applied in August, ripens wood and helps prevent die-back.

Wind Breaks

Even the toughest trees and shrubs benefit from a little artificial shelter during their infancy. What form this takes is largely a matter of taste and budget. Stone walls are a durable and handsome solution, but in a windy climate often defeat their purpose by creating turbulence. There is however enough shelter close up to them to allow for the establishment of a hedge or mixed, living wind screen. Slatted wooden fencing can be very attractive and serves its purpose well.

Where a windbreak on a large scale is called for, the very best and most economical option is a post-and-wire-fence fitted with windbreak netting. Perforated plastic cladding, usually recommended for very windy locations is too heavy, creates too much resistance, and often brings the whole fence down during high winds. A much better option is the seemingly flimsy "Titan netting", securely battened onto each fence post, where it will survive for as long as it is needed. (In the sales area of my nursery it has survived for twenty years!)

Staking

In a climate where trees seem to take forever to grow to a reasonable size, it is tempting to purchase large specimens. In all but the most sheltered of locations I would advise against this practice. In my experience, whips or small forest transplants always catch up and soon overtake the standards and semi-standards which are meant to save time. If you can't resist larger specimens, stake them meanly, and wean them off their stakes as soon as possible. Never have a

stake come up more than one third of the stem initially and reduce the stake height every year to allow movement of a tree's crown and stem to encourage the growth of firm anchoring roots. Check stakes and ties on a regular basis (winter is a good time) to prevent rubbing, chafing, or ties which have grown too tight, preventing natural stem expansion. Plastic tree ties with one or several spacers are a good choice, but even better, and more durable are pairs of tights. Black or flesh-coloured to blend in, bright pink or purple, if you want to make a statement.

Rabbit Protection

I'm not sure who introduced rabbits to the Shetland Islands, but I know from personal experience that they cause severe damage to gardens, especially trees and shrubs. On a small scale individual perforated plastic guards or wire netting enclosures are effective. When it comes to protecting a whole garden or large shelter plantings, chicken wire, buried below ground to half its height, becomes essential. This is a time-consuming and expensive undertaking, and I would suggest a much more pleasurable and highly effective alternative: cats. In my own garden I have no rabbit fencing. The garden and croft grounds run to nine acres and are kept completely rabbit-free by a dedicated tribe of eight hunting cats. (They do need supplementary feeding through part of the year.)

Management

Gardens are never at a standstill, they grow and evolve over the years. Plants might outgrow their allotted space with breakneck speed, while others only just hold their own. In a windy climate, where growth is slow, there is a tendency to plant too closely in order to create much needed initial shelter. Such plantings, if well-fed and well-pruned, can be kept going for years, but usually have a limited life span through over-competition. Closely planted trees will grow straight stems, but shed their lower branches which makes them ineffective as windbreaks. Removing surplus plants, especially weak performers, is essential for keeping your shelter plantings in good heart.

Many shrubs can be shaped or clipped to fit a given space and to provide an effective wind filter, and trees such as willows, poplars and alders can be coppiced (cut to the ground or back to a short stump) from time to time to keep them clothed in branches to ground level.

Herbaceous plantings benefit from a good overhaul now and again, and might call for complete replanting after a number of years. Individual plants might be treasured for their rarity value, but if they only just hang on to life and look miserable for most of the year, their space might be better filled with a more enthusiastic grower. Conversely those plants which are too well adapted, swallow up large expanses of ground, and swamp their neighbours, will have to be curtailed. It is up to the gardener to establish a "natural" balance through well-timed and sensitive intervention.

Reading

All gardeners are influenced by other gardeners and writing gardeners, as opposed to garden writers, who aren't necessarily gardeners. Margery Fish, especially her book *A Flower for Every Day*, made me realise how many different plants can be squeezed into a small garden, and that there is something interesting to see in every month of the year.

Beth Chatto made clear to me the importance of providing plants with suitable habitats, and has greatly helped reducing losses in my garden. I stole the idea of creating "garden rooms" from Vita Sackville-West. They're perfect for a windy climate, but in the case of my garden and its limited scale, amount to little more than closets or broom cupboards.

The works of Graham Stuart Thomas are without doubt amongst the most frequently consulted in my library. His clear and evocative descriptions, as well as notes on climate and propagation, always help me to make the right choices, especially when it comes to roses and herbaceous perennials. I first met many of the plants in my garden in the pages of his books.

Last, but by no means least, comes Christopher Lloyd. I love his infectious enthusiasm and no-nonsense approach to gardening. His *The Well-Tempered Garden* was my constant bed companion for years, and brought a turning point in my gardening life, by adding an understanding of plants to my passion, and by taking away my fear of doing something wrong or doing it at the wrong time.

Flowering Times

When deciding on a concept for this book, I did not realise the difficulties I was to encounter with a month-by-month account. Few plants perform by the calendar; some start flowering in one month and finish in the next, while others span several months. Flowering times can vary widely from year to year and according to the weather.

Shetland is said to be at least four to six weeks behind England and two to three weeks behind Scotland. This might well be true of Scotland's mild west coast, but in some years, plants in Shetland flower well before their counterparts in Scotland's eastern seaboard and the Highlands. My garden's microclimate complicates matters further by running – sometimes several weeks – ahead of other Shetland gardens.

Rather than fitting plants into an average performance window, I stick to the calendar of my garden, and mention or describe them when they delight me most or when they first catch my eye.

January

According to the calendar, winter has only just begun, but I prefer to adhere to nature's itinerary, where winter begins in November and ends in February. The saying "As the day lengthens, the cold strengthens" always holds true. Frosty winter mornings have their charms, especially if there's a dusting of snow; and fine skies in duck-egg blue and violet grey have been known to make the gardener's sap rise – just a little. January is a long and inhospitable month and the attractions of a warm house rather outweigh those of a cold garden. Yet the lengthening of daylight hours, imperceptibly at first, but notably towards the end of the month, gradually fill me with renewed energy and the feeling that spring is only just around the corner. There are signs of it everywhere: *Meconopsis napaulensis* is slowly expanding its resting buds, the Oriental poppies are up, and my patch of *Persicaria bistorta* 'Superba' has sprouted a carpet of brand new red shoots, the first willows have slipped the brown husks off their catkins and the earliest spring bulbs are beginning to show colour.

January can bring our fiercest blizzards, but it also brings calm and sunny days, often a surprising number of them, and being close to the sea, the temperature rarely plummets low enough to cause blue noses and stiff fingers during clear and frosty weather. I must admit to my shame, that after more than two decades of gardening in a rough, cool and often very wet climate, I am still largely a fair weather gardener. I like my creature comforts. Nothing will get me out there during a howling gale or a torrential downpour, but a blue sky, however pale and wintry, and the weak rays of the sun on the southern horizon, will do the trick each time.

I am not one of those gardeners who follows a week by week calendar of chores: quite often I just stroll around the garden – purposelessly, you might call it – having a good look around, getting lost in thought, entangled in new planting ideas, until my eye falls on something that needs doing, doing now, as a matter of urgency.

Winter exposes the garden's bone structure, shows up all the little faults and blemishes hidden below billowing, lush greenery during the other seasons. It reveals crossing branches and dead wood, rubbing stakes and broken tree ties. It's a good month for getting out the pruning saw.

In a garden as close to the sea as mine, shelter from wind and salt spray is of the utmost

Meconopsis napaulensis.

Left: *Phormium cookianum.*

A glimpse of the sea from the Round Garden.

Salix alaxensis.

importance, and the draught excluders providing it need care and attention. This is also the time of year, when I, and my plants, are most keenly aware of any shortfall in that department. Around the garden I have what I call, for want of a better term, a mixed windscreen. This planting is not nearly wide enough to deserve the name shelter belt, and is composed of elders, flowering and black currants, olearias, alders, pines, spruces, willows, birches, rowans, whitebeams and sycamores. As they grow taller, they create good shelter higher up, but the wind whistles through them lower down. In some this is inevitable and desirable: tall trees are handsome and do much to enhance the garden's skyline. In others the fault is easily remedied. Willows and alders can be coppiced or pollarded from time to time, and shrubs can be pruned hard to keep them clothed in leaves right to ground level.

When I started the garden I planted large numbers of flowering currants (*Ribes sanguineum*) as a first line of defence against the sea winds. They carried out their duty all along the southern front, uncomplaining and with little thanks or attention from me. They were soon hidden from view by a row of trees planted behind them, and I only became aware of them again when, one summer, I got glimpses of the sea through their bare, dark stems, an unexpected and alarming sight, as from that part of the garden, the sea could be heard and smelled, but hadn't been seen for a long time.

Ribes sanguineum soon accumulates masses of old, unproductive wood, and grows bare and leggy. The quickest method of restoration is to cut the bushes to the ground, followed by a generous feed of high nitrogen fertiliser or a mulch of well-rotted manure. All but the very old respond readily to such drastic treatment, but that leaves a sizeable gap in the defences until the shrubs have reached their former size and height again, which in their case, can take a number of years. It's much better to do the task in stages, spreading it over two or even three seasons, by cutting out a proportion of old wood each winter or early spring. Using loppers and a pruning saw is hot work, so cold weather is ideal, and I can tackle several large shrubs on even the shortest January day.

Elders (*Sambucus nigra*) can be cut to stumps in winter or early spring, and, with or without feeding, will reach eight or ten feet again by the end of that growing season. They are as tough as they come and I have seen old trees, twisted into corkscrew shapes by the wind, growing right by the sea shore, their bark covered in moss and lichens, and their branches festooned with seaweed. I am convinced that Tannhäuser's walking stick, which magically burst into leaf after decades of barrenness, was made from elder wood.

James, after cutting down an ancient, multi-stemmed (and unwanted) elder in somebody's garden, brought back the wood and stacked it, to be dried and sawn into logs at a later date. Somehow forgotten, it remained where it had been put, on a bank of sand outside the garden, dormant for two years, then, the following spring, sprouting a forest of strong, young wands. If my garden was right on the shore, or on an exposed hill top, this plant would be my first choice for creating shelter, with the Japanese briar, *Rosa rugosa*, a close second. This makes a good, deciduous hedge in the most exposed places, with single pink, white or magenta flowers in summer (according to which form you buy), and large red tomato-shaped hips which last well into winter. It has just one drawback: its fiercely suckering habit and great territorial ambition make it quite unsuitable for small gardens. Here, grafted plants can take its place. The crimson double and strongly scented *R. rugosa* 'Rosaraie de l'Haye' will grow four to five feet tall, and the single pink 'Fru Dagmar Hastrup', which is never out of flower from June to October, reaches about three feet. *Olearia haastii* is almost as resilient and evergreen into the bargain. It has oval, leathery leaves of a rather

dull green, and clouds of tiny white daisy flowers in August. Once settled down, it grows rapidly, and like the elder has a tendency to form a small, multi-stemmed tree. Both need regular pruning to form an effective wind screen or very large hedge.

Shrubs like mock orange (*Philadelphus coronarius*) and *Weigela florida* are meant to be pruned as soon as they have finished flowering in late July, but its a job I prefer to do now and not when they are in full leaf and I have to wade into an overflowing border to reach them. Devoid of leaves, their old dark branches show up clearly against the paler new wood, and it's child's play to cut them back to a strong young shoot, or in the absence of one, which is rare, right down to ground level. As their flowers, just like those of *Ribes sanguineum*, are produced on the old wood, that means losing some blossom in the summer following the operation, but that is a small price to pay for the long-term health and vigour of the shrubs. I don't prune them on a regular basis, but give them a good going-over every three or four years.

In some parts of the garden the shelter problem is of a different nature. The Back Yard, a hay meadow originally, was never meant to become part of the garden, but has now been under development for almost a decade. It is too small a space to create a shelter belt or solid windscreen, and here, the planting of trees goes on in rather a piecemeal and experimental fashion. High above the other parts of the

Part of the Back Yard shelter planting.

Diary **10th January**

There are scenes of devastation everywhere. In the Peat Garden most of the pulverised bark (carefully applied two days ago) has found its way onto the gravel path below. On the Alpine Slope several cushions of mossy saxifrages have been dismantled and scattered all over the place, and in the Back Yard, the grass is strewn with compost and wads of soggy newspaper. I tidied up as best I could with the help of a brush and rake, then, on my hands and knees, picked the litter from amongst the crocus buds.

I sometimes wonder why I like my blackbirds so much, they scratch and scrape like farmyard hens, and play havoc with my alpines in their search for worms and fat grubs. In some parts of the garden, close to paths and grass, mulching has become impossible. Yet I would not be without them at any price. The garden belongs as much to them as it belongs to me, perhaps more so, as they live in it. The youngsters still treat me as an unwelcome intruder and fly off with a high-pitched screech as soon as I appear in "their" garden, but some of the older birds, the hens especially, hardly notice my presence. They may get out of my way with a few sideways hops, then continue whatever they are doing, while throwing the odd wary glance in my direction. Three are old friends and have been given names according to their distinctive coloured throat patches: Chocolate, Blanche and Rosy.

garden, it has become a testing ground for tree species and cultivars new to this climate, with the toughest all around its perimeter, and the less so planted over parts of the interior, to create a small arboretum. A grand title for such a tiny plot, and used for want of a better term.

These young trees, planted in turf, need careful nursing and must be kept free from all competition in the early stages of their lives, which entails regular weeding or keeping them thickly mulched. I used to mulch all the trees in the Back Yard with thick layers of wet newspaper to kill off existing weeds and grass, then, piled over the newspaper, garden compost, grass clippings, leaf mould, or anything I had to hand. This worked well and kept them perfectly weed-free, for as long as the blackbirds remained uninterested.

The garden is home to large numbers of birds, year-round and summer residents, as well as migrants dropping in for short stop-overs. For their sake I don't use any pesticides, and they, in turn, do a good bit of pest control for me. That still leaves me to take care of the weeds and I use three different types of weedkiller. I could not manage the garden without them. One is a granular type, which I apply in January or February around the base of newly planted trees and shrubs to keep the grass at bay. I also use a spray, applied every March to all my paths and paved areas with a fine-rosed watering can which, used solely for this purpose, is labelled accordingly in large black letters. This keeps all the hard surfaces more or less weed-free for the whole season.

In my ornamental plantings, and in the vegetable garden, I handweed or hoe, which is a chore I enjoy, because it is an occasional, rather than a frequent or regular one. Once plantings have filled out and cover all bare soil, weeds, with one or two exceptions, pose no problem.

At one end of the South Border couch grass was brought in with a plant, and by the time I noticed it, had spread to several others. The use of weedkillers in such situations is largely ineffective, even counter-productive. Their application instils a false sense of security in the gardener: she feels she's done something to get on top of the problem, and while her back is turned, the weeds, weakened rather than killed, start their work all over again. Where weeds such as couch or ground elder grow cheek by jowl with ornamental plants it is difficult, or even impossible, to eradicate one without harming the other, and good, old-fashioned cultural methods are by far the most satisfying way of tackling them.

I lifted all the plants, cleaned them as best I could, discarded any suspect pieces and potted up the remainder, to be kept under close observation. The ground was dug over twice, with every scrap of couch root removed, also kept under observation for two years, and every blade of grass which subsequently turned up was promptly removed. This treatment left a sizeable gap in the border which I filled with an assortment of potted plants before I returned those of its previous residents which had a clean bill of health. Ground elder, again brought in as a stowaway, turned up in another part of the garden and was dealt with in the same way. Four years on, neither have returned.

But there was one weed problem in the garden which used to defeat me year after year. In the shelter plantings along the south and west boundary of the garden, falling leaves were (and still are) left in *situ* to create a weed-suppressing mulch, which they eventually do. Some trees and shrubs there are underplanted with ivies, tolmeias and other shade-tolerant ground cover. There are also large expanses of spring bulbs. Weeds never got a look-in until hairy bittercress, *Cardamine hirsuta* arrived on the scene. This is a short-lived plant, called an ephemeral, which can germinate, grow, flower, ripen and scatter vast amounts of seed within a few short weeks. It was soon prolific and hundreds of seedlings turned up all over the mulched areas. My attempts at weeding, on hands and knees, or flat on my stomach in the less accessible places,

never got the better of it, until I started using a pre-emergent weedkiller, applied dry every spring. This does not harm the bulbs or ground cover plants, but prevents all seeds, including those of the bittercress, from germinating. From this stronghold it used to make repeated bids to take over the rest of the garden and I am still fighting it on several fronts. In January it doesn't run to seed as it does in almost any other month of the year. Its fat, green leaf rosettes are easily spotted, and their peppery taste makes them a good ingredient for winter salads. This is a good month to tackle it, weather permitting …

Snow comes in two distinctly different ways, gently and vertically, creating magical winter scenes, or fiercely and horizontally, creating havoc and chaos. Freezing winds blacken and dessicate every leaf in sight, and a great depth of snow covers all. I used to frantically try and shake or brush the snow off my hedges and evergreens, as instructed by the gardening magazines, but during a north-easterly blizzard, with snowdrifts the size and shape of Saharan sand dunes this becomes an impossible task. Being a crofter as well as a gardener means there are more pressing priorities at times. In some winters sheep, buried under the snow, need to be dug out, and those as yet unburied, have to be prevented from simply walking into the garden over gates and fences. This can only be achieved by digging a ha-ha outside of the fence, alongside the garden's eastern perimeter (large quantities of snow invariably arrive from the east or north east).

Winter sheep.

Diary

The storm has abated and overnight the garden has been transformed into a dreamscape. Every twig and branch is outlined in white down, plants are wrapped in fur stoles or balance impossibly tall white top hats, the tree trunks are whitewashed, and the large rounded shapes of the rusty iron buoys in the Back Yard have been turned into iced plum puddings. A blizzard with a sense of humour. The paths are patterned with the spidery hieroglyphs left by the feet of my hopping, scurrying blackbirds. I feel fiercely protective of my paradisical winter garden: Anna, her friends, their sledges and snowball fights, even the lopsided carrot-nosed snowmen are banned. I want to preserve that pristine, untouched look for as long as I possibly can.

Anna in the winter garden.

… a blizzard with a sense of humour …

All in all not much shaking and brushing gets done on these premises. Plants have to take their chances and I am sure that some of them would not thank me for removing the only bit of insulation they have against the freezing, bitter winds. Now and again branches do break under the great weight of wet snow, which can set like concrete, and rhododendrons seem particularly susceptible. Some mend with the help of splints and waterproof tape, and those limbs which are beyond repair have to be amputated. Sometimes shrubs get squashed like concertinas and never regain their former shape. A hedge of shrubby honeysuckle, *Lonicera involucrata*, was reduced to half its height by a snowdrift one year, but looked breathtakingly beautiful as a long, white bolster.

Snow, to work its magic, needs something to fall on, plants of all shapes and sizes, deciduous ones and evergreens, especially evergreens.

Olearias and hebes feature prominently in many parts of the garden, they give it shape and substance. All do their bit, from the large, widely-branched New Zealand hollies to the green buns of tiny hebes. *Eleagnus ebbingei* makes a good winter shrub, and *Griselinia littoralis* always looks bright and fresh. This is often recommended as suitable for seaside gardens and over the years I have tried several shrubs, from a variety of different sources. Given good protection, they survived, but having them hidden inside an enclosure of hessian or windbreak netting all winter rather defeats their purpose. Those left to get on with it by themselves turned brown or lost most of their leaves. All changed when a New Zealand botanist, who had visited the garden the year before, send me some *Griselinia* seed which he had collected at high altitude on the South Island. The plants raised from it, and called 'Mount Cargill' after their place of origin, are glowing with health, and their large, rounded leaves, unlike those of their predecessors, remain unblemished all year round. They form a perfect background for *Chiliotrichum diffusum*, a tough little South American evergreen with tiny linear leaves, dark-green above, silver below, and white daisy flowers in June and July.

Another South American, *Maytenus magellanica*, is one of the handsomest evergreens I have, a slow-growing small tree with pink twigs and dark, faintly toothed elliptic leaves. Unlike other broad-leaved evergreens which

gradually shed their old leaves during the summer after they have turned yellow, it drops large quantities in early spring, while they are still green. Perhaps this is to draw attention to its minute crimson, orange-scented flowers which open at the same time, and might otherwise be overlooked?

Phormiums come from the temperate regions of New Zealand, but their broad sword-shaped or arching leaves and dramatic infloresences bring a tropical look to the garden. Both *Phormium tenax* and *P. cookianum* do well in my garden and have grown into free-flowering, imposing specimens in a short number of years. Their variegated forms are less obliging in cool, wet climates, but the green and yellow striped 'Sundance' and the maroon and pink 'Rainbow Maiden' hold their own in pots filled with sharply-drained compost. Surprisingly all my phormiums remain in a respectable state all

Griselinia littoralis **'Mount Cargill'**.

Arundinaria murielae.

through the winter, but by April, the weather has taken its toll and I remove large quantities of their old, torn and bleached leaves, by cutting them away at the base. Split lengthways into several strands, they make durable garden twine.

Two bamboos do well in my garden, and survive most winters relatively unscathed. *Chusquea culeou* from Chile, has olive-green canes and densely crowded leaves which create a rich, bottle-brush effect. It has grown into a solid-looking, five-foot thicket in a sheltered, damp corner of the Back Yard. The Chinese bamboo, *Arundinaria murielae* has a graceful arching habit, with yellow-green canes, brilliant green when young. Its leaves are long and narrow, and despite their thin texture, rarely get scorched by the wind.

Other evergreens don't pass the winter test. The leaves on *Cistus* 'Silver Pink' hang limp and sad, and *Artemisia* 'Powis Castle' exchanges its silver summer plumage for soggy, grey dish

mops. But that leaves plenty of others, and those with a good dash of yellow in their green look best under grey, wintry skies. *Olearia solandri* is just such a plant, with slender, twiggy growth and khaki-green, heather-like leaves. It grows in an exposed spot, in wet soil, but even on the coldest day it has a warm glow about it. *Ozothamnus ledifolius* creates a similar effect: its tiny, rounded leaves are dark green, but its young twigs and prominent leaf buds are yellow. This

Ozothamnus ledifolius.

young growth feels sticky to the touch, and when crushed during warm weather gives off a strong stewed-prune smell. *O. rosmarinifolius* also has small, dark leaves, needle-shaped as the name suggests, and set off nicely by white-felted twigs. Both species grow against the low wall of the Temple, our west-facing conservatory, in poor, gritty soil. Their heads of tiny white flowers, which open from conspicuous red buds, are produced in late July. They need regular hard pruning to keep them in good shape, but doing this, as recommended after flowering, rarely gives the new shoots enough time to ripen before the winter. I found a compromise which suits us (the shrubs and myself) well. I let them flower one year, then clip them over lightly. Every other year I forgo the flowers, or enjoy them in October by pruning the shrubs hard in early May.

I use the same regime on my small-leaved hebes (the large-leaved ones, with one or two exceptions, refuse to stay with me for long). Left unpruned they soon grow leggy and bare in the middle, before falling apart altogether. With regular clipping they keep their looks for many years, and their rounded shapes make them the soft furnishings of the garden. *Hebe topiaria* lives in the Sunk Garden, a dome of gentle sage-green, two feet tall and twice as wide and in early summer it is covered in countless small spikes of white speedwell flowers. *Hebe rakaiensis*, whether clipped or unclipped in spring, rarely flowers with me, but its leaves are the bright green of a Granny Smith apple. It makes a well-rounded shrub, three by three feet, but now and again, after a particularly bad winter, looks a little scorched on its windward side. *Hebe carnosula* has grown into a forest of strong, upright shoots, about a foot high, and as is the case with these shrubs, much wider. Its shell-like leaves, glaucous in summer, green in winter, are set in neat ranks and give the shoots an interesting, quadrangular appearance. It has the typical white flowers, flushed with a little mauve.

The whipcord hebes look quite different.

Hebe topiaria.

They have a conifer or heather-like quality with their feathery, upright growth and scale-like leaves. *Hebe edinensis* has been in the garden right from the start and is now in its third, or even fourth generation. Its dense bolster of foot-tall, crowded warm-green shoots are soft to the touch and could easily be mistaken for a club moss. *H. armstrongii* has the same height and habit, with wiry branchlets in a dull, olive-green, veering towards yellow. Prostrate blue junipers, turned even bluer with the cold, look good with this, and so does the red-leaved grass, *Uncinia uncinata*. This also looks striking among heathers, and makes vivid contrast with the gold-leaved ones.

I don't have a heather garden, but part of my borrowed landscape, the hills to the north and north-east, is a heather garden extraordinaire, with large expanses of ling (*Calluna vulgaris*), disrupted here and there by a stretch of grass, or punctuated by spiky, tufted sedges and bright sphagnum moss in the damper places. Nature's design, and a far better one than any I could have dreamed up on my small plot. I like using heathers as shrubs in their own right, planted singly for the largest and most vigorous, and in small groups of one kind for the less so, to knit together into one entity. Grown with other small shrubs, alpines and spring bulbs, they never take on that lumpy, restless look they seem to get when planted in a mass. I find varieties of *Erica carnea*, which by the way is lime-tolerant, and *E. vagans*, best for my purposes, vigorous and with good foliage that never browns. They will grow happily on almost any soil, as long as they have plenty of moisture and good light. Just one plant of the golden-leaved *E. carnea* 'Aurea', with its glorious tone of yellow, is enough to lighten up a small planting.

Lonicera nitida 'Baggesen's Gold' has this same sharp, fresh colouring in winter, but does not like sea winds, which spoil its graceful, feathery outline. Mine is growing into a fine specimen against a sheltered, east-facing wall. *Lonicera pileata* also prefers a little shelter. Apart from that, it isn't fussy and is one of those shrubs which

Erica carnea cultivar in bud.

Hebe 'Red Edge'.

puts up with dense, dark shade. It has a wide, spreading habit, and small, oblong leaves, neatly arranged along its sturdy twigs. Before I was familiar with its horizontal style, I planted one close to a small stone seat in the White Garden, too close as it turned out. The necessary hard pruning into old wood left it looking like a moulting hen for a couple of seasons. Clipped into a broad mushroom since, it has great dignity and presence. In cold weather the light-green leaves take on a purplish flush, to match the small, translucent violet-purple berries.

Another shrub which changes colour in cold weather is *Hebe albicans* 'Red Edge'. The plum-red edge which recedes to a fine line in summer, becomes broad and prominent in winter. Mine grows in a raised bed near the entrance to the Sunk Garden, and the drystone dyke which holds the bed's soil in place is planted with *Sedum spathulifolium* 'Purpureum'. A chance meeting, and a fortuitous one, as the colouring of the stonecrop's fleshy rosettes is a perfect match for the hebe's leaf margins.

In the same part of the garden I have a small, slow-growing form of *Drymis lanceolata* which came to me from Tasmania via the Faroe Islands. It is a pretty little evergreen, wider than high with lead-green leaves, which are a good

Sedum spathulifolium.

Drymis lanceolata.

substitute for chilli pepper, and crimson bark. Clusters of pink buds form in the autumn, expand into white stars in spring, and are followed by large, blue berries on the female plants if both sexes are grown. I tried several male plants; none flowered and all got hopelessly battered by the wind. At long last I have a groom for the bride. It came from Michael Wickenden's mail order nursery in Castle Douglas and, still in its pot, is covered in buds as I write. Behind the female *Drymis* I grow the Tasmanian cedar, *Athrotaxis cuppressoides*, which I hope will eventually grow into a small tree. It is slow-growing, and after half a decade in the garden, barely three feet high. Like the *Drymis*, it sails unscathed through all weathers. Its leaves are reduced to dark green scale-like segments, separated by tiny bands of white wadding. It looks rather like a larger, and much more solid version of *Ozothamnus selago*, a rockery shrublet which has survived in a raised bed in sharply-drained soil for over twenty years, with scant attention from me. Sometimes in a hot summer it produces a few of its cream button flowers.

Ozothamnus hookeri is a promising newcomer to the garden, impervious to wind and weather. It has an open, upright habit with long, wiry growth and narrow bands of dark, scale-like leaves, pressed close to the white-felted twigs, creating a striped effect. It shows great vigour and looks like the kind of shrub which insists on perfect drainage.

Winter wet, rather than sea wind, or a combination of the two, seems to be the enemy of many evergreens, and in the Kitchen Garden there is a stark contrast between the long, shaded border with its deep, rich, peaty soil and the raised beds where copious amounts of sand and grit have been added. The Kitchen Garden is not, as its name suggests, a vegetable plot, but an ornamental planting, named after the first ever bed dug in the garden, opposite the kitchen window. Such names, no matter how incongruous, tend to stick.

This bed has since become a long, narrow, shady border, and its great depth of soil stays damp all summer and gets soaking wet in winter. The wind whistles through it from west to east (and vice-versa) and no evergreens, apart from a dark-leaved holly, have survived there for long, and those which did, soon looked too miserable to be worth keeping.

Now, during my winter walks, I turn my back on this border and look at the raised beds opposite instead. The soil in them is well-drained and small evergreens abound, interplanted with grasses, sedums, saxifrages and the prostrate mats of thyme and *Celmisia bellidioides*.

In the White Garden I have another winter-green oasis, which gives me much pleasure at this bare time of year. *Olearia capillaris* is a rounded, four foot shrub of somewhat sparse habit, but this is an advantage, rather than a drawback, as the long intervals between its orbicular grey-green leaves allow a good view of the fawn-coloured, undulating branches. Next to it grows *Osmanthus heterophyllus* with its black-green holly leaves, and behind these stands a large old *Hebe traversii*, its bare stems, like the legs of a Victorian table, decently skirted by a green cloth of *Lonicera pileata*. To the front of this group I have a large fountain of *Libertia formosa*, with its stiff, grass-like leaves, and next to it another shrub. *Prunus laurocerasus* 'Zabeliana' is a low-growing laurel with dark-green, polished leaves, lit up by scented white tapers in spring,

Prunus laurocerasus **'Zabeliana' with** *Hebe rakaiensis* **(in foreground).**

and, some years again in autumn. The *Libertia* needs a good grooming after the winter to have it looking spruce for its June flowering, when the dark brown, arching stems rise and the three-petalled white flowers unfold.

Two large specimens of the New Zealand holly, *Olearia macrodonta* are amongst the White Garden's most impressive features at almost any time of year. After removing some of their lower branches they look more like multi-stemmed, small trees than large shrubs. This has created some nice planting spaces for vincas, snowdrops, pulmonarias and violas underneath them. It has also exposed the stems with their peeling bark and pale cinnamon wood beneath, a handsome feature.

I don't have many trees or shrubs worth growing for their bark alone, but on the Alpine Slope I have what might be a dwarf form of *Salix lucida* or *S. mackenziana*, possibly of hybrid origin and supplied as "*Salix rotundifolia*", which as far as I can make out is not a valid name. Not the least bit bothered by its precarious nomenclatural state, it has grown into a low, urn-shaped shrub and I keep it thus, by pruning it now and again. Its polished bark is a vivid, uniform, olive green and makes this little willow one of the best winter features in the garden, a wonderful background for small purple crocuses or blue grape hyacinths. Even the best are improved by good companionship, and nearby, the slender, maize-yellow twigs of Salix phylicifolia form a low, tangled thicket.

Salix hastata 'Wehrhanii', planted on the edge of the Matterhorn (one of the many raised beds in the Kitchen Garden) looks pretty in glossy maroon, and bears large crops of catkins each spring. But *Salix fargesii*, grown in the Peat Garden, is the most flamboyant of my winter willows, with red new wood and prominent scarlet leaf buds – which earned it the highly descriptive name of lipstick willow from the late Peggy Ramsay, a friend and great gardener. Its summer foliage is also exceptionally good: large and pointed and a lively shade of green.

Salix alba **ssp.** *vitellina.*

In the damp part of the Back Yard I have *Salix alba* ssp. *vitellina*, whose bare wands glow egg-yolk yellow. In the same bed, a group of three *Cornus alba*, climatically challenged and a little dwarfed, show off their crimson winter bark in front of a yakushimanum rhododendron called 'Sweet Sue'. Its old leaves are a rather dull green, but its flower buds and young leaves are closer to yellow than to green and add to its attractions.

Rhododendron yakushimanum in its wild form has been all but replaced by its numerous hybrids and few of them have the good foliage and heavy indumentum of their wild ancestor. This species is still available from a few specialist growers, and is one of the best evergreens in my garden. Its dark-green leaves, arranged in perfect whorls, are narrow, slightly curled along their long edge, and beautifully contrasted by lime-green petioles. Flower buds are a pale, silver grey at first, then deepen to orange buff.

Blue-leaved rhododendrons can look very good too, especially when teamed with golden-leaved evergreens such as x *Cupressocyparis leylandii* 'Castlewellan Gold', which in turn gives a much-needed lift to the purplish green of *Ilex* x *meserveae* 'Blue Prince'. I have a nice specimen of the apricot flowered *Rhododendron* 'Alison Johnstone', growing on a well sheltered north-facing bank with ferns, woodrushes and other contrasting greenery. Its rounded leaves, sea-green when young, and blue-grey in maturity, give away its *cinnabarinum* parentage. I have always thought that species with its long, pendant, bell-shaped flowers the most desirable in the genus, but never dreamed of growing it in our salt-laden air. I now have two young plants of *R. cinnabarinum* on the nothing ventured, nothing gained principle, one from a purple, and one from an orange flowered parent, just over two feet high and covered in beautiful waxy, glaucous foliage. With a modicum of shelter they have sailed through their first winters and seem immune to powdery mildew, a disease which disfigures them in warmer, drier climates.

Most of the large hybrid rhododendrons will have nothing to do with me and my garden, but one large-leaved species gives me much pleasure. *R. bureavii* has the most handsome foliage: pine green, glossy and finely pointed, and that is only half the story. I have planted it near the Back Yard steps, well above head height, so I can admire its leaf reverses, which are thickly felted with a startling red woolly indumentum. It is still in its infancy and might not flower for a number of years, but is well-worth growing for its impressive foliage alone. I don't know what its height, or more importantly, spread is going to be in maturity, and the approximate sizes given on labels and in books are not always reliable indicators in this climate, which can stunt some plants, while turning others into giants. Planted close to the steps, it might eventually encroach on them, which won't pose too great a problem, as rhododendrons, thanks to their compact, fibrous root systems, don't mind being moved.

I still find it difficult at times, when faced with a small plant in a pot, to imagine it as a fully-grown tree or shrub, but I am getting more careful when siting those with the potential to grow very large. Two Japanese larches, the oldest trees in the garden, were planted (during my less careful days) in impossibly awkward places, where they took up too much space and created too much shade. Moving them was out of the question, and felling them was never considered

an option, as they had grown, after many years, into handsome specimens, clothed in branches which swept the ground. A compromise had to be found. Removing a large number of their lower branches was a somewhat drastic measure, but it solved the problem and turned both trees into quite distinctive, if somewhat eccentric personalities. The larch at the east end of the Kitchen Border now proudly displays a zigzagging stem, while the one between the Sunk and the Round Garden looks like a large, long-haired, sitting cat with its tail wrapped around its body.

The "kitchen larch" has a very simple but effective underplanting, a carpet of the deep-green, low-growing fern *Polystichum setiferum* 'Acutilobum', which retains its fresh looks all winter and well into spring. I enlarge my colony a little each year with the embryo ferns it produces in the axils of its fine filigree fronds. Some other ferns still look good too and will go on looking respectable until I cut them to the ground in April. In a narrow, north-facing bed, *Polypodium vulgare* 'Cornubiense', the Cornish polypody with its finely divided pinnea, looks as fresh and green as a bunch of parsley. Our native hard fern, *Blechnum spicant* forms wide mounds of overlapping, dark greenery, and from their centres rise the fertile fronds, bolt upright like green fishbones. I grow this with the broad-leaved, pale green sedge *Carex plantaginae*. *Blechnum chilense* hasn't been in the garden for long and is said to reach three feet high in good, deep soil. Mine is only just over a foot tall, but has started to wander about in one of the shady beds in the Round Garden, a sure sign of contentment. Its pale young fronds are flushed with pink and copper on first emerging, but soon turn to a rich dark green; their hard, leathery texture giving them a slightly reptilian feel and look. I wouldn't mind having a small forest of these nobbly-backed crocodiles.

Ferns are a tough race on the whole, and the small evergreen ones make a perfect foil for all kinds of spring bulbs like snowdrops, crocuses and scillas. Long before my garden had any shelter on its eastern front I planted the hart's tongue fern *Asplenium scolopendrium* there, in a little niche between a wall and the Back Yard steps, amidst a small drift of snowdrops. It is unlike any other fern, with its broad, entire fronds in bright yellow green, and looked at from below (the bottom of the steps), displays its prominent, rust-coloured spore cases. Its rather solid look has been enlivened with a dark, small-leaved cotoneaster and the blue-grey shrublet *Ruta graveolens* 'Jackman's Blue' in front. I like the strange smell of rue, sweet and astringent at the same time, like bitter coconut. This part of the garden still lacks shelter in winter, but all the inhabitants of this small bed know how to make the best of their less than perfect situation.

The wind also whistles through a large gap in the shelter planting on the westside of the garden, not by default, but by necessity. A large gate, wide enough to allow a tractor and trailer

Asplenium scolopendrium **displays its prominent, rust-coloured spore cases.**

Diary **31st January**

I don't think I've ever felt quite as cold as I did today. The wind, the faint easterly breeze from yesterday, is veering to the south-east, bringing on a thaw. It's blowing hard, and after an hour in the garden this morning, slipping and sliding all over the place, I was chilled to the bone. I fed the birds, then tried to settle down to some writing in the kitchen. I don't know why this should be, but when the wind blows from this direction the house turns into an ice box. The curtain in front of the saucepan shelves was in constant motion, and icy draughts came from the cupboard under the window. The catflap, flapping and flapping, eventually just stayed open – horizontally. As soon as I'd locked it, the first cat appeared at the window, meowing to be let in. Ten minutes later the next one appeared, and no sooner had I let it in, and returned to my writing, the one I'd let in first, wanted to go out again. I left the flap unlocked, put on another jumper, made myself a cup of tea and pretended to feel comfortable. But it was no use. A numbing cold was creeping up my legs, and my fingers felt stiff. For a while I toyed with the idea of gloves and extra socks, then discarded it in favour of a much more attractive one: a hot water bottle, the ben (livingroom) heater turned to full, a sofa, two blankets and an old Bette Davis film.

to pass through, gives access to the byres and the hay loft. When the extension to the house was built, an area below the west gable of one of the smallest outhouses became a builder's yard of timber, sand and stone chips. Cement was mixed there and the mixer swilled out at the end of the day, creating layers of thin, hard concrete. It took several days of pick and shovel work to break up the lumps of concrete and to remove them along with the largest stones, nails and timber offcuts buried beneath them. I was left with a stony, sandy, and very exposed desert. My original plan was to build a raised bed and to fill it with wall shrubs and climbers. But the drystone gable end of the outhouse had started to "run" and had to be reinforced with an ugly, concrete buttress three feet high by two feet deep. A raised bed against this would have looked quite out of place, and aesthetics play an important part here, as the bed is the very first thing visitors see as they enter the garden. An assortment of deciduous, herbaceous plants, and a lot of massed, bright colour in summer, seemed a perfect choice at first: safely below ground such plants would come to no harm during the rough, tempestuous times of the year. But that would have meant a stretch of bare sand, a return to the desert state for almost six months of the year; and I wanted a planting which looked at least decent in winter, or preferably interesting, perhaps even a little exciting …

After a whole years' contemplation and large numbers of strategically placed container plants, I dug a little garden compost into the sand and filled the bed with an assortment of plants capable of surviving on a starvation diet, and hopefully impervious to salty south-westerlies. Most of them like my desert bed: *Cordyline australis*, the cabbage palm, grows there, as does *Fascicularia bicolor* with its rosettes of long, prickly leaves. Sedums, thyme and Corsican mint carpet the ground below the billowing, blue-green clouds of *Euphorbia characias*, and the dark swords of a purple-leaved *Phormium*. Behind this planting, on the shelf created by the buttress, I have bowls of sempervivums, pots of alpines, bulbs and dwarf shrubs. High above them, on the gable end, "Talelayu" the Inuit spirit of the four elements keeps watch.

Above: Talelayu the Inuit spirit of the four elements keeps watch. Right: View east from the South Border.

February

There is a feeling of hope and excitement in this, the third and final month of winter. The buds on the trees are swelling; the blackbirds, silent for so long, start to sing once more, and where there was bare earth in January are the plump green shoots of tulips, daffodils and colchicums. Between the hail showers, the driving rain, sleet and snow, the sun, glued to the southern horizon for three long months, looks a little less pale and distant. The winter tempests abate and we get the first "days between weathers", mild, even balmy (with a little stretch of the imagination), or unnaturally warm, as some people prefer to call them. Comfortable enough to spend a whole day in the garden without the damp and cold creeping into one's bones, and the first opportunity to shed a jacket or woolly jumper while finishing the winter pruning. The land outside the garden is still firmly in the grip of winter, the heather on the hills looks brown and dead, the sea is leaden, the pastures bare and the sheep have a hungry look about them.

The garden is a different world, like a patch of ground from some distant, verdant planet, dropped into this cold and empty landscape. *Clematis macropetala* shows green amongst its tangle of brown wire, and the peonies have pushed their round, fleshy noses through the ground. Translucent pink asparagus spears have shot up over night, fringed at their tips with the pink threads of unfurling leaves, and nestling between them, like tiny grape hyacinths, clusters of tightly-closed mauve flowerbuds. *Dicentra spectabilis*, the bleeding heart, bone-hardy below ground, but susceptible to freezing winds above, often lives to regret its early rising. Youngsters, highly susceptible to "freeze-drying", need the

shelter of a cosy, shaded niche to bring them safely through their infancy, but old matrons like mine soon make good their losses.

February brings the first primroses. Some have hardly taken a breath and produced buds on and off since the autumn, but others have a more proper sense of timing and wait until now to expand into bloom. *Primula juliae* shows a spot of mauve here and there from the very beginning of the month, takes a break when the weather turns cold, then continues until April. *Primula* 'Wanda', with violet magenta flowers, is never far behind and was given to me by my gardening neighbour, the late Joan Nicolson, shortly after we moved into the house. She had large colonies of this plant flanking the path, two broad purple ribbons, all the way from the

Primula 'Wanda' hybrid.

Left: The Back Yard in early February with Gloria and Johnson.

Primula 'Wisley Crimson'.

garden gate to her front door. My small patches don't look nearly as impressive, and the plants have a tendency to heave themselves out of the ground, showing their starchy pink rhizomes and white feeding roots. I tuck them back in with a dressing of peat or composted bark and every third or second year, I lift, split, and replant them. In damp soil or shade they rarely open a bud before March, but in the well-drained soil of the the Alpine Slope they start flowering in mid-February.

'Wisley Crimson' is another early riser, with smooth, velvet-textured petals of a smouldering garnet red and rosettes of dark, crimped foliage. 'White Wanda' flowers a little later than the type and usually chimes in at the end of the month together with the first narcissus, 'Tête-à-Tête'. This always flowers several weeks ahead of 'February Gold', which I have never known to live up to its name in my garden. 'Tête-à-Tête' has become a firm favourite over the years because of its short, wind-proof stems, its clear

yellow flowers, two to a stem, as well as its obliging nature and long season. I started off with eight bulbs in a raised bed and now, after not all that many years, must have several hundred, some in clay pots outside my front door, some growing through carpets of *Anemone blanda*, others tucked in between small shrubs. Congested clumps are divided in early May (if I remember to do so), and any surplus bulbs are planted in grass, where they go on multiplying almost as quickly as in a border. This little daffodil will grow anywhere in sun or shade, pure sand or soggy peat, and flowers from mid-February until early April.

I only have a few bulbs of the tiny, lemon yellow *Narcissus* 'Cedric Morris', which came to me from Beth Chatto's garden, where it flowers in time for Christmas. With me, the first buds appear at ground level in the middle of January and start to open a month later. I have it in two places, with snowdrops in a shady border and with *Iris reticulata* on the Alpine Slope. The green

Iris reticulata.

angular spears of this iris push through the soil at the same time and in a mild season they open a few buds this month. I have them in a range of colours, but am particularly fond of the lobelia blue, violet-scented 'Edward', and the powder blue 'Cantab'. They tend to dwindle with me, but bulbs are inexpensive and I don't mind topping them up every autumn. *Iris histrioides* 'George', which always flowers at the end of the month, has more staying power and flowers of a deep violet mauve with the typical darker falls, and a yellow meridian stripe. All these stand up remarkably well to strong winds, but the yellow *Iris danfordiae* tends to bend the upper part of its stalk and holds its flowers horizontally, not a bad arrangement.

Next to my outdoor, north-facing larder I have a very narrow raised bed, barely a foot wide, filled, for want of a better idea, with prostrate junipers. Behind it, against the house wall, is a sheltered stone ledge, just wide enough to stand small pots on. Young or newly-bought plants often do a stint on this handy

"observation ward", before I find them a place in the garden. *Helleborus lividus* first flowered here in a tiny pot. It is worth growing for its leaves alone, dark, slightly glaucous green, and intricately veined and netted in cream. The first of its green, pink-flushed flowers open at the beginning of the month. They are cup-shaped at first, then widen into saucers; gradually they darken to a dusky pink and remain on the plant all summer, while the seed pods start to swell and ripen. It is a little slow growing with me and appreciates every bit of shelter it can get. *H. argutifolius* is more enthusiastic and grows into a two foot mound of jagged, blue-green, tripartite leaves, topped from February to June with clusters of drooping, apple green bells. It lives in a shady bed of sandy soil, carpeted with "Mind-Your-Own-Business", *Soleirolea soleirolii*, a rapid surface spreader which covers the ground with a dense film of minute, bright green lentils. Doom-laden prophecies about this plant taking over my garden in the dead of night remain unfulfilled. It is not truly evergreen with me and

Helleborus argutifolius.

Soleirolea soleirolii, **a dense film of minute bright green lentils.**

after a bad winter shrivels to dry, brown cobwebs, which can be pulled off to make way for the new fresh growth beneath them. The native *Helleborus foetidus* also has a vigorous shrubby habit, with palmate leaves and long, narrow, individual leaflets. Early in the month large terminal clusters of buds open into pale green bells with a neat maroon rim. It survives all kinds of weather and flowers well enough, but tends to shed much of its foliage during January, which gives it a sad, vulnerable look. I tuck it in behind small potted evergreen shrubs to camouflage its nakedness.

Like all hellebores the above like a little lime and gritty, humus-rich soil. They also must have some shelter, to prevent their beautiful leaves from getting torn and scorched by the wind. Before my garden had any, and before I had a greenhouse, I used to grow some hellebores in large clay pots, stood outside for the summer and kept in my south-facing porch during winter and spring, a regime which suited them (and

Diary   **3rd February**

Frost has formed a hard skin on the sleet and wet snow which has covered the garden for two days. It makes walking almost impossible, and after two painful falls I returned to the house to modify my footwear. When I was a child, long before the days of municipal gritting, my mother used to strap the broad, red rubber rings, used to seal kilner jars, around our shoes to give their soles a better grip. This made walking to school in winter, even on black ice, perfectly safe for her children. It still works, but rather than the one band, doubled up, I now need two in their full width on each foot. A thin layer of ice covers all and has welded the buds of crocuses and hellebores to the ground. A sheet of ice has formed in a bowl of *Sedum oreganum* and its green and red leaf rosettes below the transparent surface remind me of flowers imprisoned in a glass paperweight.

me) well. Regardless of pot or open garden culture, *H. foetidus* is never around for long. *H. atrorubens* hort. makes a fine change from the green theme. Its cup-shaped flowers are a sultry blood-crimson and are produced in great quantities from late December until April.

These are hard times for my blackbirds, and as soon as I put out food for them, dark clouds of starlings descend on the garden. They fall upon my offerings in a frenzy of flapping wings and sharp beaks and the more food I put out, the more starlings appear.

Blackbirds and robins never got a look-in until I started to feed them separately, either at dusk, after the starlings had turned in, as they always do at sunset, or on the kitchen window sill, where they don't dare venture. Blackbirds and robins have no such inhibitions, and, not the least bit bothered by my presence on the other side of the glass, eat their fill. They are a bad influence, and I have been known to idle away whole days watching and photographing them, my elbows propped on a cushion on the window sill. There is a large population of wrens in the garden (Shetland has its own sub-species), but they never come to the dining table. They must somehow manage to fend for themselves, even during the worst of times, when the white landscape is only interrupted by the grey of the sea, and not a morsel of food is to be found anywhere.

Snow covers a multitude of sins and eyesores: it covers bare borders, old brittle stems, rotting leaves and wind-blown debris, but it never lasts long, a few days perhaps, a week on the outside. But at this time of year I don't mind expanses of bare soil. I like snowdrops best with the marbled arrow-shaped leaves of *Arum italicum* 'Pictum', or growing through the small, dark leaves of an ivy. Neither like my Kitchen Border, and there, the snowdrops look fine rising from the dark soil, or growing out of brown leaf-litter. Both the single and double form of *Galanthus nivalis* do well with me. They don't

... **hard times for my blackbirds** ...

self-seed, but soon grow into large, congested clumps with some of the smaller bulbs pushed out of the ground. These I gather and replant where there is room for more, and there always is. Immediately after flowering (in the green) is said to be the best time to divide and transplant snowdrops, but that means March, and by then there are a thousand other things to see and do, and the snowdrops are easily forgotten. Instead, I do the job as soon as they emerge in January, when their buds are still upright and tightly

Arum italicum 'Pictum'.

Galanthus nivalis.

closed, a sliver of white sandwiched between the green. Each year I lift several large clumps and replant them, in small groups, or singly where I want lots, in borders and in grass. In the Back Yard meadow, where I long to have sheets of them, I still don't have nearly enough, but in some parts of the garden they have at long last grown into something resembling small drifts. I also have one particularly fine large-flowered and long-stemmed snowdrop called 'Samuel Arnott'. It is not cheap to buy, but the bulbs increase quickly and flower freely. A great one for both picking and long-distance viewing.

Diary   13th February

After a dull grey morning, the clouds parted in the afternoon and lit up the garden for a few precious hours. It brought a glow to all the bare branches and set the Japanese larches on fire. The Kitchen Border is white again, not with snow, as it was last week, but with carpets of nodding snowdrops, in tight bud a few days ago, all the flowers seem to have opened at once. In the shade of the drystone dyke they grow as thick as grass, and amongst them the oriental hellebores are hung with clusters of large, drooping buds beneath their ruffs of greenery, dusky-pink and plum-purple, the size of pigeon eggs. The first red-legged oyster catchers have returned in time for Valentine's Day and stride purposefully across the

Crocus tommasinianus.

meadows, long beak and eyes to the ground. And in the sunk garden the grey paving stones are outlined with meandering bands of soft, hazy lilac. The silky goblets of *Crocus tommasinianus* have opened in the sun.

Just after my parents had moved into their newly-built house in 1962, my father bought a packet of "lawn flower seed". The only flower to appear on the lawn was *Crocus tommasinianus*. It has since escaped to an old apple orchard below their house where it turns the ground beneath the trees into a sea of lilac. Like the snowdrops it does not self-seed with me, as there are not many pollinating insects on the wing in February, but the bulbs my mother gave me increase rapidly and I have great fun spreading them around wherever I want more. I have them in the Kitchen Garden, and on the east side of the Back Yard, where I can see them from my study window. Planted singly, they soon fill out to form pools of colour.

Just around the corner from the raised beds of the Kitchen Garden, the east-facing gable of the byre, and the south-facing wall of a lean-to convenience (it's decaying wooden structure and internal furnishings long since demolished), meet at right angles to form a square, enclosed on two sides and accessible by a short, narrow path. Here I have yet another small raised bed, filled with peaty soil and perfectly sheltered from the sea winds. There are many raised beds in the garden, some a foot or more high, others just a few inches off the ground, such a good way to improve drainage on my predominantly wet soil.

Even some of the dullest, darkest days of winter start with a blue sky, and this bed catches every ray of the early morning sun. An ideal place for a little colony of *Crocus tommasinianus*, growing at the feet of *Rhododendron leucaspis*, one of the bed's oldest inhabitants. Its slim, lax branches are huddled up against the byre wall and have grown a little threadbare over the

Oriental hellebores.

Rhododendron leucaspis.

years, but there is still enough of its light green, hairy foliage left to keep it looking decent. At the end of the month small milky-white moons open from fat brown buds. The crocus complements it perfectly, but while the morning sun warms and opens its flowers, it can turn those of the rhododendron into brown pulp, if there has been a frost in the night. Spring-flowering shrubs with frost-tender blossom should never be planted against east-facing walls, but in this climate, compromises have to be made now and again. East in my garden means shelter from sea winds and salt, and in this case, it was either an east-facing wall or not growing this plant. All I have to do when sub-zero temperatures threaten, which isn't all too often, is to cover it with a piece of hessian in the evening. It has given rise to a hybrid called 'Snow Lady', taller and more vigorous than *R. leucaspis*, but with the same early season and bell-shaped white flowers in small, loose trusses, also a little frost-tender.

Other winter flowering shrubs need no such pampering and have a much longer flowering season. In some forms of *Erica carnea* the buds start to colour in August, open during November and December, and flowering continues well into late spring or until curtailed by my garden shears. There are hundreds of

cultivars on the market, with little or nothing to distinguish one from another, except to the eye of a heather enthusiast, and I grow no more than a handful. 'Springwood White' is by far the most lusty grower and I have seen plants a metre long and almost as wide – a wonderful sight when in flower, and still impressive without. My plants are still dwarves by comparison and just now are covered in spikes of little white bells, enhanced by their milk chocolate anthers. 'Springwood Pink' is often recommended as a counterpart, but for some reason does not like my garden. Despite a good clipping each spring, which

Erica carnea **'Springwood White'.**

Erica carnea **'Myretoun Ruby'**.

keeps all the others growing close and neat, it soon develops bald patches and after a few seasons, looks thin and worn out. 'Pink Spangles' does much better and has flowers of a light rosy lilac. 'Heathwood' is also good, with much the same colouring, and has the added attraction of purple-flushed young foliage. 'Gold Scarlet' is a white flowered winter heather with bright yellow green foliage, a combination I like. It is good with other small, dark-leaved evergreens and its young growth is flushed red and orange in spring. *Erica darleyensis* 'Margaret Porter' has bronzed leaves, a neat growing habit and an abundance of lilac pink bells from February to April. The darker varieties of *E. carnea*, with dark foliage to match, are all a little later in flowering, some wait until well into March and none are quite as strong growing as their lighter counterparts. Good darklings in my garden are 'Vivellii' and 'Myretoun Ruby', deep cerise and rich crimson respectively.

I plant them wherever a little year-round green carpeting is needed and a dash of winter colour won't go amiss. They mark the corners of raised beds, spill out of borders onto gravel paths, and stop the soil from being washed away on banks and slopes.

I use grasses in much the same way, and sedges, which like it damp and acid, do particularly well. Surrounded by pasture and hay meadows, grass seed gets blown into the garden and I have spent much of my gardening life trying to banish grass. For a long time I could not warm to the idea of ornamental grasses, but all changed when I encountered *Carex oshimensis* 'Evergold', a perfect mound of broad,

Carex oshimensis **'Evergold'**.

Carex **'Coman's Bronze'.**

arching deep green leaves with a prominent central band of light, luminous yellow. Now I have quite a few grasses. They are easy to please, add new tones and textures to the garden, make such good contrast to broad-leaved plants, and the evergreens among them are indispensable in winter.

Carex 'Coman's Bronze' was very unkindly referred to as "that dead grass" by Madeline, who used to work with me in the garden, and can prick out seedlings with the speed of lightning. She does have a point. This sedge's winter colour is a bleached brown, but cut to the ground in spring, its new growth has a lively ginger tom cat vibrancy. 'Frosted Curls' has the same hair-like leaves, not horse hair as in 'Coman's Bronze'

but something a little finer, pale silvery green, and given bounce by a light perm in its tips. Both can be clipped repeatedly during the growing season to keep them within bounds, and to freshen up their colouring, or be allowed to fling their long manes over their neighbours. I know of one gardener who grows several of these grasses in tall chimney pots with the leaves cascading over the sides. I sometimes think it would be fun to give each a different hair style, short bobs, plaits or tidy topknots.

Carex conica 'Snowline' is a departure from this theme. Its leaves are broader and very much shorter, tapering to a fine point, dark, almost blackish green, and thinly outlined in lightest grey, forms tidy little mounds, refined rather than flamboyant. *C. testacea* is also on the quiet side, a neat, foot tall clump of narrow olive green foliage, overlaid with a touch of pale orange, and good for warming up little grey leaved hebes. *C. buchananii* is similar in habit with thin, upright reddish brown blades, playfully curled at the tips. *C. plantaginea* looks more like a small, gold-leaved hosta than a sedge. Its broad, ribbed leaves are a very light yellowish green, and are held on short red stalks. Slugs are fond of it and must be curtailed. It soon forms dense colonies less than

Carex plantaginea.

a foot high and makes classy ground cover in sun or shade.

C. pendula grows into impressive clumps of broad, upright, grassy leaves, three feet or taller in rich, damp soil. Long brown tassels, dusted with gold pollen, dangle from the tips of tall, arching wands in July. An old specimen, which had grown too large for the garden, now lives among willows and alders in the boggy part of the shelter belt where it has reached a diameter of over two metres and is sought after by blackbirds as a sheltered nesting site – cats permitting.

In under a decade, parts of this shelter belt have started to resemble a young forest. It runs in an L shape from the White Garden along the eastern and southern front of the flower meadow and on the higher, drier ground where it is planted with conifers, it is almost impenetrable, and a much used secret hiding place for Anna and her friends, perfectly sheltered even during a force ten south-westerly.

Carex pendula.

Diary   **21st February**

February is a strange month for planting Spanish bluebells, especially with snow on the ground, but several large clumps, lifted in the autumn, have been lying about all winter. Some have turned to pulp with the frost already and as there is no space for them (and their incontinent seeding) in the garden, the shelter belt seems a good place. James and I took an hour to set them all amongst the birches – cold, but enjoyable work. On the way back we took a short-cut through the undergrowth (on hands and knees in places) and came across "Gloria's Garden". She's our oldest "kitten", born in July 2000, and the spot she has chosen, underneath pines and larches, is bone-dry. She's made several nice sleeping places, hollows in the moss, thin grass and fallen needles. Her dining room is less inviting, strewn with rabbit's tails and chunks of pelt and, sadly, feathers and small wings.

Shelter in many parts of the garden itself is a somewhat rare commodity in winter, and during February I spend considerable time in the comfort of the greenhouse. The annual clean and tidy up, which I start in November, drags on through the winter, gets forgotten over Christmas and has to be finished now as a matter of urgency. Tedious chores, like washing, sorting and stacking pots, and less tedious ones like checking over the permanent and seasonal residents, removing their withered leaves, top-dressing their pots with a fresh layer of compost, and giving all which have been kept dry in winter a first soaking. Those of the garden's summer guests which are a little on the tender side have their winter quarters here. *Tulbaghia fragrans* flowers in a large tub outdoors from August to November, takes a short rest, then puts out some more of its little scented bells through January and February. They are held in large, drooping umbels on long, strong stems, and in the garden, in good light, they are a pale lavender pink; in a shady corner under glass they are pure white.

Unseasonal flowers are always a bonus. A small rooted pelargonium cutting was tucked into the back of a greenhouse border some years ago and forgotten about. It has since scaled the greenhouse wall with the help of a cherry tree and is never out of flower. In winter, under grey skies, its large heads of sugar-pink flowers take on a wonderfully garish, day-glo brightness. It needs a good grooming now, and some curtailing to stop it from going through the roof.

Handling plants is always pleasant and satisfying work, and some need a little more care than others. *Mutisia ilicifolia* is still in its infancy, but potentially a large, vigorous climber with small, holly-like leaves and large pink daisies produced in July and August. It stubbornly hangs on to its old, withered foliage in the same way some clematis do. But unlike the clematis' leaves which can be shaken, brushed, or gently pulled off, those of the mutisia are welded to the stems. It takes a bit of time to snip off each one with a pair of kitchen scissors, taking care not to injure the new leaf buds or to cut through a stem. The ensuing transformation is worth every bit of time and effort.

'Cornish Snow', the first camellia, is in flower now, a small twiggy shrub, with pliable, arching growth and small (for a camellia) single white flowers. Inspired by my mother-in-law's Surrey garden and the wonderful camellias she grows against the walls of her house, I have tried to grow camellias out of doors. They did grow, in the most sheltered corners I could find for them, but failed to produce any buds, and all have since been moved to one of my greenhouse borders. 'Debbie', a double pink, starts to flower in early March, and 'Adolphe Audusson' chimes in at the end of that month with large red, semi-double flowers well-filled with gold stamens.

Camellia 'Debbie'.

Both started life outdoors, where they had looked increasingly sorry for themselves. Under cold glass they are growing into large shrubs. To pick their luxurious blooms for the house, or to give them away to friends is a great indulgence but a brief one, as their flowering never lasts for more than a few weeks. I have often wondered how Dumas' "Dame aux Camellias" managed to wear a flower on every day of the year.

My camellias will sooner rather than later outgrow their very confined space and in my foolishly optimistic moments I hope that when that day comes there will be enough shelter to accommodate them in the garden, and a climate change to bring them into flower. All gardens are fuelled by hope and optimism, but why is it that all real gardeners want the impossible and insist on growing plants they can't grow? If my reasons are anything to go by, it gives them an enormous thrill simply to have the company of such plants, it brings an edge of excitement to gardening which few other things can provide. It means inhabiting that delicious, elusive zone between the dream and the reality of the garden.

Magnolia sieboldii has lived through two harsh winters without any sign of die-back and looks luxurious during summer, dressed in large handsome, light green leaves. As it flowers on the young wood during July and August, there are no worries about buds making it through the winter, as is the case with other magnolias.

M. wilsonii has lived for many years in the Temple, in a large earthenware pot, root-pruned now and again; a small, gnarled bush rather than the large, majestic shrub it should and could be – in other people's gardens. Just now it is covered in grey, silky buds, a wrapping which falls away in two husks as the flowers emerge, cup-shaped, ivory white, nodding at first, then held upright, filled with scent and a ring of red stamens. What more could anybody ask for?

But there are more prosaic sides to gardening. On clear, sunny days the temperature under south-facing glass can rise as high as 18°, sometimes 20° Celsius or more, and plants,

especially young seedlings, need frequent watering. With this rise in temperature returns the smell peculiar to all greenhouses, a smell of warming earth and young, healthy plant growth. Vegetables like leeks, spring onions, broad beans, slow-maturing brassicas and early salad crops, sown in the first week of the month, are well under way three weeks later. They get a little extra help from a gas heater which I light when the temperature plummets. Less climatically-challenged gardeners probably sow their broad beans and cabbages outdoors in April, or even start them off in the previous autumn. Our growing season is a comparatively short one, and successful crops and a well-stocked vegetable garden often depend on an early start.

Brussel sprouts and black Tuscan kale keep us going until March, or until we grow sick of them and feed the rest to a grateful flock of sheep. I don't grow ordinary white cabbage, but grow savoy, which, boiled to death and served as a greenish yellow purée, was one of the banes of my childhood. Now I love it, cut into thin noodles, blanched in salt water and served with onions softened in butter, freshly-grated nutmeg and a dash of cream. We usually dig up leeks until the end of March, and if the season has been a mild one, and it often is, Swiss Chard 'Fordhook Giant' pushes up a few tender young shoots among its old tattered leaves all winter. The tight green rosettes of lamb's lettuce, sown last July, are beginning to expand and there are always a few green lace doilies of American landcress. This, like bittercress, is a prolific self-seeder, and once in the garden will keep itself going indefinitely. It has a peppery taste and is good eaten raw in salads; cooked in soups it makes a very acceptable substitute for watercress.

Parsnips and carrots have started to mark their locations with tufts of greenery. I never bother to lift or store root crops. With hard or prolonged frost a rarity, they can be safely left in the ground, where they stay crisp and retain more of their flavour. I manage to pick a bunch of parsley on most days of the year, but by the end of the month the weather has usually taken its toll and I have to resort to slight forcing. I pop a large, black plastic pot, weighed down by a stone, over some of the plants in a row. This warms up the soil sufficiently to bring on new growth, which quickly greens up once the pot is removed or moved onto the next patch. This also works with chives if they are slow to get started.

Large, bulging envelopes arrive this month, filled with exchange seed from several plant societies. The bulk of mine usually needs cold germination and these I sow without delay. The sowings are placed out of doors to subject them to as many cycles of freezing and thawing as winter still has in store, and this usually coaxes all but the most stubborn out of dormancy. Seed exchanges are a great source of cheap seed (a nominal fee will secure ten or more packets), including those of rare and unusual plants not available commercially. Sometimes there's been a mix-up, the resulting plants don't live up to their names or descriptions, and now and then a seed from a completely different plant finds its way into the wrong packet, but all that adds to the fun. I like surprises and always tick the box for the "distributors choice", the barn sweepings and spillings left after the seeds have been packaged by volunteers.

Over the years I have developed my own sowing routine. I use half-pots rather than trays, because they hold a greater depth of soil which doesn't dry out as quickly. I use whichever compost I happen to have available, peat or soil-based and sometimes a mixture of the two. First I fill as many pots (of varying sizes) as I think I might need and gently firm the compost with a circular mortar board, tailor-made by James. All but the largest seeds, like those of peonies (which I push into the compost), are sown on the surface and then covered with a layer of fine grit instead of soil. I vary the depth according to seed size, a thick layer for larger seeds, a mere dusting for very small ones. This goes a long way

The greenhouse in late winter.

in preventing seedlings from damping off. Primulas, fern spores and other tiny or dust-like seeds I leave uncovered. These are also the most susceptible to damping-off and other fungal diseases and I sterilise the surface of their compost with boiling water prior to sowing. Sowings which are kept under glass are then plunged up to their rims into a basin of water; those placed outside get watered automatically sooner or later.

But before I tear open the first seed packet I label each pot with a six inch plastic label, then sow the seed to prevent any mix-ups. Labels are stuck in to about a third of their length to discourage the blackbirds from pulling them up, while leaving enough space for a good deal of information: the sowing date, the plant's name, its family, country of origin, eventual size, habit, flowering time and colour. Having all this data on the label saves a lot of head-scratching and rushing into the house to consult reference works when the seedlings start to pop up or are ready for planting out.

Some of the seeds I sow, umbellifers, erythroniums, peonies, most bulbs, as well as some woody plants, will take a year or so to germinate, and during that time must never be allowed to dry out. It's a long wait, but more than compensated for when the first cotyledons (seed leaves) push through the compost the following February. Sometimes there's a tray-full, often just one or two seedlings, but all are greeted with wonder and gratitude.

The view from the greenhouse across the vegetable garden used to be a dismal one in February. Cabbages and leeks are not the most exciting plants to look at, and the bare branches of the trees and shrubs planted along the southern boundary behind them looked cold and uninviting. A large expanse of Irish ivy, *Hedera hibernica*, has given the scene a tremendous lift, and so have the snowdrops growing through it. This is a large-leaved ivy, glossy-green, and with a little dark marbling, especially in winter. I also grow the old double cream and yellow *Narcissus incomparabilis*, which flowers in March, as well as bluebells and white hyacinths, through this leafy carpet.

Broad-leaved evergreens, which can give the garden a warm and populated look in winter, were never planted along the garden's sea-front. Twenty years ago, when I first started to create shelter, I couldn't imagine that any could survive the full force of the south westerlies and south easterlies, and now that I know they can, there is no space for them. They feature large in other parts of the garden, and now and again it's time to make room for more.

'Rosaraie de l'Hayé', a crimson rugosa hybrid with a robust constitution and a heady scent, has been a prominent inhabitant of my South Border since it was planted nearly two decades ago. After a drastic pruning one spring it suddenly started to sucker, as is often the case in grafted roses after such interventions. Pulling or digging up the suckers became an ongoing job,

and one I had grown thoroughly sick of. I am keeping a wary eye on another, younger specimen of this rose in a different part of the garden, also grafted, but so far behaving well. Removing this large rose bush, five feet high and more than eight wide, took the best of a day and left a sizeable gap at the east-end of the border. Had I done the job in summer or autumn, the replacements I chose might have been quite different, a buddleia perhaps and another rose, but this being winter and the border's shrubby background devoid of leaves, I decided to plant evergreens.

In the gap left by the rose I planted *Pittosporum biflora*, a tall, slender, fast-growing shrub with small, dark narrow leaves, and next to it, *Lomatia ferruginea* which has the most gracefully ferny foliage of any shrub I know. Both have survived several winters unscathed in their pots and enjoy a good bit of shelter where they are now. The flowers of the pittosporum start as brown pin pricks along the new twigs in winter and expand to clusters of small maroon and yellow bells in April. The *Lomatia* is much slower growing and will only start to flower once it reaches adulthood. It is a member of the protea family and should eventually produce showy, pale yellow flowers, rather like spidery honeysuckle blossom.

Leaving aside olearias and hebes, broad-leaved evergreens which survive, let alone thrive in this climate, are few and far between and need careful placing. Over the years I have learned many lessons, taught me by the wind and the topography of my garden. Places which look snug and cosy to me can ironically be the most cold and turbulent. One such place was the south-west facing bed tucked into the corner between the house and porch wall, where fierce eddies flattened everything and winter losses were high, until I planted elders and flowering currants in the bed opposite to help filter the wind.

The ground behind the house rises steeply to the north and looks cold and exposed, but

Lomatia ferruginea.

many evergreens thrive there. Olearias, escallonias, *Pinus radiata* and several Yakusimanum hybrid rhododendrons survive average (which means wet and windy) winters unharmed and only look a little scorched towards spring, after a succession of force ten south-westerlies. This is inevitable, and states of perfection, expected or even demanded by gardeners in more benign climates, can't be relied on where wind-pruned shapes, stag-headed trees and browned foliage are the norm – often for a good part of the gardening year.

It makes me appreciate all those which are impervious to wind and weather all the more. *Leptospermum lanigerum*, a graceful grey-leaved shrub with feathery branch work and little white flowers, always escapes unscathed and so, surprisingly does the deciduous *Nothofagus antarctica* with its "ladderlike" growth and small dark leaves. Both live at the Back Yard's cold, northern fringe.

In other parts of the garden I am content with the green from herbaceous plants.

Cardamine raphnifolia creates large pools of fresh green cress leaves wherever there is enough moisture. The yellow-green, broad grassy leaves

Pinus radiata.

of day lilies look remarkably bright all winter and also like it damp. *Tellima grandiflora* prefers a little shade for its soft, hairy, heart-shaped leaves, which tend to blacken and decay when in direct contact with wet soil, but with a top dressing of horticultural grit between them and too much winter wet, all is well. In the variety 'Purpurea', they are backed with plum purple and are darkly-veined. In May, two foot stems carry spikes of small green, pink fringed bells with a surprisingly strong scent. *Tolmeia menziesii*, the pick-a-back plant, is better known as a house plant in the cold north, but is an invaluable stop gap in the garden. It is a rapid surface spreader and I use it a lot as a temporary weed proof ground cover while more desirable plants are being grown on. There is a variegated form called 'Taff's Gold' with leaves generously mottled and splashed with yellow, when grown in full sun, or cream when growing in the shade. Wherever a leaf touches the ground, a young plant grows out of it, hence the common name.

Slender spikes of tiny, gold-stamened chocolate flowers look pretty when the plant is grown in a large drift, and there are enough of these little spikes to make an impact. It won't flower in the deep shade under trees.

Nor will *Crocus ancyrensis*, which can always be relied upon to open the first of its flowers in the last week of February, and the last ones a month later, regardless of the weather. They are a cheerful yellow, just what is needed on a cold winter's day. Yellow always looks better with a green background, rather than against bare soil, and the tiny *Mitella breweri* is just what this crocus needs in the way of companionship. Small, rounded scalloped leaves grow into dense mounds which eventually knit together into large deep green, undulating hummocks, studded with tiny sprays of apple green bells in late spring. Large numbers of seedlings appear close to the parents and are welcome. *Mitella caulescens*, apart from its slightly larger size and paler shade of green, is similar.

Nothofagus antarctica.

Why must it rain quite so much? I remember when, during our first or second spring here, I asked Jimmy (our next-door neighbour) this very same question. He looked to the sky, then ran his eye over his near-empty kale yard and said: "The ground needs it." That might well have been the case then, but now, I think, the ground has had quite enough, and so have I. A million grey rivulets run off the heathery hills, the open drains have swollen to torrents and the lawn is squelching under my feet. My new bed, ready for planting, is all sticky mud and puddles. It has rained, without reprieve, for three days now, and the sky has closed in, heavy as lead. My spring enthusiasm has given way to flat depression and there are times when I fear this winter is never going to end.

But there are plants which don't mind the wet. In my damp, shady borders, I grow the spring or winter snowflake, *Leucojum vernum*. Unfailingly every January, rounded green noses appear, soon to be followed by large, square-shouldered, green-tipped bells. It is a robust plant with a strong yellowish tinge in both its leaves and flowers which quarrels with the grey green and bluish white of the snowdrops. The two are best kept well apart. My clumps increase freely and the bulbs will grow anywhere. They look particularly good when naturalised in grass, but the white bells last longest and shine brightest in shade.

Flowers above ground level are few and far between at this time of year, but I am working on improving matters. I have two winter flowering shrubs, *Chimonanthus praecox* and *Lonicera purpusii*, still in their pots. The wintersweet, grown under glass for half a decade, is slowly bulking out and I shall soon start it on a regime of high potash feeds and a little root restriction to coax it into flowering. The winter-flowering honeysuckle, kept in a sheltered spot outdoors, shows no hint of die-

back, which is always a promising start. Both were raised from seed and might well take a decade or more to reach sexual maturity and that much longed-for flowering stage.

No such dilly-dallying in the case of my witch hazels which were bought as grafted specimens. *Hamamelis mollis* 'Pallida' not only flowers, but manages to set a few seeds. It still looks a little sparse and stiff, but all along its bare branches clusters of pale brown buds open into whorls of narrow, bright yellow ribbons, like lemon peel cut with a "zester". The flowers have a sweet, strong scent and I like having a few twigs in a small vase on my bedside table during February. Spurned on by my success I have since acquired *H.* x *intermedia* 'Diane' with flowers of a deep, warm, cinnabar red. It is a glorious sight just now, with its flowering branches spread against the white walls of the house. Both grow on the east side of the garden, well-sheltered from salt-laden sea winds, but vulnerable to the

Hamamelis x *intermedia* 'Diane'.

freezing north-easterlies which can bring their performance to a premature end. But as the shelter in that part of the garden grows a little more substantial every year my witch hazels' season also grows a little longer.

Since the garden has developed a few sheltered, shady pockets, I have tried numerous mahonias, but none survived for long until my luck turned with *Mahonia* x *wagneri* 'Pinnacle', an impulse buy in full flower. It was destined to become a greenhouse shrub and was given a large, ornate stoneware pot. Stood outside in May it was somehow forgotten about, and when encountered again in December, it was covered in buds. It is an upright grower with warm green, pinnate leaves and young foliage flushed with coppery red in winter. Each shoot ends in

Pseudowintera colorata.

a bunch of long, arching flower spikes, densely crowded with canary-yellow bells, and with a heady, lily-of-the-valley scent. Like the witch hazels, this mahonia does well against an east-facing wall.

If it wasn't for their sweet scent, the tiny, greenish white flowers of *Sarcococca hookeriana* var. *humilis* would go unnoticed. They are produced all along the undersides of the branches on a ground-hugging, evergreen shrublet, barely a foot high. I grow it where I can enjoy it, raised to waist height in a narrow, north-facing bed near the front door.

Pseudowintera colorata is said to prefer sheltered woodland conditions, which I can't exactly provide, but it seems happy enough underneath the Japanese larch in the Round Garden. This I grow for its extraordinary foliage alone. A few of its leathery oval leaves are light green, but most are a pale, greenish cream, heavily flushed and overlaid with pink, and broadly outlined in red. These crimson margins look as if they had been applied with a very wet water colour brush, they run and bleed into the leaves in irregular patterns, so no two ever look the same.

In the Round Garden I also have *Berberis ilicifolia*, a vigorous evergreen with a narrow, upright habit and small, holly-like leaves of a dark, polished green. Unlike the *Pseudowintera* it blends in and goes all but unnoticed for much of the year, but at the end of February it sparkles. All along its branches hang little grape-like bunches of tubular, tangerine coloured flowers. I have never seen it in any other garden and Hillier's Manual describes it as a very rare evergreen species of small to medium size. Mine was raised from seed collected in Southern Chile by a Faroese horticultural expedition.

Right: *Berberis ilicifolia.*

March

March is said to come in like a lion and go out like a lamb, but it rarely does. More often than not it lashes its icy tail and roars as loudly on the last day of the month as it did on the first. It is a rare March when winter does not continue its pattern of freezing, thawing, sleet and hail past its official final day on the calendar. The land looks bleached, like a favourite garment put through the washing machine far too many times. The garden, undaunted, sparkles with new green and bright spring colours.

This is the month which puts my gardener's patience to the test and often has me hankering after a more benign climate. There are glimpses of a pale watery sky between the showers and still spring mornings filled with bird song, which lure me into tackling those major jobs which call for a lengthy spell of fine weather. Many remain half-done and I'm driven indoors again and again by the equinoctial gales. There's always the greenhouse to escape to.

Pricking out seedlings is an ongoing job and one of the problems is to find space for them all. James' study and the guest room on the first floor of the house have to be requisitioned for the tender, and those of doubtful hardiness. Both rooms have central heating and large, south facing skylights, perfect temporary quarters for young seedlings. The rest are crammed into the greenhouse.

My south-facing greenhouse is divided into two parts by transparent polycaronate panels and a door. In the western half I grow early vegetable and salad crops and raise all manner of ornamental plants from seed. Behind the closed partition door, and with a little supplementary heat on frosty nights, the young and delicate are kept snug and warm. Their hardening off process

starts in the eastern half of the glass house where vents and the door to the outside world are kept wide open whenever the weather allows. The ventilation serves a dual purpose. Two cherries, a tart 'Morello' and a sweet 'Stella' are trained against the south-facing wall. In March, this part of the house is filled with cherry blossom, and pollinating insects have free access. Few, apart from bluebottles, are on the wing in time and we usually have to help out 'Stella', which flowers first and crops miserly without assistance. I hand-pollinate the lower branches, and James, who has a better head for heights, does the ladder work.

Few gardeners in better climates would plant a sloe, *Prunus spinosa* in their gardens. But here, until quite recently, it was the only tree to provide me with a brief flutter of spring blossom, its black outline wreathed in white for a week or two each March. It took well over a decade before it decided to flower, and only ever does so on its landward facing half.

I now own two young plants of the Fuji Cherry, *Prunus incisa*. One is a twiggy little bush, the other trained into a miniature standard. Both have flowered from a very early age. The flowers are small, nodding, and appear in great profusion. The first buds open early in the

Prunus spinosa.

Left: *Ribes sangnineum* 'Lombartsii'.

Prunus incisa 'Paean'.

month, white, but held by a pink calyx, give an overall pale pink appearance from a distance.

March can be a disappointing month and it is often only now that winter takes its toll and damage inflicted weeks, or even months earlier, becomes apparent. Many precious and reputedly tough evergreens turn from winter green to spring brown almost over night, even indestructibles like *Olearia macrodonta* can look a bit of a mess (they always recover). Others are impervious. *Brachyglottis rotundifolia*, which is said to grow only within sight, sound or smell of the sea, and enjoys all three in my garden, never shows as much as a curled edge on those large, round, fawn-backed leaves, used as post cards by the sub-Antarctic whalers. It grows in a wind funnel between the house and the barn, a situation few evergreens would survive, let alone thrive in. My griselinias look almost unnaturally fresh and healthy among all the brown and grey of late winter. But the beautiful red-stalked leaves of *Daphniphyllum macropodum* hang like limp rags, despite its cosy spot in the shade and shelter of a large sycamore. This is an anxious time and I frequently check all my special shrubs, those nursed in pots for years and planted out in the most sheltered corners I can find in

Brachyglottis rotundifolia.

Ribes **'White Icicle'.**

my exposed garden. I have accumulated a small collection of broad-leaved evergreens, but am always on the lookout for more. Finding the right ones, and precisely the right spot for them, is still largely a matter of trial and error. *Crinodendron hookerianum*, planted in a shady, sheltered corner all but succumbed to the cold north-easterlies. It took two seasons to nurse it back to health and its former size. It now enjoys itself in a large pot, stood against the west wall of the house. Its long, dark, narrow leaves are a little scorched, but it lives up to its name of Chilean Lantern Tree. Its flower buds are formed in the autumn, miraculously survive the winters, and expand into long-stalked, cherry-red bells in March. Two specimens of *Embothrium coccineum*, the Chilean fire bush, also started life in pots, but now grow away lustily in the round garden, where they receive a fair hammering from the wind now and again.

But I must not get carried away by my hit-and-miss collection of dream plants, and pay due respect to the less capricious inhabitants of my garden. *Ribes* 'White Icicle' is way ahead of the pink and red flowering currants and dangles its little cream racemes above a carpet of variegated *Vinca minor*. Several vincas are on year round ground cover duty, which they carry out admirably. They have their moment of glory in March and April when they flower in periwinkle blue, mauve, purple and white. I also have a double form which is rampant and has little rosette-shaped flowers of a slatey maroon, set off by yellow-green leaves. They grow into wide mats of tangled stems which root as they go and benefit from a clipping over in late spring.

The flowering currants are among the most reliable and floriferous shrubs we can grow in this climate, and I often take mine for granted until they burst into flower at the end of the month. 'Lombartsii' is the palest of them all with pink buds and open flowers of lightest, champagne bubble pink, creating a nice, two-tone effect. 'King Edward' has flowers the shape, and colour of ripe loganberries, and 'Pulborough Scarlet' is not scarlet at all, but a rich, dark cerise. I find the darker flowered kinds not as strong-growing nor as long-lived as the common pink and the pale 'Lombartsii'.

Some gardeners harbour an intense dislike towards these marvellous shrubs – their smell, they say, reminds them of scent-marking tom cats. I do keep tom cats and find the comparison an unfair one, unfair to the shrubs that is.

Flowering currants, once established, will grow with little or no shelter at all, but a modicum of shelter is vital for some early herbaceous treasures. In the shade of an old Japanese larch, bronzed, fingered leaves unfurl in February, and hidden amongst them are tight clusters of pale buds. A few days later the stems have elongated, the leaves turned a fresh green and the buds of *Cardamine enneaphyllos* have expanded into creamy white bells. Next to it grows *Pulmonaria* 'Frühlingshimmel'. The flowers of this little lungwort look disappointing at first, with buds the pink of a washed-out flannel petticoat. Within days they change to a pale, milky blue to match the colour of an early morning spring sky. It is always the first of its tribe to flower and makes a neat, low carpet of small white-spotted leaves which mark the spot where the cardamine grows, long after it's disappearance in July.

The Christmas Cowslip, *Pulmonaria rubra*, now and again lives up to its name by producing a bud or two in December. It has plain, apple green leaves and I have two large colonies of this plant, one in the sheltered Kitchen Border and one exposed to the cold north-east. Those in shelter get into their stride in late March. The colour of their bell-shaped flowers is a soft, gentle red, halfway between a robin's and a bullfinch's breast. Those without shelter flower a

Diary   4th March

I was stopped in my tracks on the way to the Front Yard today by a sea of violet-purple flowers underneath a willow. For an instant I mistook them for crocuses, then remembered: Two years earlier I had broadcast a few "curds" of *Lathraea clandestina* over the tree's roots. There was no sign of it last year, and now there are thousands of its keeled and hooded flowers, in crowded clusters, like a mussel bed on dry land – a breathtaking sight. What a performer! From all the bits I planted only a tiny patch of flowers appeared near a *Salix alaxensis* in the Back Yard last spring. I've searched for it on hands and knees just now but can find no trace of it. The same story with all the other willows, alders and poplars I "inoculated" two years ago.

full month later, and in time with drifts of the slender, straw-yellow *Narcissus* 'Hawera'.

Pulmonaria 'Sissinghurst White' also flowers in March. It is the most vigorous of all the lungworts I grow and its large carpets of neat, white-spotted leaves contribute to the scene long after the sprays of white flowers have faded. I have interplanted it with *Scilla bythina*, a vigorous light blue squill which self-seeds freely.

Lathrea clandestina.

Crocus sieberi **'Tricolor'**.

Lathraea clandestina grows wild in Portugal and Spain. It has no green leaves and makes its living as a parasite on willow roots. It is said to be difficult to establish, and this was borne out by my initial success rate. Since then several more patches have appeared and I am thrilled to bits. The host willows are as vigorous as ever, and much enhanced by the toothwort.

Crocuses start to flower in February, the earliest even show a little colour in January, but it's the March sun which opens their flowers and warms them into parting with their delicious honeyed scent. *Crocus sieberi* 'Tricolor' is one of the first, and lives up to its name as soon as its buds expand: strong light purple, separated from the yellow base by a band of white. It responds instantly to even a few minutes of sunshine by first expanding into wide goblets, then six-pointed stars. I have large drifts of it all over my Red Bed, just inside the garden gate. *C. sieberi* 'Firefly' lacks the white stripe and has flowers of a lighter shade of purple. 'Barr's Purple' is another early riser with slender, delicate looking flowers in a pale, silvery lilac. 'Ruby Giant' is neither a giant nor ruby coloured, but a rich purple on the outside and pale mauve within, prettily veined and feathered with a darker shade. The three outer segments of *Crocus* 'Whitewell Purple' are a pale lavender, and the inner ones a clear, bright mauve. All three are cultivars of *Crocus tommasinianus* and display the same vigour and floriferousness.

Many of the smaller crocuses available from shops and garden centres are sold as "species crocus", but we are never told from which species the numerous cultivars are derived. As far as I can discern *Crocus chrysanthus* is either sole parent or involved in the ancestry of many.

Crocus **'Advance'**.

Crocus chrysanthus **'Princess Beatrix'**.

'Advance' has buds of a pearly, dusky mauve and opens into soft cream and scrambled egg tones (I've just had my Sunday breakfast). 'Dorothy', 'Saturnus' and 'Fuscotinctus' are all good cheerful marsh marigold yellows with greater or lesser degrees of external bronze feathering. Their yellow looks even brighter against a carpet of purple-leaved ajugas. 'Ard Schenk' is pearly white with dove grey basal markings, 'Romance' is a cream-backed light yellow and 'Blue Pearl' and 'Princess Beatrix' are shades of soft, lavender blue. All these small crocuses do very well with me, but in my experience need better drainage than the giant Dutch crocus. Some also take a little time to settle in. They flower freely in the spring following planting, take a season off, flower sparingly the one after, then get back into the swing of things from their third year on.

These large, beefy, bouncy Dutch crocuses in white, blue, purple and striped in those colours look good in a large expanse of grass or between clumps of emerging herbaceous plants and I try to fill every available space with them.

Diary   **17th March**

Hundreds of large white crocuses have suddenly appeared in the South Border. Clusters of buds among long, silver-striped leaves are everywhere. I must have planted them, but can't remember ever having done so. The crocus puzzle kept nagging me all day, until it suddenly dawned on me. Two years ago I turned out the contents of a large, clay pot, planted with regal lilies and a "top storey" of white crocuses. I found hundreds of small corms and spent the best of an afternoon planting them. They must have reached flowering size this year.

Acaena magellanica.

At the South Border's western edge where the ground is quite damp I grow Bowles' golden sedge, *Carex elata* 'Aurea'. This grass turns dull green in winter, but its new growth, produced early in the year, is a startling bright yellow. Next to it, for vibrant contrast, I have another grass, several mounds of the low, arching *Uncinia uncinata* with leaves of a brilliant sealing-wax red. It is a stunning combination, especially on a sunny day, and greatly enhanced by the large, satin-textured purple crocuses planted among the grasses.

Sunny days are a sticky point in the cool, overcast north and the poor crocus has a reputation to live down. "It's far too flimsy and delicate to stand up to the wind," is one objection levelled against it, "it never opens its flowers properly," is another. Both are true, very, very occasionally, when nature is particularly unkind to us in March. But that is rare. Most years March brings enough clement weather and hours of sunshine to allow those flowers to open wide enough to give a view of the yellow-throated interior and the saffron coloured, pipe cleaner stigma.

On the Alpine Slope, *Iris reticulata* (mentioned last month) is at its best now with a flower on each glassy green stem. The violet purple 'J.S. Dijt' looks striking, but on the whole I prefer the blue shades and like the light blues best of all. Their flowers have a fragile, fresh look with their undulating standards a little paler than

the rounded falls, which are prettily marked with white and orange. These bulbs have the annoying habit of splitting up into numerous small segments after flowering which remain unproductive for years before building up flowering strength again (if they ever do). Deep planting sometimes helps.

Iris histrioides 'Katherine Hodgkins' has a much more conducive system of reproduction. Its bulbs grow fatter every year before finally dividing into three or four large segments, each capable of producing a flower. At the same time small bulbils are produced at the base of the parent bulb, which can be detached and grown on. Its colour is a unique, pale duck egg blue. The falls have a central yellow blotch and are delicately veined and spotted with inky purple.

"How on earth did I ever manage to garden without?" I have quite a few plants in the category of the indispensable and *Anemone blanda* is one of them. Mats of frilled foliage appear in February, and suddenly, at ground level are the folded buds. Tinged purple with cold and stemless at first, they soon grow in stature as the soil warms up and turns them into fine-rayed blue flowers. I have several carpets of them growing through evergreen ground cover such as the cream and grey leaved *Ajuga reptans* 'Variegata'. Grown as a mixture this anemone comes in a range of blue shades with the occasional pink and white thrown in for good measure. The flowers of the cultivar 'White

Anemone blanda.

Anemone blanda 'White Splendour'.

P. vulgaris 'Lilacina Plena' ("Quaker's Bonnet").

Splendour' are slightly larger, but this might just be an optical illusion, and look lovely with Crocus 'Blue Pearl' or the pale blue *Pushkinia libanotica*. This only looks blue from a distance, close up the delicate bells, held in small spikes, are white with a pale blue line dividing each segment. I also have a few pink flowered blandas and a small group of the striking cerise cultivar 'Radar', growing through the glaucous mat of *Acaena magellanica*.

Anemone apennina is very similar to the blue form of *A. blanda*, but a slightly larger plant. Its mats of tangled rhizomes increase freely. Mine grows in a small shaded, peaty border with *Hacquetia epipactis*. As soon as this tiny umbellifer pushes through the ground it opens its bouquets of threadlike yellow flowers, held by fresh green ruffs.

I'm very fond of double primroses, and have a few in my garden, most of them raised from Barnhaven seed or donated by generous gardening friends. Initially I planted them, according to the instruction in a pamphlet on double primroses, in rich damp soil, not realising that my idea of that growing medium was very different from what the author had in mind, and my plants dwindled away at an alarming rate. Since I have learned that rich and damp in England is my idea of reasonably well-drained, my plants have faired rather better. Still, their characters differ widely and not all have a strong constitution. Two of my treasures, one powder blue, the other pearl grey, just manage to hang

onto life, while yet another with Prussian blue flowers and a striking silver edge to each petal goes from strength to strength. A dark crimson one with perfectly formed little rosettes increases rapidly in a raised bed, and a rosy lavender semi-double has made a large mat of light green and flowers its heart out in ordinary garden soil. The old lilac "Quakers Bonnet" does well and so does 'Dawn Ansell', which holds every white rose in a little collar of lettuce green leaves. They do best on neutral, or slightly

Primula 'Dawn Ansell'.

alkaline soils, and where the ground is very acid, appreciate a top dressing of garden lime in early spring.

Gold laced polyanthus is easily raised from seed and I sow it every three years or so to replenish my frequent losses. Regardless of soil, aspect and treatment, it is never around for long but has lately shown some staying power in a most unlikely place. It flowers in April and the gold lacing which outlines and divides each red or mahogany petal, makes the five petals look like ten. I grow mine with *Fritillaria michailovskyi* which repeats the brown and yellow theme, but brings a contrasting shape with its large, rounded bells, each segment curved outwards at the tip. Both live at the foot of a sandy bank, which gives them a rare combination of sharp drainage and plentiful supplies of moisture.

Beneath them, on the low drystone dyke which holds the bank in place, woolly thyme, *Thymus lanata*, has grown into wide, soft-grey mats, met by the stiff, upright foliage of *Libertia peregrina*. Its leaves are striped in khaki green and burnt orange – sometimes one is entirely orange – to match the orange seeds held by three-pointed papery stars. This is planted at the foot of the bank's retaining wall, and on its edge grows *Rosmarinus officinalis* 'Prostratus', the only one capable of surviving our winters in the

Gold laced polyanthus.

open. This makes a low tangle of crowded shoots, clothed in dark green needles. Out of the wall cascade the snaky stems of *Euphorbia myrsinites*, clad in blue-green scaly leaves and tipped with rounded, lime-green buds.

Rhodiola rosea has a similar colouring, but its growth is upright and old plants form wide, dense mounds, a foot or more across. It grows wild on seacliffs and is known as Lady's Footstool in Shetland. I have a rather good form of it with blue-grey leaves and flower heads of a rusty orange rather than the typical yellow-green. One large old plant grows out of a carpet of *Saxifraga crispa* with dark leaf rosettes and a foam of pale pink flowers.

Saxifraga geum has slightly larger rosettes, crimped at the margins and buff coloured flowers. These and good old London Pride make handsome, evergreen groundcover. I grow several cultivars of *Saxifraga umbrosa*: one is white-flowered, another has leaves spotted and splashed with yellow, and a miniature form called 'Elliott's Variety' with dark-stemmed pink flowers, above neat, hard hummocks. All start into growth early and their light green spring rosettes, with the flower buds nestling inside them, look fresh and new against the darker, older leaves.

Sweet violets belong to my group of nostalgia plants, plants closely associated with my German childhood. *Viola odorata* was the favourite flowers of my paternal grandmother. It grew abundantly in all the hedgerows and could be relied upon to open the first of its tiny flowers in time for her birthday on the third of the month. After a succession of failures with named varieties, I now, at long last, have three plants, begged from my mother's neighbour, and originally collected from the wild, in the days when such practice was commonplace. All I had asked for were tiny offsets, but what I received were three large clumps, beautifully wrapped in moss and brown beech leaves. I treasure them and hope they will make the garden their permanent home. Each is different, one violet, one white and one pink, and all have that powerful, sweet scent.

At the end of the month, when the earth has started to dry out a little, I start digging my vegetable garden, a job I always mean to do in the autumn, but with the gardener's motivation at a low-point, most brassicas standing over the winter, and the root crops left in the ground, my excuse is – there isn't much earth left to dig. Some parts I don't dig at all. Where I have grown salad greens and other short-term crops I spread a thick mulch of compost in the autumn, ready for planting in spring. These areas I cover with large sheets of clear polythene from February onwards. The soil underneath them warms up, weed seed germinates early and I can deal with the seedlings before I do any planting or sowing.

I can't say I'm very fond of digging, I find it backbreaking work, despite the use of a small, light-weight "Lady's Spade". It is also one of the dullest jobs in the garden and I can't bear to spend more than an hour or so on it at a time. Still it all gets done in time most years. On those dry and sunny March days when I should be doing my digging I often get itchy feet, and when I've seen all there is to see in my garden I drive off to see somebody else's.

Two strange little yellow daffodils can be found in many old Shetland gardens. One, quite short, has green-backed flowers with a muddled, double centre, or occasionally a flower which looks like a single daffodil, but has a trumpet stuffed densely with narrow little segments. The other is taller and has more green in its double flowers, which look strangely lopsided, even a trifle deformed, on first opening. I sent a few buds to Sally Kington, daffodil registrar at the RHS, for identification. Both plants apparently belong to what is now called the 'Van Sion Group', or *Narcissus* 'Telamonius Plenus' a race of double-flowered hybrids or sports of *Narcissus pseudonarcissus*, the little yellow daffodil still found in the wild in some parts of Britain. *Narcissus* Van Sion is mentioned by John Parkinson in his "Paradisi in Sole" of 1625, a rare and highly-prized plant in his day.

My garden was filled with them when I arrived and I still value them, for sentimental and historical reasons only. Even the smaller and more symmetrical of the two has a scruffy look about it, as its thin papery petals brown and curl as soon as the flower is fully open. All have long since been banned from the garden and look good, from a distance, in grass. They start flowering at the end of March.

The alders are also starting to flower now.

Diary   **22nd March**

I visited Nick Brett's magical garden today. It slopes gently away to the sea and is divided into two parts, one sheltered behind the house, the other, an open green yard in front. Numerous old willows grow there, their trunks and branches leaning every which way, some in soft curves, some at strange stiff angles, others snaking through the grass like moss-covered serpents. A stone's throw away are the rolling waves of the Atlantic, piles of brown seaweed heaped on the shore, and soaring, noisy gulls. The green warm smell of the garden mingles with the invigorating air of salt and iodine. In the grass between the gnarled old willows sway sheaves of daffodils, their buds still green and upright.

Narcissus **'Van Sion Group'**.

Alnus sinuata **catkins.**

The male catkins are held in bunches and remain hard and green all winter. Now they elongate and hang in long yellow tassels below the brown or maroon clusters of last year's rounded fruits. Alders like damp places and don't mind having their roots in water for part of the winter. I grow both the common alder, *Alnus glutinosa*, and the grey alder, *A. incana*, which, after a decade or more, have started to take on the shape of small trees. *Alnus viridis*, the green alder from the European Alps has, in the same span of time, grown into a well-rounded six-foot shrub. It carries large crops of handsome catkins, and its leaves retain their fresh, green spring colouring all summer. *Alnus sinuata*, the Sitka alder from Alaska, is one of the fastest growing trees I know and a good choice where quick shelter is needed on soggy ground. Its catkins are as long and fat as Cheviot lamb's tails.

In a wet and windy climate spring, rather than autumn, is a good time for planting bare-rooted shrubs and trees and my orders from

mail-order companies on the mainland start arriving at the beginning of the month. Underneath turf the land is usually dry enough to be workable for immediate planting. And there is enough moisture around, both above and below ground to make for a speedy settling in before the drying winds of April arrive. Evergreens can be a bit more tricky to establish, as they are never truly dormant, but they start to increase their metabolic rate about now, and are able to re-grow the fine feeding roots lost during the process of lifting in the nursery and replanting in the garden. They must have some shelter and a reasonably well-drained soil, as even the toughest, like lodgepole pines, get rocked loose and start leaning at precarious angles on water-logged ground.

Pot-grown specimens can of course be planted all year round, but they are never as beefy or grow away as well as those which arrive with their large root systems wrapped in straw and hessian. Where large numbers of trees are needed, those grown in root trainers establish best. They are generally of a smaller size than bare-rooted stock, but rapidly catch up. Rapid is perhaps not the best term, as even fast-growing species can take three, even four years before they are fully settled, and get into their stride.

Celandine turns the grass below the alders from green to yellow, which is a welcome sight in the pastures outside the garden, but their lacquered cups, however pretty, are less welcome in my borders, with one exception. Christopher

Lesser celandine.

Ranunculus ficaria 'Brazen Hussy'.

Lloyd's bronze-leaved 'Brazen Hussy' grows around and among the crowns of a large *Hosta sieboldii*. By the time the Hosta's leaves are fully expanded, those of the celandine have disappeared. Such double, or even treble occupation of a site is a good way to get the

Diary   **27th March**

It has rained all night, the morning is dark, with a heavy sky and thick fog cutting off the view at the garden gate. The garden is blue with chionodoxas, anemones and pushkinias. All green sparkles, the trees have expanded their leaf buds over night, there is a pale green fuzz on the larches and the older ones are studded with flowers, the females with their red spiral patterns and the males laden with pale yellow pollen. *Cotoneaster horizontalis* is dotted with green and the tips of its herring bone branches are hung with large rain drops. The blackbirds are singing and *Paeonia delavayi*, my fabulous red tree peony, is unfurling its pink leaf fringes. The earth has taken on a new, fresh look.

Ranunculus ficaria 'Christo'. The first ever double bronze-leaved celandine.

most out of the tiniest garden. 'Brazen Hussy' was a disappointment at first, as its chocolate brown leaves are exactly the colour of my dark, peaty soil and don't show up against it, a misfortune easily remedied with a dressing of contrasting blue grit.

The hussy seeds freely, and much to my delight one of the seedlings turned out to be double. The chocolate leaves are a shade lighter and the flowers perfect yellow rosettes, each laquered petal tipped with mahogany. I've named it 'Christo', after its "grandfather".

There are many March days when it is too wet and windy to venture outside, and I have to watch spring's progress from the house. The bay tree below my kitchen window shows tufts of new growth, and on the other side of the path *Cotoneaster lucidus* is covered in brand-new, shiny, bronze-green leaves. Beneath it the oriental hellebores have opened more of their buds into wide saucers of dusky purple, mauve and rose pink. One plant has white flowers with a green and pink flush and dense, dark spotting inside. *Aquilegia flabellata* has spread out its blue-green fans among the bluebell leaves, and cushions of brilliant green moss glow in the wall behind them.

Caltha palustris has colonised the central ditch of the hay meadow below the garden. Its hard round buds are still green and tightly closed, but next month it turns the ditch into a golden yellow river. The double form of this

Caltha palustris 'Alba'.

plant, grown in a damp bed behind the house, has flowered since the beginning of the month with bright rosettes of tiny, overlapping petals above carpets of rich, polished green. I also have the Himalayan form, *C. palustris* var. *alba*, with clusters of starry white, yellow-centred flowers. It has the longest season of them all and coincides with the flowering of *Primula rosea* 'Grandiflora'. When this little plant first emerges its leaf rosettes are a fleshy pink, and the buds nestling inside them look like cerise match-stick heads. As the leaves turn green, the scapes rise and the pink flowers open with neon light brilliance.

Scopolia carneolica is a plant which doesn't turn many heads, and would turn none if it flowered later in the year. Tubular bells the colour of not quite ripe aubergines dangle among whirls of rough green leaves on foot high stems. The flowers end somewhat abruptly in a straight, clean edge, as if cut in half with a sharp knife. I grow it in a little raised bed at the garden's east gate with blue primroses and *Corydalis ochroleuca*, a fumitory with luxurious mounds of light green ferny leaves and little yellow-tipped cream coloured larkspur flowers.

Towards the end of the month the great flowering of the willows begins and the first bees are on the wing. I have a lovely male form of *Salix* x *smithiana* which produces clouds of

... the garden is blue with chionodoxas.

Corydalis ochroleuca.

large yellow catkins every year. *S. alaxensis* is a newcomer to my garden, a fast and vigorous grower without the slightest bit of die-back in even the most exposed position (rare among willows). Its young growth is thickly covered in white felt, which gives all its upper branches a frosted appearance, its long, shaggy female catkins are a greyish green. *Salix udensis* 'Sekka' is planted in a prominent position on the Temple Terrace, where I can see its curled, flattened branches against the western sky. They are a polished mahogany brown, studded on their broad sides with small grey, pink-flushed catkins. With me this has grown into a large, broad shrub, but I have also seen it as a small, handsome tree. Not all of my willows flower, and some only do so sparingly. Every spring I search for the large, scented yellow catkins of the almond-leaved willow, *S. triandra*, and am thrilled when I find a few. *Salix melanostachys* flowers moderately but has the most

extraordinary catkins. They are a glowing red on first emerging, then slowly turn black. They always look a little bedraggled, like kittens caught in a heavy shower.

One of March's highlights is the flowering of *Daphne mezereum*. My shrub has undergone countless moves and is at long last happy in a raised bed, where I also grow other lime-lovers such as hellebores and soldanellas in a mixture of garden compost, sand and crushed eggshells. The bright magenta purple flowers densely stud the daphne's bare branches and have the most intoxicating scent: a strong lily perfume with a hint of bitter almond. I used to grow the white form until it was squashed by a fierce blizzard. I must remember to replace it some day.

On the Alpine Slope, large mats of *Arabis albida* (raised from a packet of mixed seed) are studded with pink, mauve or chalk-white crucifer flowers. The variegated form hardly needs its white flowers. Its rosettes of pale, cream-edged leaves have grown into large bolsters and look pretty without any floral adornment. 'Lady Greer', a tiny polyanthus with primrose yellow flowers grows here and so do a few plants of *Primula vulgaris*. I have no idea how the Shetland "Mayflooer" found its way into my garden, as the nearest wild colony is two miles away, on soil which is a good deal less acid than mine.

In March 1999, my younger sister died suddenly and unexpectedly. On the day of her

The great flowering of the willows begins.

Arabis albida.

Primula **'Peggy'**.

death, I was digging a new border on the east side of the Back Yard. I dedicated it to her, and it is always referred to as "Edith's Bed". There I have two rather unusual primulas, one of a primrose type, the other a polyanthus. The primrose was found by my friend Peggy Ramsay in the wild and I have named it after her. Its flowers are a dusky pink, dull close-up, but from a distance they take on a handsome peachy glow. The polyanthus has the same, but slightly darker colouring and has been grown in Shetland gardens since times immemorial.

My damp borders are still devoid of colour and the numerous primroses I planted there have long since been moved to drier quarters, except for 'Guinevere' which likes it damp and has grown into substantial clumps. Its light, warm pink flowers, produced both singly and carried polyanthus style on short, sturdy stems, look good against the dark, crimped leaves.

Primula **'Garryarde Guinevere'**.

Diary   **21st March**

Yesterday, the official first day of spring, I drove home from my weekly shopping trip. Weisdale valley was bathed in sunlight beneath a blue sky with billowing white clouds; oyster catchers were feeding by the side of the road. Suddenly the sea turned dark and a black horizon, just half a mile to the north, trailed curtains of snow across the land. I drove from spring straight into winter.

This morning the blue skies have returned, and I waded through knee-deep snow to reach the washing line. A pair of hooded crows, such beautiful birds in their elegant grey and black plumage, were balancing on the thinnest, flimsiest twigs of an alder, which they started to attack with great ferocity. They severed a few and gathered them in their beaks, then, as if deciding that spring had been delayed and nesting could wait, dropped

The view from my bathtub is an enchanting one in late March. A steep bank, planted with vincas, ajugas, anemones and large patches of *Primula juliae*, is spangled with blue and mauve and the first rhododendron is in flower. *Rhododendron praecox* sheds most of its leaves during the winter, which is no bad thing, as it shows off the flowers to great advantage. They hover like amethyst butterflies among the bare branches. It never ceases to amaze me how their thin, translucent petals survive the vagaries of early spring.

Weigela middendorfiana is another precious early performer, planted in the wrong place: a south-west facing bed where the wind bounces off the house wall and whirls around with great ferocity. I could have moved the weigela, but I like it near the garden's entrance as a spring

Weigela middendorfiana.

welcome. Instead I have provided some shelter for it with the help of two evergreens, tough old *Brachyglottis rotundifolia* and the graceful, tall-growing *Olearia virgata* 'Lineata'. The weigela comes into leaf early, sometimes in January, but somehow manages to preserve its spring-fresh looks until the flowers open. They are produced all along last year's wood; pale yellow blowsy foxgloves with fine orange spotting on the lower lip. In some years it produces a few more in September.

Climatic set-backs are fleeting and the garden's tempo starts to hot up from mid-March, especially if Easter comes at an early date, and with it the garden's first opening to the public. It always astonishes me how much I overlook, or make myself overlook, when the garden is for my eyes only. The nests of brown winter leaves wedged between the pots of spring bulbs, soggy prostrate fern fronds, and borders only half-cleared during my autumnal tidy-ups. Ignored for months, all come into sharp focus now. It usually takes about a week to have the garden ship-shape once more. Despite the spring bulbs and forests of young shoots, parts of it look dismal and bare, the soil compacted and heavy. I resist the temptation to loosen it, as there are always late-rising perennials and bulbs, which might become victims of my probing fork or trowel.

Instead I spread a mulch of bark or sieved garden compost, which brings instant transformation – rotting foliage, broken twigs, the whole detritus of winter – covered by a soothing brown blanket which shows up the bulbs and spring green to perfection. It also, unfortunately, shows up all the white labels like grave markers; which they sometimes are where a plant has succumbed. I've been meaning for years to replace them all with black ones, durable ones, the kind which can be inscribed with a sharp tool. Perhaps, one day, I'll get around to it. For now a little camouflage has to suffice. The garden always throws up small stones, or I bring them to the surface while digging or planting. These I place over or in front of the labels, grey stone instead of white plastic – a great improvement.

The final, and most enjoyable preparation for the great day is a re-arranging of my "Ladies in Waiting", a wide array of pot-grown plants. Many whose greenery sufficed during winter, won't do for spring and are taken behind the scenes. I scan the rows of plants in the nursery and borrow any which look their best and make a good background for the many spring bulbs I use as a welcome. When potting bulbs in the autumn I always prepare some special containers, anything which looks pretty and is suitable, shallow glazed bowls for crocuses and anemones, tall earthenware pots for tall narcissi. There might be an early-flowering shrub in the greenhouse, a blue-flushed *Cyanothus* or a *Correa* adorned with pink bells, and if the weather is clement enough, they are brought out for the day. All are grouped to complement and enhance each other, some on the ground, others raised on short wooden pillars. The garden is ready to greet its first visitors of the year.

Right: *Caltha palustris* **'Plena'.**

April

There are two kinds of April, one which comes as a continuation of all that was horrid about February and March: driving rain, hail storms, snow, sleet and howling wind which shakes the house and garden. During winter I don't mind, but with April comes expectations of something drier, warmer – better.

This is one of the busiest months in the garden. There's always some digging left to be done and more seeds to be sown. Herbaceous plants grow away apace and provide plenty of shoots for the taking of basal cuttings. Some might need dividing before they become too large; I might want to overhaul a border, or plant a new one. Work like this needs dry weather and reasonably friable soil, not mud which clogs up my tools and sticks to my boots like cement. This is where the other kind of April comes as a heaven-sent, at last a departure from the wintry theme, an April which sails in on the fresh, dry, easterly winds of a Baltic high. Once these have blown themselves out they leave cloudless skies, drying earth, and at long last, some warm sunshine.

Dicentras love my garden and they are a recurring and connecting theme in all its shady places. I don't mean the large *Dicentra spectabilis* – that flowers much later – but the smaller ones which carpet the ground with a dense forest of ferny foliage. *Dicentra eximia* is barely six inches high, with feathery grey-green leaves and stems of drooping, pink lockets. The vigorous *Dicentra formosa* is a little taller and must be curtailed now and again to prevent it from swamping its neighbours. A few of its brittle, fleshy rhizomes with one or two feeding roots attached, and planted in a damp spot, will soon cover a square yard. It has sage-green leaves and flowers of a

Left: *Fritillaria meleagris* 'Alba'.

Diary   **4th April**

Signs of spring have been around for weeks, the chorus of the blackbirds, the first patches of emerald green among the bleached grass of the pastures, and broody starlings which have started to dismantle our house. A pair has found a gap between the guttering board and the wall and has pulled out large wads of yellow glass-fibre insulation, which obviously hasn't passed the test as suitable nesting material. The lapwings have returned and in the evenings I can hear the whirring of snipes in the hills behind the garden. On the Alpine Slope *Lathyrus vernus*, the spring pea, has opened its first fragile legume flowers. This morning a willow warbler was singing in the shelter belt. And there was another song which carried strong and clear on the easterly wind. Jimmy Tait, our neighbour, is singing. A sure sign that spring has finally arrived, that the earth is warming up and the ground ready for ploughing. A sign more definite than all the bird song combined.

Lathyrus vernus.

Omphalodes verna.

dusky old rose shade. Both have become indispensable, lush and pretty for a long season, and putting up with the most inhospitable conditions.

I also grow their white forms which flower a little later, and bring a quality of purity and freshness. Their slim, pendant flowers are pale cream or white and look good with the light blue forget-me-not sprays of brunneras or *Omphalodes verna.* They feature in several parts of the garden, but being a little less vigorous than the species, occupy the choicer spots where the soil does not dry out in summer and where the wind blows in moderation. Left to their own devices, these small dicentras flower untiringly all summer, but regain much of their spring freshness when cut to the ground in late May or early June. They soon unfurl new leaves and are in bud again a few weeks later.

Dark-flowered cultivars such as 'Bacchanal' and 'Bountiful' have proved slow and difficult to establish, but the relatively new cultivar 'King of Hearts' is showing some promise. *D.* 'Stuart

Dicentra **'Stuart Boothman'.**

Sambucus racemosa **'Plumosa Aurea'.**

Boothman' is perhaps the most striking among small dicentras, with blue grey filigree leaves and flowers of a vivid cerise. It has a prominent place in one of the raised beds in the Sunk Garden where it looks very pretty with the large, violet-magenta goblets of *Tulipa humilis* 'Persian Pearl'.

The Sunk Garden is the warmest part of the garden, completely sheltered from the north, east and west, but being open to the south it receives every minute of sunshine, and the paving stones and retaining walls which soak up heat in the day act as radiators well into the evening. It takes an exceptionally wet and cold summer to make me lift and dry the tulips I grow there. Opposite the Peat Garden I have a small, east-facing bed, backed by clipped Japanese larches and dominated by a large, cut-leaved golden elder, *Sambucus racemosa* 'Plumosa Aurea'. This, cut back to two foot stumps in

March, shoots up to seven or eight feet again each year, and is clothed from head to toe in its deeply serrated yellow-green foliage, which emerges, in bronze-flushed, bright butter yellow. In spring, cowslips, brunneras and blue lungworts are in charge of this bed.

As children, my sister and I used to pick armfuls of cowslips in a water meadow not far from my parent's house. No matter how many we picked, my mother received them gratefully and filled small vases and jam jars with them to scent every room of the house. Each spring, since coming to Shetland, I longed for them, but it somehow never occurred to me to grow them in the garden, probably because they were not to be found on the plant and seed lists of the numerous mail order nurseries I dealt with in those days. I have already mentioned the surprises which might turn up in a packet of exchange seed, and a chance seedling which came up in a pan of meconopsis turned out to be the humble cowslip.

From one plant I now have many, and unlike their cousins the primroses, which need extra drainage and a little lime now and again to keep them going, the cowslips have no such fads. They grow enthusiastically in all kinds of soil and seed themselves into the bargain. Their drooping umbels of yellow flowers, each held by a long, pale green calyx, fit in anywhere and I like them best with water forget-me-nots or the airy, light blue sprays of brunneras. Their leaves, fresh and soft in spring, tend to turn coarse and dark once the flowers have faded, but those of *Brunnera macrophylla* 'Langtrees' are an exception: outlined with smudges of metallic grey they look pretty all summer.

Pulmonaria 'Mawson's Variety' has dark green, hairy leaves and deep, gentian blue flowers held by slate purple sepals, good with the pale blues and yellows of the brunneras and cowslips. I am very fond of this lungwort and also grow it with white snakeshead fritillaries, Bowles' golden sedge, and the white and lemon *Narcissus* 'Minnow'. *P. longifolia*, covered in speedwell blue just now, has grown into low wide mounds of overlapping leaves, long and strap-shaped, and heavily spotted in silver grey.

The common lungwort, *P. officinalis*, is too vigorous for small spaces and grows tucked in

Pulmonaria 'Mia'.

Pulmonaria 'Mawson's Variety' with white snakeshead fritillaries.

between shrubs and underneath trees, wherever there is room for it, and where its spotted leaves light up a dark place once the tree canopy has closed above it. Its flowers are pink in bud, then change to blue as they age, hence its common name, Soldiers and Sailors. *P. saccharata* has the same flowers, but better, broader foliage, splashed and mottled in green and palest grey, with the occasional all-grey leaf. Pulmonarias hybridise freely, and the best mixed marriage offsprings are worth keeping. Amongst my best are a vigorous grower with soft-pink flowers, and a Cambridge blue one with heavily spotted foliage named 'Mia'. All need cutting back to ground level after flowering to produce good new crops of leaves.

April is daffodil month, and because of that, a month I came to dread, and still do, but to a lesser extent. I had a brief infatuation with the daffodil in my early gardening days, when hungry for spring colour after a long dark winter, I vowed to fill my whole garden with as many different varieties as I could find. On closer and longer acqaintance I found many a bit too loud and brassy for my liking and grew tired of their company.

Daffodils (botanically narcissi) are very popular in Shetland, and they are everywhere, some in conducive settings and arrangements, as drifts of one or two kinds in grass, others (the majority) not. They are grown in large blobs or serried ranks, in jumbles of all kinds and all kinds of colours, shapes and sizes. They even turn up at road verges, large cultivars, in the harshest yellow imaginable, planted in straight rows against a backdrop of ling-clad hills, still in their mauve-brown winter dress. It makes me shudder, even as I write it down.

In my own case, the brief love affair was rapidly replaced by something bordering on hatred. I couldn't bear the sight of daffodils, and threw them out of my garden in large numbers. I still find many of the modern hybrids hideous, especially those circular combinations of white and orange, which to me, look like fried eggs on stilts. But hatred is an emotion hard to sustain, and has in turn been replaced by a much more balanced approach. I am now rather fond of

some daffodils and grow many, including a few large-flowered hybrids.

Even the most handsome ones amongst those have one major drawback: their dying, yellowing foliage hangs around forever, and most, along with *Narcissus* 'Van Sion', mentioned last month, have since been moved into grass. I still have some below the shelter trees around the vegetable garden, the bright yellow 'St. Keverne', the taller 'Carlton' with a primrose yellow perianth and lemon trumpet, and the milky-white 'Thalia', which isn't all that large-flowered, and looks nice with the darker forms of the flowering currant.

A few have been allowed to stay. The taller ones are tucked in among shrubs or grow at the back of a border, where later on, their dying is not obtrusive. The smaller ones have homes amongst clumps of herbaceous perennials, which do an admirable camouflaging job once the daffodils are past their best.

Container-grown plants, my Ladies-in-Waiting, are used in all parts of the garden, especially at both entrances to the house, and

... my Ladies-in-Waiting ...

favourite daffodils feature large in my April groupings. There is the tall 'White Lady' with long, elegant buds, a small, pale yellow cup, and broad, white suede-like "petals" drawn to sharp points. It used to be a popular cut flower in the 1920's and 30's, discarded in favour of "new and improved" cultivars, and now re-discovered in a hedgerow in Kent. *Narcissus poeticus* 'Praecox' is another white favourite with a tiny red eye, fetchingly twisted and reflexed perianth segments, and a heady scent. It flowers towards the end of April, a good month before the other poeticus narcissi.

I have an ever-growing collection of smaller daffodils: the little 'Quince' with a mimosa-yellow cup and pale, translucent perianth, 'Pipit' with small and perfectly shaped flowers and white-striped segments, and 'Jenny', a white and pale yellow triandrus hybrid. *Narcissus* 'Rugulosus' is grooved, rather than wrinkled as its name suggest, and has strongly scented yellow flowers with a flared cup and narrow twisted segments. I also grow the double form which is equally beautiful and has a full, soft, gardenia centre. On the whole I prefer the single kinds, but find 'Keats' irresistible: a tall growing white narcissus with broad, elegantly curved petals, and a tiny centre of threadlike greenish yellow segments.

I buy most of my special narcissi from Ron Scamp of Falmouth, Cornwall. His catalogue deals mostly with daffodils for the show bench and reads like the code of a secret society. Instead of descriptions you'll find abbreviations: 'Honeybird' 1Y-W (E), which translated means this narcissus belongs to division No.1 (trumpet daffodils), has a yellow perianth (Y), white trumpet (W), and flowers early in the daffodil season (E).

All daffodils in my garden grow happily in ordinary soil, in full sun or dappled shade, but the delightful white and lemon *N. canaliculatus*, found wild in the north of Italy, needs perfect drainage and a sunny spot. The hoop petticoat

Narcissus '**Jenny**'.

Erythronium 'Pagoda'.

daffodil, *N. bulbicodium*, is a great favourite of mine, and has grown into thick, grassy clumps, but produces its flared yellow bells rather sparingly. *N. bulbicodium* var. *citrinus* does a little better, especially when grown in a damp spot, and has flowers of a light lemon yellow.

Where other gardeners have drifts of daffodils in their borders, I have drifts of American erythroniums (trout lilies) in yellow, white and pink. In the shaded border of the Kitchen Garden are several large colonies of the sulphur yellow 'Pagoda', aptly named for the elegant, upward curve of its pointed petals. The flowers, several to a slender stem, are held well above the broad, maroon banded leaves. A large swathe of them, nodding in the breeze, is a wonderful sight. It does not set seed, but its white, fang-like roots increase freely. It also grows happily in thin turf and I divide it (and the others) after their leaves have died down in July or as soon as they appear in early spring.

Erythronium 'White Beauty' sets no seed with me either. When it pushes through the soil its buds nestle inside a tightly rolled funnel of leaves, like the ringer inside a bell. The leaves are a glossy green with pale, narrow banding, like the ripples left in the sand by the receding sea during a low tide. The flowers are ivory white and have a prominent red ring at the base of the petals.

I have two forms of the much smaller *E. revolutum*, one blush pink, one cyclamen pink, and both seed freely. Thick forests of tiny grass-

like shoots appear around the parent plants, broaden into small, banded blades in their second season, and take a further two or three years to reach flowering size – an event well worth waiting for. They grow near the Back Yard steps on the east side of the garden and share their quarters with *Cyclamen hederifolium*, small primroses, pink oxalis and other treasures in the shade of a lodgepole pine. The mixture of sand, peat and needle litter in this small bed also seems to suit the Canadian bloodroot, as it grows a little more substantial every year.

I have the double form, *Sanguinaria canadensis* 'Plena', with rounded, scalloped grey-green leaves and white flowers which look like tiny, full-petalled roses. Expensive to buy and said to be difficult to grow, I kept mine in a cold frame for several seasons before I dared plant it out. It has a tendency to push its pink crowns out of the ground, and I, fearful of losing my pampered darling, used to push them back in, like an anxious mother hen tucking her straying chicks back under her wings.

To the south of this small bed is a narrow, west-facing border. In April this is bright with spring colour, large mats of double white *Anemone nemorosa*, the lavender posies of *Primula vulgaris* 'Sibthorpii', wild yellow primroses and the lilac shuttlecocks of *Cardamine pentaphyllos*, held on arching stems above fingered leaves.

Erythronium revolutum.

Cardamine pentaphyllos.

Here I grow the dog's tooth violet, *Erythronium dens-canis* and if I'm lucky it might produce a tantalising few of its charming little flowers with their back-swept petals and long white, purple-tipped stamens. This European species is not nearly as prolific as its North-American and Canadian relatives with me. I have two forms, one with cerise flowers and another which looks white from a distance but is actually a very pale lilac. Tried in many different locations over the years, neither flower as freely as they could or should, but their rounded, maroon spotted leaves are a delight.

Trilliums are said to enjoy much the same conditions as the American erythroniums, but I have found them much slower to increase. I have two which I treasure: The white flowers of *Trillium grandiflorum* nod on short stalks above large, tri-partite leaves. They last for a long time, and as they age, the three broad, ribbed petals gradually change from white to apple blossom pink. *T. sessile* has leaves mottled in maroon and green, and upright mahogany flowers which look like the buds of a strange, slim waterlily. Trilliums and erythroniums are summer-dormant, and some prostrate, shallow-rooted plants like *Lysimachia nummularia*, ajugas, or the little dark, creeping fern, *Blechnum penna-marina*, planted as a second storey above their roots, keep the ground clothed once they have gone.

Tulipa tarda.

On the Compost Rock at the east end of the Kitchen Garden, *Tulipa tarda* has expanded its green, pink-flushed buds into white-tipped yellow stars, spread out above the low mats of sparkling green leaves. This is the oldest and most reliable tulip in my garden, flowering freely and increasing steadily. It isn't the least bit fussy, but prefers well-drained soil and a sunny spot. I have a nameless tulip, donated by my gardening friend Bertha Johnson, which also has great staying power. Its slim, pale-pink flowers are produced with great freedom, several to a slender eight inch stem, above sparse, narrow foliage.

Tulipa tarda grows beside a gnarled old, woody specimen of *Pulsatilla vulgaris* in a glorious clash of yellow and purple. I enjoy seeing them together, and there's enough green between them to stop the colours from biting each other. The pulsatilla is well past pension age, but still flowers spectacularly every April, its rich purple goblets wrapped in feathery down. Pulsatillas grow on calcareous soils in the wild and mine gets a dusting of lime every year. Countless others, bought from a variety of sources have inexplicably failed to establish, but a healthy batch of seedlings, raised from Scottish Rock Garden Club exchange seed, has sailed through two winters and looks set to flower as I write.

Cytisus x *kewensis* has also reached pension age. Planted at the top of the Compost Rock, its twiggy growth cascades over one of the large, upright boulders which give the bed part of its name. The other part is derived from the area behind the boulders, which was used as a compost heap by our predecessors. Unlike other brooms, which have come and gone, this shrublet, planted in 1979, shows no signs of ageing. Bright yellow buds open into slightly scented primrose yellow pea flowers all along its arching branches. The only attention it gets from me is a light clipping after the flowers have faded. Winter-flowering heathers, some hebes, helichrysums and shrubby artemisias get the same treatment at the end of this month or the beginning of the next.

Apart from the winter-flowering heathers, some of which are still going strong, small flowering shrubs are hard to come by at this time of year. *Berberis* x. *stenophylla* 'Corallina Compacta' is a notable exception with neat, dark serrated leaves and small tubular bells which change from coral red in the bud to orange vermilion in the open flower and last well into May. *Berberis empetrifolia* is another good dwarf evergreen, a prostrate shrublet with dark, needle-like, spine-tipped and maize yellow bells at the end of April. I find it hard to believe that this is one of the parents of *B.* x *stenophylla*, a large, graceful evergreen (semi-evergreen in full exposure), with arching growth and generous crops of small, apricot yellow flowers in early May. Its other parent is *B. darwinii*, smaller than its vigorous offspring with broader leaves and orange flowers from red buds. It is slow-growing with me and looks a bit of a mess most springs, not a shrub for a prominent position.

This is such an exciting time of year and in my daily search for new buds and flowers the handsome spring foliage of some plants is easily overlooked. In the Kitchen Garden, the leaves of *Acer pennsylvanicum* are a soft, luminous green against the red twigs and will soon be joined by long, drooping racemes of green flowers. *Hosta fortunei* looks striking with the pale green spears of its new leaves emerging from their mauve sheaths. *Sorbus aria* 'Lutescens' does indeed, as is often mentioned in books, bear a fleeting resemblance to a magnolia with its white-felted goblets of slowly expanding leaf buds.

To choose at least a few of one's plants primarily for their foliage pays off. Flowers, in most cases, are a fleeting affair, but the leaves remain on a plant for its entire growing season, all year round in evergreens. The leaves of many plants in my garden, especially in their fresh spring colouring are as good as, or better than the flowers. *Caragana arborescens* is an extraordinary sight in spring and could easily be mistaken for a much larger version of *Cytisus* x *kewensis*. On first emerging, its rounded pinnate

Sorbus aria '**Lutescens**'.

Valeriana phu '**Aurea**'.

the dark, tiny-leaved *Cotoneaster microphyllus* and blue-green *Rhododendron lepidostylum*. I've left the most striking until last: *Valeriana phu* 'Aurea' eclipses all with a glorious eruption of luminous butter yellow.

In the damper parts of the Back Yard spring always arrives late and at long last the black cottonwood, *Populus trichocarpa*, wafts its

leaves, still bunched and folded all along the branches, are a bright sulphur yellow. The yellow pea flowers appear when the leaves are fully expanded and have turned to a bright, golden green. It is underplanted, for foliar contrast, with

Diary   13th April

Snow has covered the ground for a day and a night and has melted away as quickly as it fell, but the garden is still in the grip of a fierce north-easterly wind, which chilled me to the marrow and bombarded me with hailstones. Plants take this kind of weather in their stride, and seem to generate their own heat. In the shaded Kitchen Border there is a neat circle of brown earth around every clump of foliage, while the bare patches of ground are still white. Large flocks of chaffinches and redwings have blown in on the wind and look settled for the time being, much to the annoyance of the resident blackbirds, who watched from the wings, in both senses of the word, as the redwings got down to an impressive act of formation feeding in the South Border. Who needs pre-emergence weedkillers with a flock of sharp-eyed, seed-guzzling birds around?

Snow in April.

Fritillaria meleagris.

bittersweet, resinous scent once more. This is discernable all year round in the leaves and sticky leafbuds, but carries strongly on the air as soon as the first young leaves unfold in spring. *Malus* 'John Downie' sulked for years in its windy home but has at last accepted the inevitable and decided to make the best of it. Its grey branches are thickly clustered with pink buds.

We do get "weather" well into April – and beyond, and some gardeners like to go on about it endlessly, complaining about the cold and wet and telling me that snow has never come so late. They might well be right, but the advance of spring continues undaunted, and every April, along with its many delights, brings snakeshead fritillaries. I only knew *Fritillaria meleagris* from illustrations before I grew it in my garden, and still, every spring I watch with fascination the spectacle of its emerging flowers. First the buds lie closely folded to the ground, pale and faintly tessalated, then slowly they rise, pointed like snake's heads, glittering and chequered until fully expanded into large, square-shouldered bells.

Most of mine were raised from seed and now they in turn seed themselves, into the most likely and unlikely places, equally happy in rich, moist peat, sharply drained sand and naturalised in grass. The majority I grow as a mixed lot of light and dark shades with the occasional white, but over the years I have done a little selecting,

by simply lifting bulbs in full bloom and grouping them according to colour. The whites together are lovely, some a pure, milky shade, others with faint green chequering. I also have some dark, glistening purples and a rather striking raspberry pink, which starts off disappointingly with buds of bleached mauve-grey.

Fritillaria pyrenaica is equally obliging and has the same large bells, but a little more rounded at the shoulders, and with the individual segments curled outwards at their tips. The flowers are a rich dark chocolate brown, overlaid with a waxy purplish bloom, and when tipped up, reveal an interior of lacquered yellow. This dark colouring, though stunning (at least for gardeners like myself who love such colours in flowers), can get lost in the garden and tends to look sombre all by itself. It needs other colours to lift it and set it off. One group rises from a carpet of gentian blue *Scilla sibirica*, another grows in front of *Carex solandri*, the New Zealand golden mountain sedge. But my favourite combination has the black bells mingling with pale yellow *Narcissus* 'Hawera' behind a cushion of an old-fashioned Dusty Miller style auricula with yellow-eyed maroon flowers. There is a yellow form of this fritillary, found in the wild, said to be just as easily grown, yet inexplicably rare in cultivation. After a lengthy search, I now have two bulbs, as yet unflowered.

Fritillaria pallidiflora also does well with me. Its stout, two foot stems are lavishly clothed in

Fritillaria pyrenaica **with supporting cast.**

Bergenia ciliata.

broad sea-green leaves and at their apex hang several large bells of palest, translucent yellow. *F. acmopetala* is a little more difficult to please, but has flowers of a most extraordinary colouring. Through the outer, apple green segments show the inner, brown ones, creating broad, curved stripes. I grow it in the Round Garden with *Bergenia ciliata*. The frost-tender leaves of this plant get reduced to pulp in colder gardens, but stay fresh and green in mine if cushioned from the wet soil surface by a layer of sharp sand. They are light green, fringed with long white hairs, and a perfect foil for the heads of clear pink flowers with their dark, contrasting cup of sepals.

When I started my garden I planted several bergenias, as I would hostas, in rich, damp soil and shady places, and lost them all. Since I have seen large carpets of their rounded, leathery leaves in Beth Chatto's gravel garden, I have given mine well-drained soil and now have several which do very well. 'Morgenröte' has flowers of a light cerise produced generously in April, and more sparingly all through summer and sometimes into autumn. 'Admiral' flowers in March and April only, but has the most exciting winter foliage of them all with whole leaves turning a vivid crimson. Their size does not

Rhododendron yakushimanum.

stand up to comparison, but otherwise the vernacular "elephant's ears" describes these leaves rather well, and mine, at the end of winter, just like the ears of older elephants tend to look a little torn around the edges.

There are two small shrubs in my garden whose flowering is eagerly anticipated each April. One has been with me from the very beginning and has survived my ignorance and the chaos of the garden's early days, for which I am very grateful. *Daphne retusa* was planted as a tiny rooted cutting and has over twenty years grown into a low, wide dome of darkest green. Among its small, leathery leaves hide clusters of purple buds which expand into white stars during the last days of the month. On a still, drizzly day they fill the east end of the Kitchen Garden with their heady scent.

My acquaintance with *Pieris japonica* 'Debutante' is a brief one by comparison. I found it in a supermarket, in full flower, and couldn't resist. Having planted and lost several of these evergreens in the past, 'Debutante' was destined to grace the Temple until I found out it came from the wind-swept, rain-drenched Japanese island of Yakushima. Still a tiny shrublet, it has neat, oval, bay green leaves of a hard texture and long, arching racemes of faintly-scented white lily-of-the-valley flowers. The pink buds are produced in the autumn and look prominent all winter. It shares its home in the Peat Garden with a compatriot, *Rhododendron yakushimanum*, which carries its flowers in small, dense trusses, carmine pink in bud, light, clear pink when fully open, then gradually fading to white.

On the Alpine Slope, *Erysimum* 'Bowles' Mauve' has produced buds since February. It starts to flower in late March, not mauve as the name suggests, but a rich, violet purple, above grey green leaves. It has two tulips as neighbours, the orange 'Shakespeare', and the slender, graceful *Tulipa turkestanica*, with narrow foliage and several flowers to each stem. As its straw coloured petals open, they reveal a yellow

... one nameless aubrietia ...

centre and striking black anthers. The *Erysimum* tends to be short-lived, a term which brings an immediate, negative reaction from many gardeners: they consider such plants not worth the bother and thereby deprive themselves of many first-class garden plants. 'Bowles' Mauve' is such a plant, and one I would not be without. Keeping it in my garden involves little effort, as cuttings taken in summer root with the greatest ease. In my ordinary soil it lasts no more than a couple of seasons, but with extra drainage its life span can just about be doubled.

Arabis procurrens 'Neuschnee' always looks a little threadbare when grown in soil, but in the dry gravel of paths it forms tight, dark green mats, smothered in white flowers. The mossy saxifrages will grow almost anywhere and come into their own now; their bolsters are spangled with small white, pink or red cups. But some of the other easy alpines, said to grow in any ordinary soil, will have nothing to do with my garden. The little alpine phloxes and helianthemums pack up almost as soon as I plant them, but flourish in gardens not many miles from here on that most sought after and elusive of growing mediums: a neutral, well-drained sandy loam.

Aubrietias, which swallow up whole rockeries in other parts of the country, curl up their toes as soon as they look at my garden. All like lime and got some for as long as they lingered, but it made not the slightest difference. I do have one nameless aubrietia now, begged from a gardening friend, and I treasure it as much as other gardeners would the rarest flower. Cuttings root easily, and several plants in the crevices of a dry stone dyke become a hanging garden of lavender-mauve each spring.

The common, deep blue grape hyacinth, *Muscari botryoides*, again rampant in other gardens, rarely lasts longer than a season or two with me, and I have long since stopped replacing it. But I have a pale blue, strongly scented muscari which is soundly perennial and I think might be *M. azureum*. The initial bulbs arrived as a flowering gift in a pot and have never looked back since I planted them out in light sandy soil. *Muscari ambrosiacum* does well in a mixture of sand, soil, and leaf mould and starts flowering in early May, a strong, tall grower with long grassy foliage and good heads of scented milky-blue flowers on one foot stems.

Corydalis solida springs a surprise on me every year. I have several small groups of it, but never see it emerge or grow. It suddenly appears and I always come across it in full flower. It makes a low carpet of rue-like grey-green leaves and has short spikes of larkspur flowers in dusky shades of pink and mauve all month, then disappears as quietly as it came. *C. cava* is a much larger plant, nearly a foot high and sometimes much wider; its luxurious foliage is a glaucous green and the flowers, in long, lax spikes, are a good shade of mauve. I also grow the good old yellow fumitory, *Corydalis lutea*, which would take over my garden with its seedlings, if I'd let it. All these plants with their translucent, glassy stems and thin-textured lacy foliage have a fragile, delicate look about them, but are remarkably robust. They get scorched by high

Euphorbia cyparissias 'Fen's Ruby'.

winds, but always recover. Only a hurricane will get the better of them.

The early spurges are looking good now. *Euphorbia cyparissias* has swallowed at least a

Diary   **19th April**

Three days of glorious sunshine, clear blue skies and a crisp, but gentle breeze to dry the ground. (Who could ask for a better birthday present?) I have spent every daylight hour in the garden, nose to the ground (sounds a bit like nose to the grindstone, but is exactly the opposite). Time has flown and I have enjoyed myself immensely, happy as a child in a sand box, starting and ending each day with a leisurely walk around the garden to find every new shoot and bud that was not there the day before. Pottering about is such a good descriptive term for this kind of laid-back gardening: moving plants which were in the wrong places, a little handweeding, very little digging, clipping some of the hebes, planning a new shaded border for the Back Yard. And best of all: the first al fresco lunches and afternoon teas on the deck chairs in the Round Garden. What perfect bliss. All the early clematis are out and *C. macropetala*, which has swallowed up the porch roof, is hung with thousands of dusky blue lanterns.

square yard of gound with its blue-green bottle brushes and lime-green bracts. Some gardeners avoid this plant because of its wandering habits, but I can never get enough of it and don't find it a nuisance. I also grow the remarkable 'Fen's Ruby' with pinkish stems and soft "needles" of a dark, bluish green. The tips of its bottle brushes are strongly flushed with red and give an extra glow to the lime-green flower bracts.

Those stems of the shrubby *E. characias* which are going to flower bend at the tips in winter and retain their nodding position until just before the buds open, a brilliant yellow green with little beady brown eyes in broad, cylindrical heads. It needs sharp drainage to survive a Shetland winter, and so does another shrubby species, *E. mellifera* from Madeira and the Canary islands. This has never flowered for me but is well worth growing for its stunning foliage alone.

Euphorbia palustris, as the name suggests, likes it damp and has flowers of a sharp, acid yellow, which start to colour in April and last until July. This wonderfully fresh and vivid shade is one of my favourite colours and I like combining it with purple, mauve, lilac and lavender. *Primula denticulata* provides all these shades and I prefer its cool blue tones to its reddish ones. The leaves of this plant, which look handsome and restrained enough during spring, can grow to an enormous size after flowering. I cut mine to the ground in June to stop them from becoming too overbearing.

Clematis macropetala, like all spring-flowering clematis, is best pruned immediately after flowering and should have received this treatment from an early age. Slow to start with, the secateurs never went near it, and once it had settled in, it was simply left to get on with the job. Some remedial action in recent springs

Euphorbia palustris with *Primula denticulata* (in foreground).

Clematis alpina 'Willy'.

keeps it (just) within bounds, but over the years it has grown to an enormous size and in places it sags like an old mattress. A hard and thorough pruning into its old wood is what's needed, but I am worried that the patient might not survive such drastic surgery.

Clematis macropetala 'Markham's Pink', flowers just as freely, and is trained against a low, north-facing wall, which it is scaling with some speed. 'White Moth', planted at the same time against the same wall still looks sparse and there are never more than a handful of moths on the wing each April. Being a form of *Clematis alpina* I had expected it to be more vigorous, perhaps it just needs another season or two to find its feet. *C. alpina* itself does well with me and so does the violet blue 'Frances Rivis', which clambers through a large weigela. *C. alpina* 'Willy', for want of a more suitable home, was planted against a very exposed, south-facing wall. It takes wind and weather in its stride and flowers in a pleasing, light shade of pink. The cultivar 'Ruby' is just as vigorous and lives up to its name.

In April there is still plenty of light in all those places which will be in deep shade once all the trees are in full leaf, and plants growing beneath them have to make the best of a short growing season. Where a month from now all will be green, touches of gentle colour run through my shady borders.

There are carpets of wood anemones in blue, white and yellow. *Anemone nemorosa* 'Vestal', a double white, does best with me and small groups are easily enlarged into drifts by breaking off small sections of its brittle, tangled rhizomes after flowering and replanting them immediately. The lilac *A. nemorosa* 'Allenii' is also a fast worker and its newly-opened flowers have a becoming pink blush, but the powder-blue 'William Robinson' is rather slow to increase.

Anemone ranunculoides is closely related to the wood anemones, a vigorous grower with generous amounts of foliage and flowers of a bright, clear yellow, easily mistaken for a lesser celandine from a distance. It has given rise to a paler coloured hybrid, *Anemone* x *lipsiensis*, a little taller than its parent, with primrose yellow flowers. All these share their quarters with vincas and ajugas, London pride, small geraniums, striped lamiums, spotted lungworts and the polished orbicular leaves of *Asarum europaeum*.

... moving plants around becomes an ongoing chore ...

These ground cover plants go on doing their bit and help to keep down the weeds long after the anemones have bowed out.

Primroses, prominent since March, continue all through April and often well into May. One of the most vigorous is 'William Genders', an old cultivar with an abundance of cherry pink, small-eyed flowers, produced both primrose and polyanthus style.

In a damp climate plant growth is exuberant, sometimes a little too exuberant, and I am often asked what kind of fertiliser I use. The answer is none. I simply return what I remove. Leaves, soft prunings and the remains of herbaceous plants are composted with a little lime and dried blood or fish meal and then used as a mulch, applied in spring. There is never enough to go around and where I run out, I substitute composted bark. Plantings of alpines

receive a topdressing of blue horticultural grit, tiny chips of granite, known locally as washed quarry dust. This eventually gets worked into the soil during weeding and planting and needs topping-up every second or third year.

Some parts of the garden also receive a dusting of lime from time to time. Gardeners on acid or neutral soil tend to provoke the envy of those gardeners whose alkaline soil prevents them from growing ericaceous plants such as rhododendrons, and I am often told how very lucky I am. In parts of my garden the soil consists of little more than raw peat and is extremely acid (below pH 5). Even plants which don't mind acid soil can't get the nutrients and trace elements they need, they soon look starved and turn their leaves a hideous shade of yellow. I don't test my soil, nor do I apply lime on a scientific basis, by making good deficiencies in a

The Round Garden in April.

carefully measured way. I simply apply it when and where I think it is needed and always guided by the looks of my plants.

Compost for the vegetable garden is made separately out of weeds, the larger prunings (chopped up), shredded paper and cardboard, sheep manure and kitchen waste. With sheep, cats and dogs to feed, there never is much of the latter. Nonetheless, kitchen waste can be smelly and its mixture of teabags, black banana skins and mouldy orange peel is always unsightly. I scatter it immediately with a handful of sulphate of ammonia, which helps to break it down quicker, and a camouflaging layer of wood shavings. Egg shells, a good source of lime, can take an age to disintegrate, a process considerably speeded up by baking and crushing them first. I gather mine in a small metal tray which sits on top of the Rayburn (Shetland's answer to the home counties' Aga), and after a day or two, they can be crushed into fine shards.

Towards the end of the month, if the soil is dry enough, and once all the digging is completed, I start planting out the first vegetables. Leeks, spring onions, peas, broad beans, lettuce and a range of brassicas from February sowings have hardened off in the cold frames. Its a job I enjoy and one that makes me feel virtuous: putting food rather than another bunch of flowers on the table.

Moving plants around, edibles as well as ornamentals, becomes an ongoing chore in April. From the greenhouse to the cold frames, from the cold frames to the garden. Some, like the vegetables, planted out, others, in pots, trays and pans, stood out for the time being. When there's a storm forecast, the order is reversed, those still moveable go from the garden back to the cold frames and those from the frames into the greenhouse, never finding enough space as some have grown in the meantime. Then, once the weather has settled down once more, we start all over again. Its a bit like musical chairs – with the weather playing the tune.

Diary   28th April

The month has rushed past, there are piles of work to be done, and I am not nearly ready to move into May. The trees are flushing and the first ferns are unfurling their fronds. Suddenly, the whole garden is green and luxurious. The blackbirds' song has been joined by the cooing of the collared doves from the shelterbelt, and the buzzing of bees and bumble bees. They love the willows and their pollen-laden catkins, and seem especially fond of *Salix hastata* 'Wehrhahnii'.

My precious new trug has been demoted today. Earmarked for genteel activities such as gathering roses and picking peas, and standing empty since my birthday, I have requisitioned it as my new tool box. Everything fits perfectly: a pair of secateurs, two trowels (one wide, one narrow-bladed), twine and scissors, pruning saw, knife, garden wire and pliers, a bag of labels, pencil and sharpener, and my essential knee pads and rubber gloves. I believe I shall *look* more genteel from now on, carrying my essentials in a brand new trug rather than a battered old bucket.

Salix hastata '**Wehrhahnii**'.

Right: *Primula* '**William Genders**'.

May

ost years May brings a "Little Summer" with clear blue skies, hazy sunshine and a fresh breeze to put a dry skin on the newly-cast peats. It also brings the first long, warm evenings, warm and long enough to renew our summer habit of after dinner strolls in the garden. With them comes a change in the light peculiar to those parts of the earth which are close to the poles. After sunset the air takes on a pure, crystalline quality which intensifies all colour and makes the gardeners a little light-headed.

The garden is fully awake again, the ash trees *Fraxinus excelsior*, bare for many months, have at long last expanded their dark brown velvet leafbuds and even the most prosaic of all trees, the sycamore, has its moment of glory now as the large leaf scales open into shrimp-pink "magnolia blossom" for a few brief days before the leaves emerge.

May, longed for since January, always arrives too suddenly, finds me overwhelmed and unprepared. Only yesterday I was pottering in the garden to my heart's content, moving plants around from dawn to dusk; now they are advancing fast and very soon will resent such interference. I have been deprived of my playground. I have to let them get on with their business, stand by and watch.

Still, May is a hectic month in the nursery and the garden, with everything growing at breakneck speed, and one job chasing another. For once vegetables take precedence over flowers and I get all my sowings done in the first week of May, unless there's a late blizzard, which has been known to happen. If the soil is still wet

Left: ... May is a green month ... . Above: The vegetable garden in May.

and cold I cover it with a snug layer of "Agrifleece", held in place by metal pegs. This is like very thin white felt, dense enough to trap the warmth, but porous enough to allow rain and light through. Sowing the vegetables is a well-rehearsed ritual. While I am adventurous in the ornamental garden, here I am a traditionalist, set in my ways. I use the same old and well-tried varieties year after year if I can get them, and sow radishes as row markers with all the slow germinators like parsnips and spring onions. Once all is done, those neat beds with their finely raked brown earth and straight rows of sowings bring a deep sense of satisfaction and achievement.

A final chore is keeping the cats off my fresh sowings, which used to be a headache in the past, involving, with varying degrees of success, all kinds of contraptions: plywood board, upturned margarine cartons, forests of sticks. Since my friend Gunnar Appel has let me into his secret, all I do is sprinkle my sowings with coffee grounds, which works a treat as long as I remember to top them up now and again.

Lambs also take precedence over flowers. There are years when the lambing goes like clockwork and years when everything seems to go wrong.

I have a Red Bed in my garden, not as a fashion statement, and planted long before hot colours became all the rage, but as a political one, and as a permanent celebration of May Day.

Diary

I have hardly looked at the garden for the last few days with the lambing in full swing and its share of complications. "Pot Noodle", christened thus by Anna, the tiniest lamb ever to be born on this croft, is a white ram lamb, the length of my hand, with brown ears, tail and socks and in need of several supplementary feeds a day. His mother, rather long in the tooth and far too old for motherhood, has barely any milk. A first time lamber is refusing to "breastfeed" altogether and kicks and butts viciously each time her lamb comes near her. James has tethered her in the front yard and I have to go and restrain her several times a day to give the lamb a chance to feed.

As if all this was not trouble enough, a lamb born yesterday morning was found spreadeagled and stone cold last night. We gave it all the usual remedies, a stomach tube feed, a sip of brandy, vigorous rubbing to get its circulation going and placing it in a warm oven (without garlic and rosemary). Lambs, even those at death's door, respond rapidly to this combination therapy and are usually on their feet within the hour, but not this one. We tried everything, but the lamb just grew weaker and weaker and by three o'clock in the morning we decided to let it die in peace. I wrapped it in a towel and cleaned some mucus from its mouth and, miraculously, it made a feeble attempt to suck my finger. We coaxed it into taking a tiny amount of milk from a bottle, freshly milked from the bursting udder of its mother. It could barely lift its head and would not have survived a night in the byre so we took it to bed with us to keep it warm. There is little a good night's sleep won't cure and the lamb, still a little unsteady on its feet, has been reunited with its mother this morning.

A headless James with double trouble.

The Red Bed one year after planting.

International Labour Day is inextricably linked with my German past and universally celebrated on the first day of the month, except in this country, where it gets conveniently squeezed into any date or is replaced by something called "Spring Bank Holiday". Quite an unsuitable label for this feast day and one sure to make Berthold Brecht turn in his grave.

It is quite apt that this bed should be linked to Labour Day, as much hard labour has gone into its creation. To make room for the extension to the house a large hole had to be scooped out of the Back Yard. Topsoil thus removed, was spread wherever it was needed, and a good bit of the subsoil was deposited (in a large mound) where the Red Bed is now. The stony, yellow clay had set like concrete. Peter Hamilton, who worked with me in the garden at the time, spent hour after hour with pick and shovel, loosening up the clay and removing the largest stones. Then we dug in copious amounts of garden compost, sand and peat, to open up its texture

and to give it a little substance and nutrition. For trees and shrubs we dug large holes and replaced the subsoil with the same mixture. Parts of the bed are still ill-drained, while others, those higher up the slope, are a little impoverished. This is no drawback and allows me to grow plants which like widely differing conditions, all together in a small space.

The Red Bed is on the western boundary of the garden and slopes gently away to the south-east. In May it is ablaze with scarlet tulips, vermilion wallflowers and the magenta drumsticks of a late flowering *Primula denticulata*. It has a background planting of purple-leaved shrubs such as *Sambucus nigra* 'Guincho Purple' and *Berberis thunbergii* 'Atropurpurea'. There are purple-leaved fennel and the large reddish leaves of the beetroot plantain, *Plantago major* 'Rubra'. All these plants, rather dark and sombre in themselves, create a pefect foil for red flowers, make them glow and smoulder. The bed has a large clump of the red and yellow *Kniphofia*

Kniphofia 'Atlanta'.

'Atlanta', which has its red and yellow season in June, but displays handsome coral buds in May. Small groups of candelabra primulas thrive in the damper areas, the silvered magenta *P. pulverulenta* and the scarlet vermilion 'Inverewe' which flower at the end of the month with the violet *Iris* 'Margaret Holmes'.

At the edge of the bed *Ourisia coccinea* from the island of Chiloe spreads out mats of bright green crinkled leaves and holds up spikes of scarlet waxy bells. This is sometimes a little shy flowering, with just a sprinkling one year, then a satisfying crop the next. There's no such dilly-dallying with the Chilean fire bush. Two specimens of *Embothrium coccineum* are my pride and joy and, after a hesitant start in 1996, are growing into fine trees. The larger of the two has flowered spectacularly since its 2001 debut, and the second followed suit two years later. Their spidery vermilion "honeysuckle" blossom looks startlingly exotic amidst the garden's less unexpected May flowers.

The Red Bed, planted aptly on the first of May 1992, is right next to the garden's entrance, and is thus often overlooked by visitors who tend to walk straight past it. But they can't fail to see it as they leave the garden. And if they leave it on the evening of a sunny day, they are enchanted. Backlit by the setting sun all the vibrant reds take on a stained glass brilliance.

I enjoy my garden's visitors, but I also like the days when the garden is closed and I have it all to myself – or think I do.

The damp borders in the Back Yard are the slowest to warm up and the last to come back to

Embothrium coccineum.

The most dreadfully embarrassing thing happened today. I was "writing" my weekly column for *The Shetland Times*, as I often do, in the garden, while weeding the South Border. Getting carried away a bit, I started talking to myself in "article speak", pretending to be Christopher Lloyd and trying to imitate his voice and accent. I looked up, and there, across the dyke, standing in the Kitchen Garden, was the motionless figure of a woman. My first impulse was to creep away silently and hide in the greenhouse, but just then the woman turned and our eyes met. "Oh there you are," she said, "is your garden open today?" There was no escaping now.

When Anna came home from school I positioned her where my visitor had stood, while I repeated my Lloyd impersonations in the South Border. She instantly destroyed my hopes for a sound barrier or bad acoustics in that part of the garden. "Of course I can hear you Mam, but why are you trying to sound like a man on the radio?" Too late now to ask my long-departed visitor to bear with me while I go to switch it off.

Cardamine raphnifolia.

shell pink flowers. The concertina-folded leaves expand into large, lightly pleated umbrellas in May. In the same bed I grow the double form of the cuckoo flower, *Cardamine pratense* 'Plena' with substantial heads in a fresh, lilac pink. Its leaves look like larger and slightly darker versions of bittercress and are often mistaken for it by inexperienced weeders.

Few gardeners would bother growing *Ranunculus acris*, the meadow buttercup, but I am fond of a pale variant called 'Sulphurea'; and its double form with tall, well-branched stems and small yellow rosettes looks very pretty. I prefer this airy, graceful arrangement to the much larger and more solid double flowers of *R. constantinopolitanus* 'Plenus', which grows just over a foot tall and has handsome fingered

life in spring. By May they are transformed. The large green pools of *Cardamine raphnifolia* are smothered in mauve flowers and *Myosotis scorpioides* 'Mermaid' has begun its sky blue season, which lasts until November. This water forget-me-not will grow almost anywhere as long as the soil is reasonably damp. The *Cardamine* too must have plenty of moisture, as in ordinary soil it flowers without much enthusiasm and is barely worth growing. The lined rhizomes of *Darmeria peltata*, the water saxifrage, lie above the soil like small, grey-green elephant's trunks. Pink, hairy stems rise from them in late April and open into loose umbels of

Darmeria peltata.

Cardamine raphnifolia **with** *Ranunculus constantinopolitanus* **'Plenus'.**

leaves, marked with pale grey. Both start flowering at the very end of the month. I still give a wide berth to the double form of the creeping buttercup, *R. repens* 'Plenus', as the single form is a pernicious weed in many Shetland gardens. *Ranunculus lyallii* from New Zealand, is the aristocrat of the genus and the most magnificent buttercup in my garden, with its rounded, leathery basal leaves and two-inch

Euphorbia palustris.

wide flowers of a pristine white with wavy-edged petals and lemon yellow stamens, displayed on tall, sturdy branching stems. To look magnificent it needs wet ground, where it will reach the great height of three feet. On ordinary garden soil it needs supplementary watering during dry spells.

Acid-yellow *Euphorbia palustris*, mentioned last month, has now been joined by the first pink campions and the purple candelabras of *Primula poissonii*. The stems of the later candelabras (I have a mixed bag of seed-raised plants) are starting to elongate now and show off their tiers of silver-dusted buds. *Osmunda regalis*, the royal fern, takes pride of place amidst a large carpet of blue water forget-me-not, where its symmetry can be admired from all sides, from the moment the pale orange green croziers unfurl, until the fountain of fertile fronds rise from the centre of the plant in July.

Molinia caerulea 'Variegata', reduced to grey stumps every autumn, is now, once again, flushed with spring green. Its feathery new growth is a delight of gentle yellow-green, striped with cream. Later on its hazy purple flowers are held well aloft on dark, hair-like stems.

Our native water avens, *Geum rivale*, is a handsome plant with its dark, leafy mounds and nodding pale apricot flowers held by maroon calyces. I also grow the pale yellow 'Lionel Cox', which flowers a little later. 'Leonard's Variety' is another excellent cultivar with nodding cups of a pale, creamy pink, flushed and veined with copper and burnt orange and contrasted by reddish stems and sepals. All three luxuriate in wet ground, but also make good garden plants in ordinary soil.

The dormant crowns and young leaf-buds of *Gunnera manicata* are highly susceptible to frost and I have lost several in the past through lack of winter protection. I now have a strong, vigorous plant (mulched with leaves and fern fronds during the winter), and from its shaggy brown buds pleated hairy leaves begin to unfold in May. It has the largest leaves of any plant suitable for a temperate climate, carried on two metre stems and almost two metres wide. Mine has some way to go before reaching its gigantic

... orchids, inexplicably rare in some years ...

adult proportions. Two of its tiny cousins also live in the wet part of the Back Yard. The prostrate khaki-bronze stars of *Gunnera hamiltonii* are a good contrast for the yellow foliage of *Lysimachia nummularia* 'Aurea'. *Gunnera magellanica* has shiny, rounded leaves, pleated like paper fans and fat burrs of crimson flowers in late summer. It increases by runners like a strawberry.

There is a change of mood in our hay meadow below the house as the blue haze of the spring squill fades and makes way for the great flowering of the orchids. We have two species growing there, the heath-spotted orchid, *Dactylorhiza maculata* in delicate appleblossom and sugar pink, and lovely carnation and campion shades. There's also a sprinkling of the northern marsh orchid, *Dactylorhiza majalis* ssp. *purpurella* with purple flowers. In some years both are inexplicably rare and confined to just a few locations, while in others they expand over a wide area.

The meadow is a glorious sight and I pay a visit to my orchids every day, and every day I find a few new ones where there were none the day before. They keep flowering well into June and turn the meadow's green carpet into a sumptuously embroidered quilt.

There is a small, steep south-west facing slope right in the middle of my garden where our predecessors kept their peat stack. The ground, acid loam with an iron hard pan underneath is buried beneath peat, both the fibrous brown sort, conducive to plant growth, and the black, hard lumps which are not. It was heavily infested with dock and couch and half-hearted attempts to clean it up were usually abandoned. It became a horticultural headache and remained "next year's project" for well over a decade, until I finally cleared and planted it in 1997. It is quite open to the easterlies and north-easterlies, a situation which is going to be remedied once the shelter trees planted along its ridge start to grow.

Just now it houses a wide range of peat-

Ranunculus amplexicaule.

loving plants on a trial and error basis, a number of ericaceous shrubs and, as tall plants never look quite right on a bank, a lot of low-growing ground cover. *Romanzoffia unalaschcensis* vanishes in July, then re-appears in September and keeps its fleshy, scalloped leaves green all winter. They soon form wide mats and in late spring, disappear below the rounded white flowers. *Calceolaria tenella*, the tiniest of all the slipper flowers, covers the ground with a light green film, spangled all spring and summer with little yellow pouches on thread-like stems. Underneath these filmy mats I have planted the bulbs of *Hyacinthina amethystina* (a minute relative of the large, beefy hyacinths I grow in pots to scent the house in winter) with narrow grassy leaves and, at the end of May, a sea of Cambridge blue flowers, in neat, short spikes. I have two small buttercups growing in this bed, *Ranunculus amplexicaule* with lance-shaped glaucous foliage and large white, cup-shaped flowers, and *R. gramineus*, with the typical small bright yellow flowers of the tribe and broad, grass-like leaves in a strikingly contrasting blueish green.

A favourite amongst May's tiny treasures is *Polygonatum hookerianum* with fresh green leaf rosettes and large stemless lilac bells, which open into five-pointed stars. The little creeping fern *Blechnum penna-marina* has fronds of a dark, bronze green which hardly show up against my soil, but interplanted with the polygonatum they become visible and in turn show it up to great advantage. Despite breaking up the hardpan with a pinch bar, the drainage at the foot of the slope is still poor. A state of affairs which suits the shallow-rooted greater butterwort, *Pinguicula grandiflora*, to perfection. Its basal leaf rosettes are like bright stars cut from thick, sticky, apple-green felt. In May, dark, slender scapes rise and carry large, long-spurred violet purple flowers. This is a colour combination I am very fond of and the butterwort has become a firm favourite in no time. It is also a favourite with my blackbirds who tear up and scatter the leaf rosettes. Perhaps they are attracted by the little flies stuck to the leaves, as the plant is insectivorous.

Anemone multifida lives a little further up the slope where the drainage is better. Its dark

Anemone trullifolia.

greenery is livened up by a fleeting display of cream cups, which are swiftly followed by large, long-lasting pale seedheads, made of tightly curled "lambs wool". *Anemone trullifolia* has a much longer season with the first buds opening in May and the last ones two months later. It makes low mounds of dark, strap-shaped leaves, cut into long fringes at their ends and has large pale blue flowers with widely spaced, rounded petals. There is also a white form which is just as easily grown in retentive, acid soil.

May brings the scent of rowan and whitebeam blossom. To shelter my Peat Garden I have planted three Chinese rowans: *Sorbus koehneana*, *S. prattii* and *S. setchuanensis*, small graceful trees with elegant pinnate foliage. *Sorbus chamaemespilus* comes from the European Alps and belongs to the whitebeam branch of the family. It is slow growing, has dark, glossy, entire leaves and corymbs of pretty pink flowers in spring.

Several small rhododendrons are at home on this peaty bank and one of the smallest I grow is *R. campylogynum* 'Myrtilloides Group', a ground-hugging shrublet smothered in tubular dusky mauve bells with a waxy, grape-like bloom. 'Crushed Strawberry' and 'Salmon Pink' are equally lovely in subtle, subdued shades of pink, again overlaid with the same bloom, glowing and translucent when back-lit by low, slanting sunlight. Another very small rhododendron is *R.*

Swedish whitebeam flowers.

Rhododendron 'Ramapo'.

impeditum, shaped like a broad mushroom, barely a foot tall, with tiny blue-green round leaves to match and, at the end of every shoot, a little cluster of amethyst blue flowers. 'Ramapo' has the same colouring, and despite its more upright growth rarely suffers any wind or salt damage.

The winter-flowering heathers are an asset again now, with their young shoots in vivid yellow, orange or bronze. Their April pruning always leaves them looking vulnerable, like someone who has just emerged from the hairdressers', pink-eared and self-conscious after rather a drastic short back and sides.

While rhododendrons love my acid soil, most do not take kindly to sea winds and salty air, and for that reason some of mine are huddled together in one place. The great gardener Margery Fish had a "Ditch Garden" where she grew shade and moisture-loving plants. My garden has an open drainage ditch, which collects the water from the byre roof to its south and the run-off from a steep bank to the north. The sea winds from the south and west pass over this byre roof, leaving the ditch and bank snug and sheltered. A perfect, but restricted space for rhododendrons – apart from the soil, or rather lack of it.

At the foot of the byre wall and among its stones thick layers of raw peat had built up over the years. Watered from the gutterless roof above, they make a perfect growing medium, but on the bank opposite there was hardly a scraping of

Diary   **19th May**

A whirlwind weekend, the house packed with visitors for James' 50th birthday, and no time for gardening or writing. I wish I'd photographed his face when his sisters (Helen and Alice) and best friend Bernie walked in "unexpectedly" (a closely-guarded secret which involved many clandestine telephone calls and white lies). The weather was glorious on the day and we partied into the small hours, drinking Champagne and dancing Samba on the Temple Terrace.

Guests always get preferential treatment, and having only one bathroom meant Anna, James and myself turned (temporarily) into the great unwashed. I settled in for a good, long soak after everybody had left and enjoyed the view from my bathtub, dominated by three wonderful rhododendrons. 'Winsome' with its blood-red funnels and dark, bronzed leaves, 'Alison Johnstone', a concoction of soft apricot and yellow above blue green foliage, and a nameless blowsy, sugary pink. Between them the vivid green of foxglove leaves, the flowering woodrushes in the byre wall, the white hearts of *Dicentra spectabilis* 'Alba' and a carpet of dark blue Ajuga spread out beneath them.

The Rhododendron Valley.

dark earth above hard-packed yellow subsoil. Large planting holes for the rhododendrons were, rather like those in the Red Bed, dug out with a pick and shovel and filled with a mixture of peat, sand and leafmould. Broad buckler ferns, with their feet in the ditch, grow along the byre wall and I use their withered fronds as a mulch for the rhododendrons, to build up a little humus above their roots. I don't know the names of them all, but the white 'Tibet' kicks off the season on the first day of the month, closely followed by the blush pink 'Osmar'.

Now, with a little more shelter I also have larger rhododendrons in other parts of the garden. Two are worth growing for their leaves alone. *R. lepidostylum* has glaucous blue foliage, which takes on subtle greengage tints in the winter. It grows into a low, spreading shrub and has lemon yellow flowers in late May and early June, often half-hidden amongst the new growth. *R. campanulatum* is one of the most striking shrubs in my garden. Its large, oblong-elliptic leaves are a deep laurel green with pale orange undersides and mauve petioles.

'Bow Bells', a dome-shaped Williamsianum hybrid with the orbicular leaves of this species, grows on the east side of the Kitchen Garden and carries loose trusses of clear pink bells. Behind and above it grows the white May broom, *Cytisus praecox* 'Alba', a tall shrub with arching growth, turned into a fountain of scented cream pea blossom each May. *C. praecox* has flowers of a pale primrose colour and the variety 'Allgold' is a deeper shade of yellow, but I like the freshness of the white May broom best. It is not a long-lived shrub and must be replaced before it grows gaunt and bare; it also needs secure staking in windy gardens. I preserve its youthful looks for as long as it is possible by trimming back its new growth after flowering with a pair of sturdy kitchen scissors.

The shady beds of the Kitchen Garden have a white and yellow theme just now. Of all the globe flowers in various shades of yellow and orange, I like a selection of the native *Trollius*

Trollius europaeus 'Superbus'.

europaeus known as 'Superbus' best, an elegant plant with cool, lemon yellow flowers. I grow it with *Ranunculus aconitifolius* 'Flore Pleno', the white bachelor's button. Its tiny white rosettes in airy sprays are like a bouquet of gypsophila to the trollius' yellow globes. I also have the "difficult and slow-growing" cream flowered *Trollius cultorum* 'Alabaster' which is neither with me and grows equally well in sun or shade, but needs plenty of moisture.

Two small members of the papaver family are great for lighting up dark corners, a job taken on later in the season by the Welsh poppy, *Meconopsis cambrica*. *Hylomecon japonica* could easily be mistaken for a pale, hairy version of ground elder, until its large yellow, silk-petalled flowers start to open. *Stylophorum diphyllum* makes basal clumps of deeply serrated leaves and carries crop after crop of clear yellow poppies.

Ranunculus aconitifolius 'Flore Pleno'.

This looks charming with *Omphalodes nitida*, a more rampant relative of the better-known *O. verna*, which keeps the stylophorum company by producing a few sprays of its forget-me-not flowers all summer.

Whenever I create shelter from the prevailing southerlies I also create shade in my south-facing garden. Rather than a problem, shade is a great opportunity, as all the little woodland plants which would perish in the open, grow safely when tucked underneath trees and in-between shrubs. At the eastern boundary of the garden I have a narrow bed which gets very little sun. There the new shoots of *Disporum sessile* 'Variegata' rise like pale asparagus from the earth in spring. As the stems lengthen and arch over, they display dangling cream bells and leaves broadly striped with cream. It grows with the dark mats and tiny pale green bells of *Mitella breweri*, the silver marbled leaves of cyclamen, and the great favourite of all children: *Arisarum proboscideum*, the mouse plant.

Arisarum proboscideum, the mouse plant.

Diary   **24th May**

I have just come in from the garden, drenched to the skin, my fingers stiff with cold. A fierce easterly has kept us all awake for most of the night. Anna, frightened alone in her room, moved in with us, and camped on the floor, wrapped in two quilts. The wind whistles through the chimneys and the house feels cold and draughty even with the central heating turned to full. This morning I rushed out to rescue what I could, carried pots of plants into the greenhouse until it could hold no more and covered my precious Canadian bloodroot with a plastic freezer tub, weighed down with a large stone. The whole garden is in motion, the trees are groaning, every branch and twig whipped into a frenzy by the hurricane force winds. Plants lie flattened against the ground, their pale leaf reverses exposed and torn. The ground outside the porch is strewn with a confetti of leaves and flower petals. And on the door step, like a peace offering, a tulip, long-stemmed and dew-fresh, picked for me by the tempest.

Disporum smithii is a plant of perfect symmetrical growth. All its stems, set with many pairs of warm-green leaves, arch gracefully out from the centre, their undersides hung with slim ivory bells. The closely-related Solomon's Seal, *Polygonatum multiflorum* has a much more haphazard way of growing, sending up shoots here, there and everywhere from its thick, wandering rhizomes. It has the same arching stems and leaf pairs as the disporums but is a much taller plant with greenish white flowers. Mine grows through a colony of sweet woodruff, *Galium odoratum*. This makes wandering, but easily curtailed, forests of hand-long, wiry stems, set with whorls of narrow, bright green leaves and pretty heads of starry white flowers. Its leaves

are odourless when fresh, but exude a sweet scent when dried or infused in liquids.

As a child I consumed large quantities of woodruff-flavoured icecream and sherbet, but as my tastes have become more adult I prefer May Punch: A bunch of freshly-picked woodruff is infused for a few hours in a bottle of light, white wine and a little sugar to bring out the flavour, then strained and topped up with half a bottle of well-chilled champagne (sparkling springwater will do if you feel frugal). This spring cocktail has a light green colour and a distinct, delicate and refreshing flavour. It is best enjoyed al-fresco – weather permitting.

Many years ago I read a book called "The Essential Earthman" by the American gardener and writer Henry Mitchell. Lent to a succession of gardening friends it never returned, but I clearly remember one sentence, which went something like this: "Wherever human beings garden magnificently there will be magnificent heartbreaks."

My gardening hardly fits into the magnificence bracket, but the heartbreaks do, just now and again, when the fierce spring winds forget that they belong to March and not to May. They shake the barely expanded leaves off the trees and can turn young, tender shoots black within hours. Tulips, with their brittle, succulent stems, always come off worst and I have long since stopped growing some of the taller and more susceptible varieties. Those I still grow all have a supporting cast of herbaceous plants or low shrubs to lean on when the wind blows them sideways. The inky purple 'Recreado' is planted among pink dicentras, the scarlet *Tulipa praestans* 'Tubergen Variety' with a large group of *Erysimum* 'Bowles Mauve', and pink 'Gordon Cooper' leans against my sweet bay (*Laurus nobilis*), outside the kitchen window.

I have a soft spot for lily-flowered tulips and their graceful outlines. All are tall and I grow a wide range of them in four-litre pots. They do duty around the front and back door and I also use them for "cheating" by popping them, their

Lily-flowered tulips in the Round Garden.

container well camouflaged, into beds which need a temporary chromatic lift.

Some of the smaller tulip species do well in raised beds where the drainage is good and the shelter of small shrubs creates little sun traps. Two of the best are the striking scarlet *Tulipa linifolia* and the apricot-flushed yellow *T. batalinii* 'Bronze Charm'. But the most prolific and showy is 'Little Beauty', bright magenta with an indigo-stained white throat. These also look good grown in old-fashioned, fluted clay half-pots.

Tulipa sprengeri always escapes the spring gales by postponing its flowering to the very end of the month, or even until June. It is an elegant, slim-line tulip with long, graceful stems, narrow leaves and flowers which open to a bright vermilion scarlet from pale buff-orange buds. Like *Tulipa tarda*, mentioned last month, it has great staying power, is unfussy regarding aspect and soil, but increases its small bulbs fastest in well-drained soil.

New life is stirring in the ferns, one of the great, slowly-unfolding dramas in the May garden. After the old, tattered straps have been cut away from the Hart's Tongue Fern, *Asplenium scolopendrium*, the tightly-curled new fronds sit huddled like a cluster of pale snails at ground level, before slowly expanding into broad, glossy green, wavy-edged ribbons. The leaf buds of the golden-scaled male fern *Dryopteris pseudomas* are covered in golden brown shaggy "fur" before they turn into magnificent plumes of luminous yellow green. This is perhaps the showiest fern in my spring garden and beyond, as the fronds remain a rich warm green all summer.

Tulipa 'Little Beauty'.

Hart's Tongue Fern.

Onoclea sensibilis runs happily in boggy soil in full sun, its pale fronds flushed with tawny orange. I used to grow *Matteuccia struthiopteris*, the ostrich plume fern, in a shady border, where much of its beauty was wasted, as I could only see it from one side. Moved to an open bed with rich damp soil, it shows off its green shuttlecocks to perfection. The numerous forms of the soft shield fern, *Polystichum setiferum*, look graceful and luxurious with their airy fronds of finely spun green lace. Good contrast to these mossy or lacy textures comes with *Polystichum acrostichoides*, the Christmas fern, and its "ladders" of smooth, polished green.

After many years in my garden, the adiantums or maidenhair ferns still delight and surprise me. A more fragile looking plant than the tiny Himalayan *Adiantum venustum*, with its black, hair-like stalks and flimsy filigree greenery, could hardly be imagined. Each winter I fear for its life, yet each May, without fail, it unfurls its delicate young fronds and so does its slightly larger cousin, *Adiantum pedatum* 'Aleuticum' which has the same ethereal quality.

Another small treasure is *Asplenium trichomanes*, the Maidenhair Spleenwort; unlike the adiantums, this is evergreen with tiny, rounded "leaflets" arranged in neat rows along its thin, dark stems.

I like the strong contrasts between fern fronds and the calm solidity of large hostas with their mounds of rounded, overlapping leaves.

Polystichum acrostichoides.

Hosta fortunei in both its plain and yellow-margined from and *H. sieboldiana* 'Elegans' form large colonies while blue-leaved 'Halcyon', 'Wide Brim', blue green with a broad edge of cream, and 'Frances Williams' with large green and primrose yellow seersucker leaves, are good as background or specimen plants. Small-leaved cultivars such as 'Thomas Hogg', pale-edged dark green, and handsomely twisted, white-centred *H. undulata* var. *univittata* provide vigorous seasonal groundcover.

All are beautiful when their young, tightly furled leaves first emerge from the earth, but one is outstanding: *Hosta fortunei* var. *albopicta* has scrolled leaves of a luminous butter yellow, edged in palest green. These pale margins gradually darken and the yellow turns to soft primrose as the season progresses.

Towards the end of the month *Aquilegia flabellata* opens its first buds. They are mauve, delicately washed with purple and green like a water colour sketch on wet paper. A touch of these subtle shades remains in the cream and lilac flowers, held above luxurious mounds of glaucous, fan-shaped leaves. There is also a cream form with shorter stems and more greyish leaves and several dwarf forms. They lack some of the elegance of the taller ones, but are perfect for windy locations. Unlike other columbines, which are a promiscuous race, these come true from seed.

The large cream flowers of *Aquilegia fragrans* appear at the same time and exude a fresh, crisp citrus fragrance. My cross between this and *A. flabellata* has resulted in seedlings of true hybrid vigour, much larger than either parent (a cuckoo raised by a pair of meadow pipits), with plants three feet high and almost as wide, large luxurious leaves and flowers of a pale ice blue with the strong scent of their fragrans parent.

Aquilegia discolor is the tiniest columbine in my garden, less than ten centimetres high, and revels in dappled shade where the soil has been lightened with sharp sand and spent potting compost. The blue, cream–centred flowers are in

Aquilegia discolor with *Ranunculus amplexicaule*.

perfect scale and are set off by pea green leaves. *Semiaquilegia ecalcarata* enjoys the same condition and dangles maroon thimbles on wiry branching stems above carpets of ferny leaves.

I also have large numbers of the old-fashioned granny's bonnets, singles, and tucked and pleated doubles, in a wide range of colour. They need curtailing by cutting off their stems

Semiaquilegia ecalcarata.

immediately after flowering, or their offspring will take over the whole garden. A tall plant raised from exchange seed as *Aquilegia recta* "Edelweiss" has bronzed foliage and large flowers of luminous chartreuse yellow. It too comes true from seed, which it produces in copious quantities. I have it in coarse grass and as an edging to some of the beds in the vegetable garden. 'Nora Barlow' is a delight with its cream, green and pink "hedgehogs".

The beautiful, bi-coloured, long-spurred hybrids flower a month later, but never last long with me, except for 'Crimson Star', which perpetuates itself with the odd seedling or two, showing a little pink or apricot variation on the original white and red theme.

In the south border, which has its main season from July to September, I grow a few spring-flowering Shetland stalwarts: *Geum* 'Borisii' with never more than a sprinkling of orange-red saucers, and the much more rewarding *Veronica gentianoides*. This makes neat, low mats of pointed, shining evergreen leaves and carries slender spikes of pale speedwell flowers. *Geum* 'Georgenberg' has flowers of a light, blunt orange, freely produced. These contrast vividly with the airy purple sprays of *Geranium pyrenaicum*.

Geranium phaeum opens its first buds towards the end of the month. Above tall, leafy clumps sit short spikes of dark flowers, their maroon, satin-textured petals lit by cream stamens. This is a great companion for the pale yellow pea flowers of *Thermopsis villosa* or the pink pompoms of *Allium schoenoprasum* 'Forescate'.

May just wouldn't be complete without auriculas. I adore them, but sadly can't grow them. Two small patches in the garden, one maroon, one violet, only just keep going despite all the preferential treatment they get. "Old Dusty Millers", show auriculas, and Barnhaven doubles all, sooner or later, dwindle away. They simply don't like growing on peat, regardless of how much sand, lime and well-rotted cow manure I provide them with. Pot culture, in a

Thermopsis villosa.

mixture of sterilised loam, coarse sand and garden compost, is the answer. I now have a small collection which delights me. They hold prominent positions amongst my Ladies-in-Waiting and grace the south-facing window ledges of the house.

Along with the spring flowers arrive the insects which like to feed on them. Aphids, thrips and capsid bug rarely cause any significant damage, but the tiny leaf-guzzling caterpillars of tortrix moths can reach plague proportions and defoliate trees and shrubs almost over night.

I have long since stopped using insecticidal sprays in the garden, though I still use them very occasionally in both my glasshouses. Since the shelterbelts around the garden have grown up and trees and shrubs inside the garden have reached a more substantial size, great numbers of

Diary   28th May

The caterpillars have arrived again. They spin the new leaves of shrubs and trees together and, safe in their green tents, set about devouring them until there is nothing left. All the new growth on *Cotoneaster lucidus* has taken on a sickly brown look and I was going to prune back the young shoots and burn them this morning, to get rid of the caterpillars, but someone else has beaten me to it. I watched for nearly an hour from the kitchen window as a female blackcap set about meticulously pulling caterpillar after caterpillar from their green hideouts. She returned several times during the day and when I checked the bush in the evening I could not find a single one. A lot of the work done by my garden fauna goes unnoticed. The other day, while searching for some pots below the greenhouse staging I came across a spider's web studded with winged greenfly.

migrating birds arrive each spring and autumn. Shelter is rare in this tree-less landscape and entices the birds to settle in for a good spell and

Garden auriculas.

to feed to their heart's content. They take care of the pests and I take care of the weeds.

I would have to do a lot more hand weeding were it not for the numerous dense carpets of ajugas. They are such obliging plants, happy in sun or shade and content in any kind of soil, or even without it. They have their moment in May when the short stems, closely set with coppery purple bracts and whorls of lipped blue flowers, rise from their basal leaf rosettes. *Ajuga reptans* 'Atropurpurea' has glossy copper leaves; 'Burgundy Glow' is a delightful concoction of pale green, pink and cream and 'Variegata' has sage green leaves marked with generous cream splashes. The most vigorous is the white-flowered 'Alba' with dark, bronzed and crinkled foliage, excellent groundcover in even the most difficult places. *A. reptans* 'Catlin's Giant' is another fast worker with large glossy rosettes and tall spikes of a good, deep blue. 'Purple Torch' is a pinkish mauve, but 'Pink Elf' has flowers of a clear, light pink. 'Braunherz' is a blue-flowered German cultivar with perhaps the most striking foliage of them all, a deep, varnished maroon, which takes on beetroot tints in winter. *A. pyramidalis* is the most impressive in flower, with tall, substantial spikes of intense blue.

Ajugas are great cover for spring bulbs and ideal candidates for tapestry planting. *Chrysosplenium davidianum* will hold its own amongst all but the most vigorous, and lights up the dark theme with its pale hairy leaves and loose heads of soft yellow saxifrage flowers.

On one of my steep stony clay slopes I have fountains of the tawny orange grass *Carex* 'Coman's Bronze' rising from large mats of purple-leaved bugle. *Papaver rupifragum* has seeded itself there and *Euphorbia cyparissias* has formed running colonies. The silky apricot poppies look stunning against the lime green of the euphorbia and the copper and blue of the ajuga.

Epimediums are a delight now with their young foliage marbled with bronze. *E.* x

Chrysoplenium davidianum.

versicolor 'Sulphureum' is a vigorous plant with yellow, white-spurred flowers and has formed sizeable patches over the years. The German 'Lilafee' has lilac and white flowers from deep purple buds. Their fragile, delicate looks hide a cast-iron constitution. *Vancouveria hexandra* could easily be mistaken for a large, beefy epimedium with the same wiry stems, marbled leaves and cream flowers. A large carpet of it in the shade of two Swedish whitebeams, takes over once the early spring bulbs have gone.

But May is a green month, with green in a thousand different shades and hues from the emerald of new grass to the fresh, light tones of young leaves in the trees. These greens are the very essence of spring, of new life and rising sap and I never tire of them and their endless

Vancouveria hexandra.

Iris pseudacorus **'Variegata'.**

variations: the cream-striped swords of *Iris pseudacorus* 'Variegata', the pale hairy scalloped leaves of *Meconopsis villosa*, soft to the touch and gentle on the eye, the large ribbed and glossy hearts of *Myositidium hortensia*. The little Japanese woodlander *Peltoboykinia watanabei* would be worth growing for its name alone and is a delight with dense clumps of overlapping palmate leaves, flushed bronze and pale orange. Another plant which looks striking in May is *Astilboides tabularis*. Its coiled new shoots are densly covered in soft white bristles, and the large rounded leaves are pale green, dimpled in the centre and scalloped around the edges.

Diary   31st May

The redpolls have returned. I couldn't believe my ears when I heard them call to each other this morning. Last year a pair of mealy redpolls made the garden their home and gave us an anxious time. Poppy "the killer whale", our black-and-white cat has been known to pluck small birds out of mid-air. The redpolls escorted her on all her walks, one on either side, swooping low, too low for safety, while trying to frighten her off with high-pitched alarm calls. The cat just ignored them, didn't think these tiny birds a meal worth the effort of stretching out a paw. They raised a brood of five and after the leaves had fallen off the hawthorn we found their tiny nest.

The second equally surprising and much appreciated return was that of *Glaucidium palmatum*, moved last year from a tiny gap between two fast encroaching rhododendrons to a more open position. For weeks this spring I checked its new site, but all I encountered day after day, was the large white plastic label. Finally I could wait no longer and, leaving a wide margin of error, carefully dug out a large lump of sodden peat behind the label with a small fern trowel and found – nothing. Given up for dead, and suitable mourned, here it is, in *front* of the label, in all its glory.

Right: *Glaucidium palmatum.*

June

At Sixty Degrees North, June brings a rare delight to the garden, when, during the days of the "Simmerdim", the sun barely dips below the horizon, and an Arctic glow illuminates my garden at midnight. Plants are bathed in a mysterious soft light, white flowers hover, pale and ghostly, in mid-air or dance above their leaves, all yellow glows; blue grows translucent, red turns to black velvet and all green sparkles. This is a most exhilarating time, and humans as well as animals, delirious with joy, have been known to succumb to a touch of midsummer madness. It has been said that birds fly upside down, sheep roll over cattle grids, owls hoot at noon, and salmon leap onto dry land. It is difficult to lull the children to sleep with the sun still high in the sky long after bed time, and the most passionate of gardeners have been known to stay up all night.

June's weather doesn't always live up to expectations, and after the delightful spell of May's little summer, can be disappointingly cool and damp. Thick fog shrouds the islands for days on end and makes it impossible for aeroplanes to land, delaying the mail and midsummer visitors.

All is lush and luxurious with not a patch of bare earth in sight. In the vegetable garden juicy radishes are ready to pull, the first lettuces have been cut, and brown soil has given way to neat rows of greens. With all danger of frost past, the greenhouse is almost empty, its mobile inhabitants enjoying their summer holiday in the great outdoors. Field crops, always last on the spring agenda, become a pressing priority now. Winter cabbage needs to be planted, and swedes and main crop carrots give good yields from an early June sowing. Some years we also grow a

Left: Hostas are unfurling their large seersucker leaves.

All is lush and luxurious.

few rows of Shetland kale, a strain of cabbage kept going in the islands for centuries.

After spring's abundance, some of the garden's shady places are all-green once more, and if June is exceptionally cool, nature holds its breath for a week or two before getting into its stride again. I have two plants which bridge this

Shetland kale.

Diary   **2nd June**

The garden is rushing from spring into summer and I am dead-tired. We walked home from Jimmy and Ellen's at half past three this morning after putting the world to rights and discussing the intricacies of crofting and gardening in Shetland – with the help of a bottle of malt whisky. It was a wonderful morning, still and blue, mist rising from the fields and not a cloud in the sky. Jimmy gave us a large bundle of kale plants. His, set in April, have grown to an enormous size already. There was no time to lose. I stayed up, planted all two hundred of them, then did some much-needed weeding in the Sunk Garden.

I'd never worked in the garden at this time of day before. The silence was extraordinary – not a breath of wind, and a dewy freshness to every leaf and blade of grass.

gap between late spring and early summer. *Hesperis matronalis*, known as Sweet Rocket in Shetland, seeds itself freely where I want it – and where I don't. Several old plants have grown into large, woody stands, three feet tall, among the shelter plantings to the south and west of the garden and flower in early June with rounded heads of strongly-scented white or pale lilac flowers. Honesty, *Lunaria annua*, a biennial, seeds with even greater freedom and the forests of young plants can become quite a nuisance in the wrong place. I have both the white and purple-flowered kind, weed out what I don't want and leave the rest. Their bleached papery seedcases are a welcome winter feature.

There is another plant which often bridges the June gap. *Celmisia spectabilis* with its strap-shaped, silver-grey leaves, looks impressive all year round, but charms in early summer, when white-felted buds open into large, pristine daisies. I have it in several locations in the garden, and in a large stoneware pot at the gate, to greet my June visitors.

Lunaria annua **with golden elder.**

Celmisia spectabilis.

June is the month of the blue poppies and there are many in my garden, planted and well-placed by the gardener, and self-sown, and often better placed, by themselves. I first saw *Meconopsis betonicifolia*, many years ago, in a famous Scottish garden, great numbers of it massed into an island bed where it looked stiff and awkward, and the blue flowers, under an equally blue sky, were drained of colour. Such

dignified plants need a dignified, all-green setting and a little dappled shade to intensify their colouring.

In a small bed, opposite the Peat Garden, they are hidden from view and only become visible as you stand right in front of them. An expanse of glorious sky blue, their tall stems are set with large, wavy-edged saucers against a backdrop of soft-textured green from a clipped Japanese larch behind them. In the same bed I have the arching blades of *Luzula nivea*, a large expanse of *Hosta fortunei* var. *albopicta* and *Dicentra spectabilis* 'Alba'.

As well as *M. betonicifolia*, I also grow *Meconopsis* x 'Lingholm' (fertile blue group) with large lampshades in a brilliant peacock blue. Despite their liking for peaty soil and a cool, damp climate, blue poppies are a far from common sight in Shetland gardens, and doubts have been cast on their perennial status. The secrets of success are simple: never let a young

Meconopsis x 'Lingholm'.

Paeonia delavayi.

plant flower before it has developed more than one crown; if you do, it will die after flowering. Always plant in humus-rich, but well-drained, soil. To keep old plants in good heart, divide them roughly every three years, as soon as they have finished flowering.

This fabulous plant is easily raised from seed, sown in late winter/early spring, or as soon as ripe in August. In my garden, self-sown seedlings have turned up since I have abandoned the long-handled Dutch hoe in favour of handweeding in all my borders. A trowel, used on hands and knees, is a much more discriminating tool.

Tree peonies flower this month and are one of June's great delights. The very first shrub I raised from seed was *Paeonia delavayi*, destined (like so many others) to become a pot-grown inhabitant of the Temple, as in my early gardening days I could not imagine a thing of such great beauty surviving outdoors. It has now grown for many years in the shelter of a Swedish whitebeam at the east side of the Kitchen Garden. In May hard, round buds appear among its large, glaucous fingered leaves and a month later they expand into bloom. The flowers, beautifully poised on short, curved stalks are shallow bowls of Chinese lacquer red, suffused with coral and vermilion and filled to the brim with stamens of a tarnished, orange gold. Such beauty has to have its downsides. It is a rather lanky shrub, sparsely branched and looks black and gaunt when leafless in winter. Perhaps this is mine rather than the peony's fault, as I have never dared to prune it hard.

P. delavayi var. *ludlowii* has equally stunning foliage and smaller, clear yellow flowers, with petals of a thick, waxy texture. This had outgrown its allotted space in the Kitchen Garden, was cut to the ground and moved to new, and less sheltered quarters in the Back Yard, where it has subsequently grown into a nicely shaped bush.

June brings many such rare treasures.

Notholirion bulbiferum, a member of the lily family has sent up five-foot stems of dusky mauve, sparsely clad in long, narrow foliage and set with wide-mouthed lavender bells all along their upper halves. The flowers have cream-tipped petals and elegantly curved cream stamens. It is monocarpic and dies after flowering, but always leaves plenty of seed and some small bulbs around the parent plant. These will take at least two years before they reach flowering size, and plants raised from seed can take three or more. This makes it easy to keep a succession going and to have some in flower every June.

Lilium mackliniae used to be a member of the *Nomocharis* tribe when first discovered in Burma, but has since been re-classified as a lily. It is not only breath-takingly beautiful, but easily grown and long-lived in moist, but well-drained peaty soil. It's height varies, sixty centimetres (two feet) when there's ample rainfall, half that in a dry spring. Dark, leafy stems carry several white, pink-stained flowers at their apex, hooded flared bells, scrolled, waxy and thick-textured as if carved from ivory or marble. To see those first buds open makes my heart leap every June. Its small bulbs increase but resent disturbance. The plant is easily raised from seed and flowers after four or five years – an event well worth waiting for.

Nomocharis are closely related and have the same habit of growth, leafy stems with four or five exquisitely beautiful flowers at their apex. They are painfully slow to increase, and as with the lily above, seed is the best option. The nodding saucers of *N. aperta* are a clear orchid pink and a dark-spotted centre adds to their attraction. *N. pardanthina* has flowers of a light, clear pink. The three outer segments are uniform and smooth-edged while the three inner ones are fimbriated and paler towards their crimson-spotted basis. A truly flamboyant display.

Lilium oxypetalum var. *insigne* also started life

Lilium mackliniae.

Nomocharis pardanthina.

Thalictrum aquilegifolium.

as a *Nomocharis*, and looks a bit like a poor relation living in reduced circumstances (plain dress, rather than ballgown). It has been in my garden since 1987, flowers freely and increases well. Each bulb produces a large, hooded bell of sombre lilac on a foot-tall, leafy stem. Mine looks good with *Thalictrum tuberosum*, which grows to roughly the same height, has grey-green filigree foliage and large (for a meadow rue) four-petalled cream flowers with a powder puff of yellow stamens.

Thalictrum aquilegifolium reaches lofty heights of five or more feet and its branching stems carry wide, flat heads of violet-mauve or creamy-white flowers consisting of nothing more than bunches of coloured stamens, creating a starry thistle-down effect. I grow them in rough grass with dark columbines and, for strong contrast, in front of a golden-leaved elder.

Olearia 'Henry Travers' is a little slower growing than some of the other New Zealand daisy bushes and worthy of a choice, sheltered spot. It makes a medium-sized, tallish bush with dark, narrow, serrated leaves, white-felted on their reverses and very effective in a breeze. Unlike other olearias which produce their composite flowers in corymbs of varying sizes, 'Henry Travers' displays them singly on short petioles and for good reason. They are large, as much as two inches (5cm) across, with long, lavender ray florets and striking purple centres. It is one of the loveliest shrubs in my garden and a marvellous sight when in full flower.

Some of the June-flowering alliums are my pride and joy, but were my despair not all that long ago. There is nothing quite like the great violet globes of *Allium christophii* or the deep lilac spheres of *A. aflatuense*, but both, sooner or later, started to dwindle on my heavy, peaty soil. Now, with a fat little cushion of sand or grit spread below the bulbs at planting time, I have persuaded them to stay. Even with this preferential treatment they don't increase and I buy a few more bulbs every autumn to enlarge my colonies. *A. hollandicum* 'Purple Splendour' has survived several winters in ordinary soil and is showing great promise. I have it in several parts of the garden, but like it best mingling with the flamboyant *Euphorbia griffithii* 'Fireglow'.

Other alliums are much easier to please. Near the steps which lead from the lawn down to the Temple Terrace I have a group of the subtle, but impressive *Nectaroscordium bulgaricum*, a tall grower with a starburst of cream, purple and caramel bells. Like most alliums, this is bare-stemmed by the time it flowers and I have it tucked into a gap between *Sedum spectabile* and *Phormium cookianum*.

The foliage of most ornamental onions is nothing much to write home about, but there are a few notable exceptions. One such is the spring-flowering *A. karataviense* where the typical spherical inflorescence, green and white at first, then changing to lavender and grey, rises

on a short, stout pinkish scape between a pair of broad, tongue-shaped leaves. These are sage green, overlaid with a waxy purple bloom, ribbed with fine parallel lines and look pristine for as long as the flower does. The rampant, yellow flowered *Allium moly* also has good, substantial foliage, reminiscent of lily-of-the-valley leaves, but glaucous grey rather than green. They are its major asset in my garden as flowers are only grudgingly produced. It grows enthusiastically in sun or shade, wet or dry.

The leaves of *A. schoenoprasum*, better known as chives, are good to eat and their flowers give colour and a little kick to salads, and that's where their uses usually end. They are highly ornamental plants with generous crops of mauve flowers and handsome parchment seedheads and should not be confined to the vegetable garden. There's a pink cultivar (mentioned last month) as well as a rather good white form which shows up well in shade and opens its large, clover flowers from purple-stained green buds.

Two smaller species do well in the sandy soil

Allium hollandicum 'Purple Splendour' with *Euphorbia griffithii* 'Fireglow'.

of the Alpine Slope. The bright blue *A. caeruleum* is viviparous and produces small bulbs instead of seeds from its fading flower heads. It is outshone by *A. cernuum* with its starburst of carmine purple bells. From just one bulb to begin with and with a little help from the gardener, I now have several small colonies. Sadly some gardeners are put off by the smell of ornamental onions, which is only discernable close-up or if the plants are crushed or bruised.

There is a group of bulbs which gladly puts up with the prevailing stodge in my garden: Camassias like it rich and damp. Their leaves, like those of most alliums, have often withered by the time the first buds appear, and the tall spikes of starry flowers look a bit lost by themselves, but tucked in between herbaceous plants, they are marvellous. *C. leichtlinii* ranges from cream

Camassia leichtlinii.

Diary   **18th June**

Disaster has struck the garden and all the birdsong, blue skies and sunshine can't lift my black mood. I'd noticed in May that some of my Asiatic primulas had failed to make much progress, but didn't bother to investigate. We've had no rain for over a week now, and this morning I found a whole bed of candelabras spread-eagled. I lifted them all, effortlessly, and found, amongst their root remains the tell-tale curved grubs of the dreaded vine weevil. And that was only the beginning. Too depressed to do any work in the garden I visited Joan Nicolson (my neighbour). She was kneeling on the path, dividing and replanting *Primula* 'Wanda' and offered me a large clump – it was dripping with weevil grubs.

Not only will my garden never be the same again, I've obviously passed this dreadful pest on to hers.

through ice-blue to the deepest campanula shades, and enjoys itself between irises and hostas in the damp borders of the Back Yard, and the shorter, darker blue *Camassia quamash* is very much at home in a patch of grass which will later be shaded by the big leaves of a gunnera. They also look good behind the fine chervil leaves and cream tassels of *Aruncus aethusifolius* or the broad, glossy, white-edged foliage of *Luzula sylvatica* 'Marginata'. The large bulbs of this plant are said to have formed part of the North American native diet. Mine haven't increased sufficiently yet to give them a try in the kitchen.

I used to have a great passion for Asiatic primulas, especially the candelabra types, and raised hundreds from seed until, in the mid 1980's, weevils decimated their numbers and cooled my passion. For almost a decade I grew none, but now, with the help of slow-release pesticides mixed into potting compost, and

Diary   **19th June**

I didn't sleep much last night, and this morning, as soon as decently possible, headed down the road to Joan Nicolson's once more. I found her in the same spot, splitting primulas – and squashing fat white grubs. (She's well into her seventies, but out in her garden every day of the year.) With my heart hammering I asked her for how long she'd had them in her garden. When she answered: "For as long as I can remember," I managed to resist a strong urge to hug and kiss her, but couldn't repress a gleeful, almost shouted: "Isn't that great!" When she threw me a puzzled look, I stammered: "I mean it's great that you can still grow all these primulas despite the weevils."

Lifting and cleaning every primula in my garden seemed an impossible task yesterday. Now, on the wings of vindication, it looks decidedly feasible.

Primula helodoxa.

parasitic nematodes watered onto the garden in June and September, I have started a new collection, some as before, raised from mixed seed, but also a few of the species. *Primula bulleyana* has orange candelabras composed of large individual flowers and a good dusting of white farina on stems and leaves. The crimson-*P. wilsonii* var. *anisodora* smells of aniseed when crushed. Its flowers are small, and the tiers widely spaced, but its colour is rare amongst candelabras and a few plants look good amongst the predominantly orange and apricot hybrids and also go nicely with the pink shades of *P. japonica*. *Primula helodoxa* is an impressive tall plant and carries several large tiers of fragrant, lemon-yellow flowers.

In a climate as damp as this one, they don't need a bog or a waterside setting and are quite happy in ordinary garden soil, where their leaves don't grow quite so large after flowering.

At the east end of the Kitchen Garden, in the needle litter of an old Japanese larch, I grow *Primula alpicola* with flowers in shades of cream, primrose and dusky mauve, and a warm, foody scent of vanilla, nutmeg and honey. It is one of the most easy-going of all the Asiatic primulas, prolific in flower, with old plants carrying thirty stems or more, and great for picking. It will grow anywhere and self-seeds free into dry gravel paths.

Primula secundiflora is nearly as easy (it will draw the line at the gravel path) and just as

Primula alpicola.

prolific. Its colouring is more definite, clear magenta bells in large drooping clusters open from dark buds dusted with silver farina. The foliage of *P. sinopurpurea* looks as if cut from pale green suede and is as good as the flowers. These are carried in loose umbels, two or three to a stem, their cool, fresh lilac accentuated by a white eye.

Quite often, during the spring rush, plants I have raised from seed have to vacate their spaces in the cold frame, to make room for the new. There is rarely time to select a perfect spot in the garden, and as most are as yet unflowered, it can be difficult to find conducive surroundings for them. Most are simply planted where there is a vacant piece of ground. Some remain, others are moved, often several times, until I have found just the right neighbourhood for them. Many plants are good solo-performers, and some look fine, in harmony with their surroundings, where they have been "stuck in". There are many such happy coincidences in my garden, plant combinations which are as good, or better than the ones I've dreamt up. Still, most are contrived and bringing them about counts amongst the most exciting and pleasurable of all gardening activities.

Some gardeners carefully plan their borders on graph paper during the winter, then plant them just as carefully and strictly to plan the following spring. I envy them their foresight and power of visualisation. In my experience plants which look good next to each other on paper don't necessarily do so in the flesh, they might grow shorter or taller than described, or their flowering fails to coincide.

Instead of precise planting plans I prefer to use long lists of suitable plants for a particular location, made suitable by their liking for a given soil or situation first, and then according to shape, tone, habit, texture, colour of leaves and flowers. I don't always get it right first time, especially when the planting contains plants I am unfamiliar with. They might outgrow their space rapidly, or not fill it at all; their flower

colour, known only from a catalogue description might not live up to my expectations or jar with the colours around it.

Diary   **26th June**

I must have walked around the garden at least a dozen times today, with a trug-ful of *Primula sieboldii* in full flower. They are a delight with their fringed petals in pastel pinks and lilacs, but wherever I tried them they looked wrong. Finding the right place for them seemed an impossibility until I spotted the first flowers of *Meconopsis quintuplinerva* (Farrer's harebell) in the Peat Garden. Its subtle lavender bells looked drained and dingy next to its neighbour, the whiter-than-white *Cardamine trifolia*. I lifted it, replanted it further down the slope and filled the space it left with my primulas, a great improvement.

Primula sieboldii.

The Spanish *Saxifraga trifuricata* also has whiter-than-white flowers and is often mistaken for a superlative mossy saxifrage by visitors. Rosettes of dark green, deeply fringed leaves grow into large bolsters, firm yet springy to the touch, and make impressive features. In damp and shady places they tend to sag a bit with time and need to be pulled apart and re-planted now and again. In well-drained soil and full sun they are much slower growing, but remain tight and solid.

Paeonia veitchii 'Woodwardii'.

In June clouds of small white flowers on much-branched wiry stems hover above them. A fine show in itself but also a fitting neighbourhood for plants with large, showy flowers, but not much foliage to support them. *Incarvillea mairei* fits this bill. The huge cerise magenta trumpets are quite out of scale with the short scapes and sparse basal leaves of this plant. The flowers open wide at the mouths to reveal thick, white chalk marks radiating from the yellow throats, and are replaced by long, pointed, purple-spotted seed pods which look impressive until they split open in September. In a group by itself the *Incarvillea* looks clumsy and incongruous, but behind a green bolster and veiled a little by the white saxifrage flowers, it is a picture. I also grow it in front of *Paeonia veitchii* 'Woodwardii', a small species with good foliage, bronzed when young, and clear pink saucers, held, two or three to a stem, on short, nodding pedicles.

I have already mentioned nostalgia flowers. Some belong to June and are inextricably linked with my Catholic childhood. Every May and June my sister and I used to walk for miles most Sundays, and so did everybody else who had two healthy legs. The whole village walked, in a slow-moving procession in time to the prayers and chants of nuns, priests and altar boys, and the sounds of the brass band and church choir. The night before, streets and pavements were scrubbed clean, makeshift altars erected, trestle tables draped in best linen, and silver crucifixes, taken from the privacy of farmhouse bedrooms, were hung on barn doors. Life-size blue and white clad plaster virgins were brought down from attics, dusted and placed on green rugs, intricately woven from bracken fronds.

Processions were a popular pastime during my childhood, and for all I know still are, in honour of the Virgin Mary, to bless the crops in the fields, and to celebrate the birthdays of

Dicentra spectabilis.

and a dark, almost sinister-looking columbine with pleated flowers of a blackish maroon and bright yellow stamens. I also remember the evocative smell, evident as soon as the cloth was lifted the following morning, not a scent as such, as none of these flowers have any perfume, just a peculiar, but pleasant, flowery smell.

I now grow the blowsy *Paeonia officinalis* 'Rubra Plena' in the Kitchen Garden, a floppy old thing which needs the support of short peasticks to keep its large heavy flowers upright. There is something incomparably opulent in those wide cups, crammed full with satin crimson petals, and I love to bury my face in them, even in the knowlege that there are always earwigs lurking in their depths. The *Dicentra*, a good bit taller at three feet (90cm), grows behind the peony, pink and white hearts dangling from arching stems. With them I have a large plant of *Geranium maculatum* which flowers at the same time with clouds of pale lilac discs above the mounds of hairy, fingered leaves.

Chrysanthemum leucanthemum, the marguerite of my childhood, grows in the meadow behind the house and in the vegetable

minor and major saints, of which there are many in Catholic Bavaria.

Dressed in our first communion whites, my sister and I carried baskets filled with strewing flowers and no matter how hard we tried to eke them out, they never lasted the course. They were picked the night before, covered with a cloth and kept in the cellar. I remember the precise contents of my baskets to this day: white, yellow-centred marguerites, crimson peony petals, the rounded lockets of *Dicentra spectabilis*,

Chrysanthemum leucanthemum **with black Tuscan kale.**

Paeonia officinalis '**Rosea**'.

garden with black Tuscan kale, a clear case of mutual enhancement. I have yet to find a black columbine.

I also have the double pink and equally floppy *Paeonia officinalis* 'Rosea', which flowers a little later. The single red and non-floppy *P. officinalis* does well in a shady border where it seeds itself about and its dramatic greenery and scarlet seed pods add a touch of excitement in autumn. None of the lactiflora peonies will have anything to do with my garden.

Peony flowers fade away as quickly as they come and leave June to the irises, poppies and geraniums. I wish I knew all the correct names of the many irises in my garden which have lost their labels over the years. There is no doubt about *Iris chrysographes*, which I grow in both a blue and violet form, their falls delicately marked with gold. There is even less doubt

about *I. chrysographes* 'Black Form'. No other flower gets as close to black as this one, with its broad velvet falls and smooth satin standards, a strong contrast to the apricot tissue-paper flowers of *Papaver rupifragum*. The double form of this poppy has flowers composed of several "crumpled silk" layers.

Iris setosa is an excellent foliage plant with

Iris sibirica **cultivar.**

broad, sword-shaped leaves, handsome from the minute they appear, stiffly upright and stained purple at the base, then arching at the tips as the wedgewood blue flowers unfurl from inky-purple buds. The dwarf form of this, barely a foot (30 cm) tall, has the same broad, grey-green foliage, and flowers of a sophisticated lavender-grey.

Iris 'Desert Dream', is a vigorous plant, with large flowers of palest yellow, overlaid with orange-buff and beautifully veined with a warm, reddish brown. *Iris sibirica* has been in my garden from its very beginning and has put up with many moves, as its flowering is brief and its large grassy clumps take up a lot of space in a border afterwards. It revels in moist, peaty soil in the Back Yard and I cut it to the ground after flowering to refresh its tired looks. I have several different colour forms ranging from white through various shades of blue and purple, and all are un-named. It needs full sun as well as moisture to flower freely. Of all the irises in the garden, this species has the most intricately

marked flowers and I never tire of admiring the Persian carpet patterns on its falls.

The yellow flag, *Iris pseudacorus* grows abundantly in Shetland's coastal wetlands and I am content to enjoy it there. But I rather like its pale yellow form 'Pallida' in my garden, whose luminous flowers show up over great distances.

Most of my Oriental poppies are seed-raised and most are red with a greater or lesser dash of orange; some have black ladybird spots at the base of their petals. I also have a few named varieties: 'Black and White', which speaks for itself, a good red called 'Türkenlouis' with fringed petals, the delicate pink and somewhat frilly 'Victoria Louise', and the strangely grey-pink 'Cedric's Pink'.

The individual flowers of *Papaver orientale* only last for a brief spell, but to watch those great, rounded buds swell and split and see the crumpled petals emerge like butterflies from

Papaver orientalis **'Victoria Louise'.**

Diary   **11th June**

It's June and I should be in the garden. Torrential rain keeps me indoors. Even the dogs, always eager for a long walk, were glad to return to their warm byre after a quick morning round. I felt sorry for the lambs, standing still and hunch-backed in the fields, their dripping wool neatly parted along their spines to reveal a line of pink skin. An eery silence has descended on the garden, even the ever-chattering starlings are silent and look miserable. Just before the rain started we had a long bitter cold spell with freezing easterly winds blowing straight in from coldest Siberia. My mother, who is here on holiday, is convinced this was a late visit from the Ice Saints: Pancratius, Bonifatius, Servatius and Cold Sophie, who bring a chill to German gardens from the 12th to the 15th of May each year.

Ourisia coccinea.

their chrysalis is one of the great spectacles of mid summer. In a cool climate it takes several days for the sun to iron them and then another spectacle takes place, the slow expansion of the petals, revealing at their centres, a ring of quivering, blue-black stamens.

The flowers of irises and Oriental poppies are fleeting, just how fleeting often depends on the weather, which, even in June, can be unpredictable, with cold, windy snaps and heavy rain, which, once set in, can last for days. I always feel sorry for garden visitors who arrive on such days, and if they're not too numerous, I ask them into the house for a hot drink and to dry off.

Ourisias which shrivel away to nothing in warm climates, love this kind of weather. The leaves of *O. macrophylla* are dark-green, crimped and slightly scalloped around the edges and make very good evergreen groundcover. The white flowers are borne candelabra-style in tiers up the stem, held by black pedicles, and backed by the light green cocktail umbrellas of the calyx. It, and the red Chilean *O. coccinea* (described last month), gave rise to the salmon pink hybrid *Ourisia* 'Loch Ewe', which flowers a little half-heartedly, but looks good when grown in a sizeable drift. 'Snowflake', the smallest ourisia in my garden, grows in pure peat, roots as it goes and produces fresh green rosettes of broad, pointed leaves, notched with deep maroon. The short stalks are also dark and in stark contrast to the drooping heads of snow white flowers.

Like most white ourisias, this hails from New Zealand and has a rather flamboyant compatriot neighbour, *Bulbinella rossii*, a member of the lily family. Before flowering it could be mistaken for a large sap-green leek with ascending layers of broad, strap-shaped leaves. From their centres rise strong two-foot

Bulbinella rossii.

(60cm) stems, their upper half closely packed with little star-shaped flowers of a luminous maize yellow. Its home is some of the sub-Antarctic islands between the South Pole and the South Island of New Zealand, where it grows with an enormous, dusty pink *Anisotome*.

In my garden the *Bulbinella* has to make do with the less spectacular *Anisotome lyallii* from Stewart Island, a lusty-growing member of the carrot family, with dark-green celery leaves and large, domed heads of white umbellifer flowers. It is evergreen, and continues to grow during mild winters, while turning an occasional leaf, composed of many individual leaflets, bright yellow to good effect.

I also grow the much smaller *Bulbinella hookerii* with narrow bronzed foliage and small conical heads of soft orange. It enjoys the same soil as *Lithodora diffusa* 'Heavenly Blue', peaty, acid, but free-draining. This prostrate, evergreen shrublet is much admired when covered with gentian-blue stars in June and July. I also grow the white form, which has flowers of a

... the Sunk Garden comes into its own ...

skimmed-milk blue and a season which stretches into August and beyond.

In all the shady places foxgloves send up their tall spires and the first buds begin to show a little pink, mauve or milky-white. At the end of the month they begin to reveal their dark spotted throats. Some of the hostas only break dormancy in early June, now their great ribbed or seersucker leaves are beginning to expand. Lupins feature in almost every Shetland garden. Their bright candles flank paths and tower high above drystone dykes, lighting up the landscape. I know some magnificent stands in the north of the Shetland mainland, which are still going strong after more than two decades, yet with me they barely last two seasons. They soon grow woody, their crowns fall apart, flowering becomes sparse or stops altogether. Some years, when I feel I can't do without them, I raise a batch from seed, preferably in their separate, named colour strains, if I can get them. Sown in June, the seedlings are wintered in cold frames,

planted out the following spring and rarely flower before August in their first year.

Lupinus nootkatensis from Alaska, bears scant resemblance to the well-known Russel hybrids. It only grows to about three feet (90cm) and all through June its mounds of silver-green foliage are covered with short, loose flower spikes. In books these are often depicted as blue and white. The form I grow is more striking in its combination of light blue and bilberry mauve. It is naturalised not far from my garden, along Tresta Burn, a stone's throw from the sea.

From late May onwards the Sunk Garden comes into its own. It is a small paved area, surrounded by raised beds, and planted in a restrained, tone-in-tone colour scheme of pinks, purples, soft blues and all the shades in between, with the odd stab of scarlet and crimson to liven things up. Mats of purple thyme and pale pink *Antennaria dioica* grow between the paving slabs, where *Crocus tommasinianus* flowered in February. Grey-leaved sedums and large

Aquilegia vulgaris **var.** *stellata.*

cushions of sea pinks, *Armeria maritima*, cling to the retaining walls, mauve-pink in their wild form, bright cerise in 'Vindictive'.

Columbines feature large in the Sunk Garden, and *Aquilegia vulgaris* var. *stellata* still holds its pink or white saucers aloft, long after the granny's bonnets have finished. No matter how soon I cut them to the ground, some already ripe seed always escapes. The seedlings, once the long roots have gained a foothold in stonework, are hard to remove, and so are those of meadow rue. I mean to weed them all out ruthlessly, but now and again they earn a reprieve by seeding themselves in just the right place, in front of the blue-leaved *Rosa glauca*, or where the flame-red of an Oriental poppy adds a touch of drama to their mauve and lilac haze.

The cherry-pink lockets of *Dicentra* 'Stuart Boothman', on the east side of the Sunk Garden, have now been joined by the round, magenta flowers of *Geranium cinereum* 'Subcaulescens'. The fat pink spikes of *Stachys officinalis* 'Rosea' rise behind mats of pale pink sea campion and a dwarf form of *Geranium endressii*, with neat mounds of foliage and generous sprays of little chalk-pink cups.

I have two more sea campions growing on the Alpine Slope, 'Robin Whitebreast', a neat, grey-green cushion with white flowers and light apple-green calyx and the large, tangled mats of *Silene uniflorum* 'Plena' with double white flowers the size and shape of spray carnations on long, trailing stems.

The dusky-maroon *Geranium punctatum* is often confused with *G. phaeum*, but easily distinguished from by the five dark spots on its jagged leaves. It has a long flowering season and needs a light background to show it off to best advantage.

Hardy geraniums play an important role in

Geranium sanguineum **var.** *striatum.*

almost every part of the garden, and when grown in a large variety can be had in flower from June until September. *Geranium macrorrhizum* with its tangle of brown stems and rounded aromatic leaves is indispensable in shady places, where it forms large, more or less evergreen mats. It will grow without attention for many years, but is all the better for an occasional splitting and replanting. The flowers are a blunt shade of mauve in the species, a bright magenta in 'Bevan's Variety', white with a prominent red calyx in the form 'Album', and a soft pink in 'Ingwersen's Variety'. 'White-Ness' is a smaller and slower-growing plant with pure-white flowers and pale green leaves.

They self-seed and most of the seedlings have a knack of placing themselves exactly where they're needed, in dull corners, at the base of a north-facing wall where spring bulbs have left a gap, and in a scraping of soil where a path widens to make room – for a geranium. They look best in large groups of one colour and the pink form shows up well from a distance.

The prostrate, creeping *Geranium dalmaticum* could almost pass for a dwarf form of 'Ingwersen's Variety'. A hybrid between the two, *G.* x *cantabrigiense*, is intermittent in size and has flowers of a clear lilac pink. *G.* x *magnificum* has the largest flowers of them all, intricately veined and a rich violet purple above mounds of light, hairy leaves. *G. himalayense* is another good violet blue, and better with back-lighting from the setting sun, which it gets in one of the terrace beds across from the Temple. It has a creeping rootstock and needs a place where it can be allowed to roam free. *G. himalayense* 'Birch Double' has small (half the size of the former), rosette-shaped flowers in a muddle of purple, lilac and mauve, and with me only runs in light, sandy soil.

Rhododendron ponticum.

Many of the smaller cranesbills provide colour in raised beds and on the Alpine Slope. Magenta *Geranium sanguineum* and its pretty pink form *striatum*, a mixture of seed-raised *G. cinereum* with ferny leaves and flowers in strong, crushed-raspberry shades, and the light pink, purple-veined 'Ballerina', are among the best.

The rhododendrons have finished their flowering and whenever I find the time I do a little dead-heading and pinch back a shoot or two to keep them growing compact and leafy. *Rhododendron ponticum* is much maligned for its indestructibility and free-seeding habits, and considered no more than a weed further south. In my garden it is a star. At the end of June large trusses of light, clear amethyst flowers open above the dark green leaves, fresh and luminous at dusk and dawn. Gardeners who avoid this plant should take a close and unprejudiced look at it, as its beauty rivals and surpasses that of many hybrid rhododendrons. As much as I would like it to, it does not seed with me.

Clematis montana spent more than a decade in my garden, producing strong, twining stems, copious amounts of leaves, shoots half a mile long, but strangely, not a single flower. *C. montana* 'Tetrarose' which replaced it, has covered the gable wall of the byre in no time and has now started its progress across the roof. From every leaf axil clusters of round buds open into four-petalled mauve-pink flowers and fill the garden with a sweet vanilla scent. A great mid-summer spectacle.

Diary   **22nd June**

Yesterday James, our friend Robbie Pearson and I set off for Ronas Hill (Shetland's highest peak) to greet the midnight sun and look for one of Shetland's rarest plants, the mountain azalea. We left Tresta at 9pm under blue skies and there was still some hazy sunshine as we started our ascent. By the time we reached the summit all was shrouded in thick mist and we decided to wait for it to clear before setting out on our search for the mountain azalea.

We sat for ages, huddled and cold against one of the cairns and ate the picnic we'd brought. By two o'clock the fog had grown so dense we could barely see each other, let alone any landmarks to lead us back to the car. We walked for hours, probably in circles, hopelessly lost. I'm sure we waded through the same endless peat bogs again and again. It was a frightening and exhausting experience. Robbie urged us to return to the summit, while James kept repeating: "Follow the compass." Unsure whose advice to follow, I sat on a stone to await the arrival of the rescue helicopters. They never came and I don't know how we eventually found our way back to the car. We came home to a garden glittering with dew and bathed in morning sunshine, and the first three-petalled blossom on *Libertia formosa*.

Right: *Libertia formosa.*

The Kitchen Garden from the west ...   © Derek Fell

... and from the east.   © Derek Fell

The Damp Borders.   © Derek Fell

Lea Gardens from the west.   © Derek Fell

The White Garden.

© Derek Fell

The South Border from the west ...   © Derek Fell

... and from the east.   © Derek Fell

Part of the Round Garden.   © Derek Fell

View of the Sunk Garden.   © Derek Fell

Garden Entrance. © Derek Fell

Temple Terrace. © Derek Fell

July

We should have moved into summer by now, and sometimes we have, but in a maritime climate the weather can remain changeable, and seasons can vary greatly from one year to the next. When the air fails to warm up, some of my gardening friends get restless and the older ones (in both senses of the word) turn gloomy and nostalgic: "When I was young it never rained after the end of May, all the lochs dried up and the corn was cut in June. In all my years I've never seen such a cold/dull/wet/windy July, we'll get no summer this year," is what they tell me.

We always do get some kind of summer, perhaps not the one we want with (at least) twelve hours of sunshine a day, rain once a week, only during the night, and never at weekends. Some years summer does not arrive until August, or comes in carefully measured doses; warm, sunny days dished out in tiny portions like precious caviar. Each morsel is savoured to the full and commented on in great detail. The weather, a much-loved topic, plays a major role in island life.

Cool, damp weather does not harm the garden; if anything, it has a beneficial effect, the grass stays green and plants grow larger and flower for longer. The constant stream of garden visitors continues and those from warmer and drier climates often comment on how lush and

Left: Cabbage white feeding on *Geranium palmatum*. Above: ... In a cool, damp climate plants flower for longer – the South Border in early July.

luxurious plants grow in my garden. They complain of heat waves, hosepipe bans, shrivelled begonias and browning lawns, describe the drought of last year in great and harrowing detail, then compare it in even greater and more harrowing detail to one the year before.

The weather, it seems, is also a popular topic elsewhere. "Aren't you lucky?" they say to me, and there are times when I wouldn't mind swopping some of my lush and luxurious plant growth for their heat, sunshine and brown turf.

Cool weather also delays the flowering of some plants, and the laburnums, already going over in England, start to flower now. *Laburnum vulgare* is a surprisingly tough tree, and ancient, gnarled and wind-pruned specimens can be found in many Shetland gardens. *Laburnum* x

Kitchen Garden in early July with *Laburnum vulgare*.

wateri 'Vossii', planted as a grafted standard, graced the South Border for one brief summer before succumbing to a south-westerly.

L. vulgare, planted as a seed-raised sapling at about the same time in the Kitchen Garden, and trained into a semi-standard, took several years before it started to flower, which it does to this day, freely one year and sparingly the next. Stiff and sparse in youth, it has since developed a handsome wide crown and in its good years, the rain of yellow racemes is a splendid sight. *L. alpinum*, the Scottish laburnum, has a graceful, slightly weeping habit, but flowers grudgingly some years, or not at all. It too has grown into a well-shaped tree and as part of the western windscreen more than earns its keep.

In a damp climate herbaceous plants can put on phenomenal amounts of growth in a very short time, leaving the garden bursting at the seams. In the past this very lushness often spelled death to many newcomers, especially young shrubs, planted where there seemed to be ample space in spring, only to be engulfed and smothered by the more vigorous and older border residents a month or two later. Nowadays I fatten up my newcomers in the vegetable garden or in pots until they are strong enough to join the throng. Pot-grown plants have one great advantage: after a thorough soaking they can be planted at any time. Mine are plunged into buckets or basins with the water level coming right up over the rim of the pot and are left there until no more air bubbles rise from their compost. I leave them for at least an hour, even if I'm in a hurry, and overnight, if I'm not.

Container-grown trees and shrubs can be planted all-year-round, provided the ground is not frozen hard or water logged. This makes summer the perfect planting time for maritime regions and who can resist those bushy specimens in garden centres, wide or tall enough to create an instant garden? I could not, and many of these large trees and shrubs I planted grew a little shorter every year, some died back to stumps or died altogether, others were blown out of the ground, and many were rapidly overtaken by those of the same species, planted while still small and young. Not the instant effect I had hoped for.

Large shrubs and tall trees, for obvious reasons, are more susceptible to wind damage, especially when raised, as is often the case, in a much more benign climate.

But there was another reason for my numerous failures: vigorous trees and shrubs rapidly outgrow their containers, and if they've become potbound somewhere along the line, their roots often continue on that lethal spiralling route, which eventually brings about their demise. I now purchase all my large trees and shrubs bare-rooted or preferably with a wrapped rootball, during their dormant season. Those only available as pot-raised specimens I transplant in the autumn, after carefully teasing their fine feeding roots, then spreading, and if necessary pruning the larger ones, to ensure good future anchorage.

Still, pots have their uses, and many members of my ever-growing collection of cacti (desert as well as forest types) and tender succulents have dwelt happily in the same one for a decade or more. Come rain or shine, from spring to late autumn all are crammed onto two old wooden work benches at the garden entrance. They share their quarters with sempervivums and some of the smaller grasses, such as the blue *Festuca glauca*.

They delight me with their cornucopia of shapes, colours and textures whenever I pass them, which is several times a day: strings of beads, flat rosettes, saw-edged swords, cascading scalloped leaves, prickly spheres and furry towers in green, grey, blue, cream, tawny orange, pink and rose, some banded, striped or speckled. Some I enjoy for their "leaves" alone: the stiff, frosted grey foliage of *Puya caerulea*, the broad primrose bands on *Agave americana* 'Marginata', and the black-purple rosettes of *Aeonium arboreum* 'Zwartkop'. The latter is easily propagated by cutting its "giraffe"-stems into sections and planting them into a gritty compost

Cacti and succulents summering outdoors.

Aeonium 'Zwartkop' with **Echeveria pulvinata** behind.

mix. Numerous new rosettes sprout all along the severed bits, and root with great ease. Some I give away to fellow enthusiasts, others vanish without my consent.

I have several cacti of the mammillaria tribe which flower in April under glass. In the great outdoors buds appear in May, the first flowers open in late June, and continue their jewel display well into July. *Lampranthus* species and cultivars also start performing in late June and my specimens are smothered in large, fine-rayed daisies for many weeks. Their colour range is marvellous and includes purple, magenta, mauve, cinnabar and Chinese reds, as well as pink, clear, fiery orange and gentle apricot. They need copious amounts of water and soon signal any irrigation deficit by switching their fleshy, needle "leaves" from green to pink or red. I love those rosy tints, and after flowering often let them suffer – just a little. I don't have names for any in my tribe, but know that old plants grow

unproductive and are best renewed from cuttings every three or four years.

Sedum sieboldii is deciduous and, probably frost-hardy enough to survive a Shetland winter, could be tried in a raised bed. Like the *Lampranthus*, it too responds spectacularly when hit by drought, and turns a glowing crushed-strawberry shade. Its variegated form counts amongst the most striking plants I know. The rounded fleshy segments have a rich cream central zone, bordered with jade-green and margined with claret. Both forms produce rounded, pink flowerheads in early autumn.

Echeverias produce sprays of small red or orange flowers, but impress all year round with their wonderful leaf rosettes, blue-grey in *E. glauca*, pinky-bronze in *E. gibbiflora* 'Metallica' and blood-tipped green in *E. harmsii*. The exception in my collection is *Echeveria pulvinata*. Its small green rosettes are nothing much to write home about, but its July season, when the whole plant is smothered in large urn-shaped flowers of a zingy vermillion red, is truly glorious.

But succulents are only one aspect of the extensive Lea Gardens pot-culture department. Shrubs which refuse to flower in the garden often do so with their roots restricted and can lead long and healthy lives in large tubs. Containers in themselves can be highly ornamental and enhance the plants grown in them. Terracotta pots, once a little weathered, never look out of place, and glazed stoneware bowls can be colour-matched to their inhabitants.

Rather than spacing plants, especially shrubs, too closely for instant effect, as I used to do, I now leave sizeable gaps between all those with the potential to grow large. Suitable pot-grown plants are then sunk into the soil, and their pot rims camouflaged with a little bark mulch. Anything goes as far as I am concerned, from leucojums in February to nerines in October, and several of my houseplants, including a magnificent variegated *Aspidistra*, have been on border duty now and again. "Cheating" can be great fun.

Melianthus major is a great "plunger" and easily raised from seed. Everything about this South African plant is impressive, from the speed and symmetry of its growth, to the glaucous pinnate foliage and individual serrated leaflets. It is reasonably hardy here, but the whole plant can collapse into a soggy heap after a hard frost. Wind also takes its toll and, left in the garden, even in a sheltered spot, it tends to lose its pristine looks in November. Grown in a large pot, it can be wintered under glass, and brought out again in June. In pure garden compost, it reaches four by four feet in a ten litre pot, and gets cut to the ground every second year in April to prevent legginess. No other foliage plant in my garden looks as luxurious and tropical as this one.

When I first longed to have a garden (a quarter of a century ago) I dreamt of filling it entirely with lilies of all kinds. I started with the "easy" Asiatic hybrids, as many cultivars as I could find, planted randomly all over the place. Some did well, but the majority vanished after a year or two. Badly drained soil had a lot to answer for, and so did the little dark subterranean slugs, which gnaw through the shoots of many bulbous plants before they get a chance to push through the soil. I now have a handsome collection of Asiatic lilies, all grown in large clay pots, where they come to no grief.

Asiatic hybrid lily.

Split now and again, and top-dressed with rich garden compost each spring, they flower magnificently every year.

Two, miraculously, also thrive in the garden. Bright citron 'Sunray' doesn't increase, but holds its own in the South Border. 'St. Blazey' is a vigorous plant which increases freely and can be found in many old Shetland gardens. Its six-pointed orange-red stars make a splash in the Red Bed every July, regardless of the weather.

There's one late treasure whose appearance (always nerve-rackingly late) is eagerly anticipated. *Arisaema candidissimum* never appears above ground before the end of June, and after three years in the garden, just manages to hold its own. Faithfully, every July, it produces just one leaf and a solitary flower. The perfect green-striped white spathe, held on a mottled-red scape, is hooded at first, then opens out and draws to a fine point, revealing the snake-like spadix and an interior of undulating pale pink bands.

Melianthus major.

Diary

A clear bright sunny day at long last, and far too hot to finish the pricking out in the greenhouse as planned. I picked the last of the 'Stella' cherries – and ate most of them. The fruits on apple 'Mantlet' are swelling nicely, the first should be ready in a month's time. I potted all of the Barnhaven primulas, which made a lot of space in the coldframe, then did some pricking out after all, in the shade of the potting shed.

Tortoiseshells have settled on *Lithodora diffusa* 'Heavenly Blue' which is still flowering its heart out. Too early to get out the secateurs, but mustn't forget to cut it back, as I did last year – and the year before. The garden is in full sail and brimming with colour – except for those places where I grow my treasures. I don't know why this should be, but most belong to spring and early summer, and once they've finished, even with a few incidentals planted to bridge the gaps, parts of the garden look a little dull and thin.

Apple 'Mantlet'.

No matter how well placed, individuals can rarely compete with those large expanses of just one plant, which give the garden its rich, mature look in July. In the Kitchen Garden this is

Arisaema candidissimum.

created by clouds of *Geranium macrorrhizum* (described last month), the mounds of overlapping hosta leaves and a large drift of *Persicaria bistorta* 'Superba', with its forest of pink bottle brushes. In the rose border between the Round Garden and the vegetable plot, *Viola cornuta* is in full command, the individual plants woven into large sheets of white and pale lilac. Both forms turned up as chance seedlings in a pan of primulas more than a decade ago. An unsolicited, but highly appreciated gift from the Hardy Plant Society. Looking back, I find it hard to imagine how I ever managed to garden without them. The scented flowers hover above the plants like a swarm of butterflies from May until November and their tangled mats of light green stems and leaves make good groundcover.

A visit to the Red Bed brings a complete change of mood, a free-for-all against a background of *Rosa rugosa* 'Rosarie de l'Hay', which produces its scented, double crimson flowers from late June until well into August. I

Persicaria bistorta 'Superba'.

Lilium 'St Blazey' with *Knautia macedonica*.

love mixing the blue reds from one end of the spectrum with the yellow ones from the other end, and the orange-centred, scarlet *Lilium* 'St. Blazey', planted in front of the rose, provides one of these strong, vibrant contrasts. *Knautia macedonica*, planted in the centre of the bed, has threaded its long, lax stems through all its neighbours. Its flat, button flowers are a clear dark crimson and mingle with scarlet *Lychnis chalcedonica*, feathery purple fennel, and blood-red opium poppies. Some of these I raise in pots under glass, and some I sow directly into the bed in April, to give a long succession. At the edge of the bed herbaceous potentillas in shades of scarlet, crimson and strong orange grow through orange-brown *Carex buchananii* and beetroot plantain, while mats of *Dianthus deltoides*, with little magenta or blood-red flowers, spill over the border's margins. Phormiums add height and drama and *Berberis* x *ottawensis* 'Superba' with its rich purple foliage brings out a glow in all these red and orange shades.

The planting is at its best now and by the end of August it has just about run to seed. That's when I wade in with secateurs and shears and remove sackfuls of spent vegetation. And that's when the doubts start to creep in – perhaps this planting needs more structure, a bit more winter interest, or a complete replanting? But I mustn't be too greedy; getting five months of glorious colour (starting with crocuses in March) out of a small patch of ground is no bad thing.

There's no shortage of flowering shrubs in July, and much maligned *Weigela florida* is often at its best early in the month. Unruly and shapeless it might be, but it always does me proud, wreathed in pink blossom for several weeks. Its branches do grow every which way and trying to prune it into some sort of shape is a complete waste of time. *Spiraea nipponica* 'Snowmound' shares the same season and makes a suitable companion. Planted in front, it hides

Weigela florida.

foliage plant in light shade, where the green and yellow variegated leaves don't get scorched or bleached. *Weigela florida* 'Variegata' has inherited none of the ungainly habits of the species and is very slow-growing with me, a well-rounded two-footer (60cm) after half a decade, with rich green leaves edged with a broad band of cream. It refuses to flower in my garden and the same goes for many varieties of *Philadelphus* I have tried. Those with double flowers only perform sporadically or not at all.

Good old *Philadelphus coronarius* and *P.* x *lemoinei* are singles and scent the whole garden with their sweet, cloying perfume. I have a yellow-leaved form of *P. coronarius*, which needs protection from both wind and sun. *P. coronarius* 'Variegatus' has leaves broadly and irregularly margined with white. It too benefits from a sheltered site where it keeps its spring-fresh looks all summer.

It is rarely mentioned that the flowers of most olearias are perfumed. They have a sweet honey scent, grudgingly given in cold damp weather, but flowing freely on a warm day. Their

most of the former's legginess with its dark, dense, arching greenery and clusters of white flowers, freely produced all along its branches. *W. f.* 'Foliis Purpureis' has a more twiggy habit, and can be kept growing close and rounded, and usually wider than high, by regular pruning. Its leaves are a soft, dusky purple and clusters of small, mauve-pink flowers open from reddish buds. *W.* 'Briant Rubidor' is new on the scene, with rose-red flowers in early summer and a second flush in September. It makes a good

Olearia macrodonta.

great flowering gives the whole garden a festive bridal atmosphere, billowing white clouds are everywhere, some bushes completely smothered in blossom with not a leaf in sight. *Olearia macrodonta* is the most magnificent of them all, with the oldest crown-lifted, and towering high above the rest. They are a glorious sight when covered in their broad heads of small daisies. Pale brown seedheads follow and last well into the autumn. *Olearia ilicifolia* has the same fiercely-toothed (they bark, but don't bite) leaves, long and narrow, in a light greyish green. I haven't had it for long, but it looks like another tall, robust grower and seeds itself freely.

Near the entrance to the Kitchen Garden *Rosa* 'Bourbon Queen' is trained as a climber against a low byre wall. It flowers for just three weeks, but makes the most of it, its branches weighed down by large, double pink roses, which are strongly perfumed. *Olearia* x *mollis* is

planted next to and somewhat underneath it. This, like many daisy bushes, has a tendency to grow sparse and leggy and I keep it bushy by pruning it every second spring. Like all olearias it can be cut back hard, and breaks readily from old wood. Its flowers are produced in small rounded heads and in enormous quantities. It's oval, wavy-edged leaves, white-felted on both sides are a great asset and look pristine all year round. *O. moschata* has an upright (to three feet), twiggy habit and round grey leaves. It is one of the best olearias for planting in wind funnels and close to the sea; where others shed some of their leaves, this one retains them all through the winter.

Olearia nummularifolia brings a welcome change from the grey-green theme. It looks more like a shrubby sedum than an *Olearia*, until the flowers give the game away. Its tiny, rounded, fleshy foliage is a shining olive green and

Rosa 'Bourbon Queen' with Clematis seedhead.

Diary

13th July

A cloud of rooks turned up suddenly this morning, swooping and dipping low outside my study window; an untimely visit, much too early for their autumnal potato raids. They also behaved differently, their aerial acrobatics were accompanied by a deafening noise and followed by a loud thud against my study window. Their throaty, agitated calls continued for some time and I decided to investigate. The rooks took off as soon as I turned the corner of the house and, expecting to find one of them lying dazed or dead, I encountered, at arms length, and barely visible, motionless on a pile of stones, a long-eared owl. For a moment its round, orange eyes met mine, then it took to the air, silently and vertically. Its glide across the garden seemed effortless, just one wing beat to lift it over the byre and down into the White Garden, where it settled in a sycamore.

arranged in dense rosettes all along the branches. It is rather slow-growing and does best in a sheltered, but open position.

Vita Sackville-West had barn owls in her White Garden, and mine was, like countless others, inspired by it. It lies on the east side of the garden and is divided from north to south into two long, narrow borders by a paved walk which ends in the garden's southernmost corner, at a low stone seat known as "The End of Civilisation". A narrow path curves around the seat and leads, across a stile in the fence, to the L-shaped shelterbelt and the wilderness below the garden.

White gardens have long since gone out of vogue, but I like the pristine, fresh look of mine, retained on even the hottest summer day; forming a cool oasis amidst all the more colourful parts of the garden. Large numbers of the plants I grow have white flowers, not because I sought them out, but because many, like the olearias, do well in this climate. White can be a hard colour to place in the garden, an art I have not quite mastered yet. In conjunction with soft shades like pale yellow, certain pinks

... towards "The End of Civilisation".

and light blue, it looks right, but when used with strong colours like red, purple or deep blue, it can make a border look as if a large hole had been cut into it, especially if the white is used in a solid expanse.

My White Garden was going to be a Himalayan version, with white forms of rhododendrons, *Meconopsis*, candelabra primulas, and the long white trumpets of *Cardiocrinum giganteum* towering above them all. It somehow never came off. Only one of the white rhododendrons, 'Cunningham's White', made it, weevils got the white candelabras, *Meconopsis betonicifolia* var. *alba* didn't grow for me until many years later, and the cardiocrinums remain stubbornly unflowered.

It still has a white theme, with touches of pale blue and yellow here and there. It is also a garden for all seasons with more than its fair share of evergreens: olearias, hebes, privet and junipers. Between them are sheets of white violas, dicentras and vincas, white foxgloves and martagon lilies, phloxes, soft blue *Lupinus nootkatensis*, the stately *Campanula latiloba* 'Alba', white meadow cranesbill, white-edged luzulas, blue-leaved hostas and regal lilies in large clay pots. June and July are the months when I enjoy my white garden best and I often visit it at dusk, when the fading light turns its flowers into luminous, floating rafts.

Along its eastern front are the flattened remains of a dry-stone dyke with pockets of raw peat between the stones, wringing wet in winter and bone-dry in summer. Few plants are happy there, but southernwood, *Artemisia abrotanum*, thrives and so do a few self-sown ferns and aquilegias. Against this dyke in the bays between shrubs I have a very pretty form of *Polemonium caeruleum*, named 'Liebchen' because of its many endearing qualities. A seedling which miraculously escaped the Dutch hoe reaches waist height in good soil and produces many spikes of large, powderblue cups from late June to late August. Its foliage is of a particularly light, fresh green. It does not seed around, and stays

Polemonium caeruleum **'Liebchen'.**

exactly where I put it, a rare quality amongst polemoniums.

Polemonium reptans 'Lambrook Mauve', less than a foot (30 cm) high and with a long flowering season, is also well-behaved, too well-behaved in places. Recommended to me as a fast worker, ideal for covering banks, and used for this purpose in various parts of the garden, it is setting about the job with a singular lack of enthusiasm, but its neat mats of bright greenery and mauve flowers are always welcome. *Polemonium foliosissimum* has loose, arching sprays of lavender flowers, overlaid with slate purple, and *Polemonium carneum* produces copious quantities of pale flesh pink cups, fading to a silvery lilac as they age.

If allowed to seed incontinently or planted where the soil suits them rather too well, some geraniums, polemoniums, persicarias, campanulas and other lusty growers, can become a nuisance. But with a little judicious and well-timed curtailing, cut to the ground as soon as their flowers have faded, they give the garden its backbone of continuous colour. They make up the chorus for the individual and more flamboyant performers, and their enthusiastic growth covers every inch of bare soil. Once they have knitted together into large expanses, weeds don't stand a chance and from now on the garden, apart from a little snipping and dead-heading here and there, looks after itself, and just as well.

During July the house starts to fill up with visitors, and often remains filled until the end of August. Friends and relatives, like migrating birds, head north and have to be fed, watered, entertained, and shown the sights. This is what I enjoy doing, and having house guests always brings a welcome break with routine. The garden rushes ahead without me and just now and again, I long for the days of early spring, when I had time to wander through it several times a day, to admire and record every flower as it opened its first bud. Now the fleeting ones might escape my notice altogether or I come upon a plant which has done most of its flowering already, quietly, and without due admiration.

Diary   17th July

I haven't seen the garden for days and was grateful for a long, leisurely stroll this morning, in the company of my friend Lillian Tait. The walk turned into a journey of discovery, a look through her painter's rather than my gardeners' eye. She uses tropical plants in her paintings and is particularly interested in plant structure. Now and again she put on sunglasses to "switch off" colour and concentrated on form, shape and texture alone, fascinated by the gossamer veils of *Stipa tenuissima*, the broad fans of iris

leaves, the sky-piercing swords of New Zealand flaxes, and the fleshy symmetry of succulents. I in turn was fascinated by the way she "grew" plants in her ink sketches with a few, sure strokes of her pen. She pointed out the perfect urn-shape of a young, multi-stemmed whitebeam and it was she who spotted a transformed *Geranium palmatum* in the Round Garden, long before I did.

Geranium palmatum.

A long way from its warm Canary Island home it survived three winters and has grown into a luxurious dome of deep green, fingered leaves, now, for the first time, topped by a magnificent bouquet of mallow-pink flowers, perfect against a backdrop of silver cardoons. Two other cranesbills in the same part of the garden are rather more subtle in their flowering. *Geranium lambertsii* 'Swansdown' has long, leaf-clad, trailing stems, which it weaves through its neighbours or flings over the path. From each leaf axil rises a short stalk, holding a nodding, pink-veined white saucer. *Geranium renardii* also has white flowers, which look pearl-grey from a distance, due to their dark veining. Its sage green leaves, deeply lobed and textured and as soft as kid, are a great asset.

Opposite the Round Garden, in the South Border, a slow, but dramatic change has taken place. In a large, or even not so large garden, highlights can be carefully timed, and not every part needs its share of flowers at every season. While the Kitchen Garden, the shaded shelter plantings and the Damp Beds were colourful from April to June, the South Border has taken rather a backseat, with just a few early floral highlights here and there.

It was planted for a great summer climax and aspires to this state of splendour in early July. It has a background of shrubs, both evergreen and deciduous. Its centre piece is a golden-leaved whitebeam, *Sorbus aria* 'Chrysophylla' with leaves of a luminous, light yellow. Next to this grows *Escallonia* 'Apple Blossom' with small, dark leaves and clusters of blush-pink funnels. There is more gold from *Sambucus nigra* 'Aurea' at the west end of the border, and next to it a large specimen of *Rosa moyesii*, with every one of its long, arching wands wreathed in single blood-crimson flowers. *Lilium pyrenaicum* with its waxy yellow turks' caps enjoys itself there and its small colony expands a little every year. This

Campanula lactiflora.

lily really belongs to June, but sometimes strays into this month. It used to grow in every Shetland garden I am told, but has now become inexplicably rare.

At the border's eastern margin a large stand of seed-raised *Campanula lactiflora* in a soft medley of lilac, mauve and lavender mingles with *Chrysanthemum maximum* behind a huge mop of *Carex* 'Coman's Bronze'. Behind the stand of bellflowers the tall, branching stems of *Geranium psilostemon* rise in a mushroom cloud of black-eyed magenta.

A dark, almost purple form of *Campanula latiloba* grows with the large pink cornflowers of *Centaurea* 'John Coutts' with its jagged silver-green leaves. *Rosa* 'Agnes' is still going strong from a mid-June start and opens its soft, yellow, scented flowers from perfectly-shaped, slender buds. Its bare legs are skirted by the striped

Rosa moyesii **in the South Border in early July.**

Geranium psilostemon.

Campanula trachelium **with** *Lysimachia davurica.*

blue *Geranium pratense* 'Striatum', *Campanula persicifolia*, a nameless fuchsia-pink sidalcea and the flat, still-green plates of *Sedum spectabile*.

Campanula trachelium, the nettle-leaved bell flower. It has rather coarse leaves, but substantial spikes of violet purple, lilac, or white flowers. Its darkest form contrasts well with the light yellow of *Lysimachia davurica*. *C. rapunculoides*, said to be a pestilential weed, is no such thing on my heavy, acid soil. I have in fact had great difficulty getting it established. Slugs are inordinately fond of it and have killed several specimens in the past. I now have it growing in a shady bed, to the south of the vegetable garden where it can roam freely, if it ever decides to do so. It is a graceful plant with slim spikes of starry violet bells.

The meadow cranesbills are at their best now, and I have already mentioned the white form, which looks best in shade, where its

flowers look large and luminous. *Geranium pratense* 'Plenum Caeruleum' has small double and somewhat misshapen flowers in lavender and lilac. *G. p.* 'Plenum Violaceum' occupies a prime spot (which it is rapidly outgrowing) in a south-facing raised bed. It has the longest season

Geranium pratense **'Plenum Violaceum'.**

One of today's visitors, while eyeing the deck chairs in the Round Garden, asked if I ever found time to sit in them. I answered with a defensive: "Yes of course," and she and I knew fine well that I was lying. I haven't sat in the Round Garden since May, and after my visitor left I got down to a bit of defiant hand-weeding, stubbornly humming a line from an old Warren Zevon song: "… I'll sleep when I'm dead …". I enjoy working in the garden. Why should I slump in a deck chair when I'd much rather weed, plant, take cuttings, update my notebook? I can rest when I'm old and grey (if I ever reach that blessed stage). Just now, I want to submerge myself in my all-consuming passion, the garden and its plants – whenever I find a moment. I know its hard on James, and if he wasn't doing most of the cooking in the summer, we'd all have starved to death by now. But I know that he loves the garden as much as I do, and most of our pre- and post-dinner conversations these days take place in botanical Latin …

Eryngium bourgatii **behind** *Astrantia maxima*.

of them all, and lasts well into August. Each little flower is like a perfect, full-petalled rose, rich lavender blue, around a purple-tinged centre.

Blue features prominently, a theme which is continued and intensified by *Eryngium bourgatii*, one of the few South Border plants in need of staking (in a wet season). It has impressive basal foliage, grey-green and deeply cut, with conspicuous white marbling. The cone-shaped flowers in their fiercely-spined collars are a startling steel blue. It grows with Bowles' golden sedge, and the soft orange, mahogany-backed bells of *Hemerocallis* 'Golden Chimes', the only day lily which flowers reliably in my garden. This is the damp part of the border where water runs along the track of an underground drain, and sometimes, after heavy rain, comes to the surface.

Astrantia maxima is very much at home here. It came to me from the late Bella Henderson's garden at Orbister, when it was still *A. helleborifolia*, a specific name which described its tripartate leaves rather well. It increases rapidly and each spring I hack away several large chunks, and by the end of each summer it has reached its previous circumference once more. Its quivering pin-cushion flowers are surrounded by papery, pointed bracts and the whole inflorescence changes colour as the season progresses. Buds open green and white, deepen to pink and finally change to a dusky rose. Like all the astrantias it is good for picking and drying.

I also grow several forms of *Astrantia major*, the cream-variegated 'Sunningdale' and 'Shaggy' with long, irregular green and white bracts. The colouring of *A. major* 'Rubra' is variable, and the best of mine, raised from the 'Ruby Wedding' seed mix are a deep, ox-blood red before they darken to maroon.

Geraniums, astrantias, all these plants with round flowers and a rounded habit benefit from the strong verticals of verbascums and *Veronicastrum virginicum*. Two German cultivars of this plant, 'Weisser Riese' (White Giant) and 'Rosa Riese' (Pink Giant) grow to just over two feet (60cm) and flower freely. The species, which is blue, will, strangely, have nothing to do with my garden, while *V. v.* 'Pointed Finger' queens it over the South Border from the end of June until late August. It reaches six feet in a good season, with whorls of narrow foliage and long, substantial spikes of bright lavender blue flowers, all curved towards the south.

A large, biennial mullein seeds itself in the South Border. The seedlings soon form impressive rosettes of grey-felted leaves, handsome features in winter and spring. Despite

Veronicastrum virginicum with *Lilium* 'Sunray' and *Achillea* 'Cerise Queen'.

Eryngium alpinum.

their long taproots, young plants, found in the wrong place, re-established well when moved during a damp spell. The tall stems, also grey-felted, carry slim candelabras of sulphur yellow flowers, which look good with the blues of the campanulas, geraniums and eryngiums.

Eryngium alpinum has the largest flowers of its tribe and the most vibrant colour, an irridescent blue with violet shading and wide, soft calyx frills. Unlike the others, which are not particular about soil and aspect, this likes good drainage and a sunny spot.

Eryngium tripartitum and *E. variifolium* are also good plants, striking in both foliage and flowers. *E. agavifolium* needs the scene to itself and I grow mine in a large stoneware pot to show it off to best advantage. It is evergreen with fiercely serrated basal rosettes and sends up stout, five-foot stems with well-branched heads of grey green flowers.

Towards the end of the month the shrubby potentillas come into their own. They might well be bread and butter shrubs and avoided by the most snobbish of gardeners, but they are hard to beat for sheer floriferousness and length of season.

Yellow is the potentilla's predominant colour and one of my favourites is 'Elisabeth', with primrose yellow flowers over grey-green foliage. 'Longacre' is also yellow, a luminous, but gentle sulphur shade, and one of those low, spreading shrubs which are ideal for covering

Diary   **26th July**

Today I discovered John Walterson's secret garden in Scalloway, set back from the road and quite hidden from view by tall hedges. There was a simple, but highly effective planting of large, canary yellow potentillas. Rather than clipped into a hedge, as is usually the case, the individuals were widely spaced and allowed to grow into their natural shapes, several of them, planted in a curved row, their undulating, graceful outlines and wide-flung branches, dividing a lawn from a gravel drive.

steep banks. 'Primrose Beauty', a lusty grower with a long season, and the dwarf 'Tilford Cream' describe themselves. The white, grey-leaved *Potentilla* 'Manchu' is good for this purpose too, twiggy, almost prostrate, but a little slower growing.

P. rhodocalyx, rather than holding its flowers up to the sun, as all the others do, has them nodding all along the branches, small white cups, held by a star of crimson sepals. A very becoming arrangement on a scraggy-looking upright shrublet, which no amount of pruning will improve.

In the Round Garden, the purple spikes and grey-green leaves of the indispensable *Cheiranthus* 'Bowles Mauve' mingle happily with the tomato-red flowers of *Potentilla* 'Red Ace'. Even in full sun, these rarely get bleached (a cool climate has its advantages). I am not so fond of the pink and apricot ones, as they tend to look washed out after a long, sunny spell, but I like 'Grace Darling', which keeps its warm, glowing peach pink. A perfect match for the *Verbascum* mentioned earlier.

A large group of *Potentilla* 'Tangerine' in the Red Bed is used as a climbing frame by the rampant *Geranium procurrens*. It has flowers of a smouldering magenta with a small black eye and clashes magnificently with the orange flowers of its host. In the autumn I pull up sackfuls of its long trip-wires. They root like strawberry runners and I always leave a few plants to start their work all over again the following year.

In the Kitchen Garden martagon lilies dominate the scene. Raised from seed, their colours vary from dusky pink to deep magenta-purple. Amongst their thick-textured reflexed flowers and stout stems the pink lace of *Pimpinella major* 'Rosea' looks fresh and feather-

Potentilla **'Primrose Beauty'.**

Pimpinella major **'Rosea'** with *Campanula persicifolia* **'Alba'.**

light. This is also good with the white form of *Campanula persicifolia*.

No garden is complete without its share of climbers, and when I started mine I had romantic visions of roses smothering every wall.

Coppery pink 'Albertine' has been with me for many years and flowers well enough, but does not count amongst my favourites; while its buds are long and elegant, the loosely-double flowers, once open, look lop-sided and lack substance. It suffers badly from powder mildew in a dry summer. Many climbing roses have come and gone over the years, and I must admit to having been less than kind to some of them. Where other plants which didn't live up to expectations get a second chance, another season or two to prove their worth, climbing roses have rarely had that option, as I don't care much for their bare and thorny looks in winter.

On a south-facing wall, where many roses had tried and failed, *Clematis* 'Hagley Hybrid' becomes a waterfall of large pink stars this month. It has in recent years been joined, unsolicited, by the "Scottish flame flower", *Tropaeoleum speciosum*. This scales great heights and turns up in the most unexpected places, which has some gardeners instil it with magical properties. Its brittle fleshy roots can travel considerable distances, but within reason; plants which turn up miles from the others are undoubtedly bird-sown seedlings. In my garden I like it best planted all along a shady wall, where its scarlet nasturtium flowers look particularly vibrant.

July would not be complete without at least a brief mention of the genus *Watsonia*. More and more of its members have found their way into my garden of late. Related to the better-known *Crocosmia*, they have a charm all of their own, and a much wider colour range. Most were raised from seed (first smoked over the barbecue to break dormancy) and remain unflowered to date, but three species have proved soundly perennial and flower freely: The buff-orange *W. meriana* cv. *bulbilifera* prefers a rich peaty soil and is easily propagated from its numerous stem bulbils. *W. pillansii* lives on a sandy bank and throws up slender spikes of striking vermilion-red flowers from late July. These grow to about two feet (60cm) with me. The long-tubed, widely spaced flowers of *W. angusta* are red in bud, then change to a pale orange. This is a vigorous plant, reaching three feet (90cm) in a damp, but free-draining soil.

Still unfamiliar with their names, I'm often at a loss when asked by visitors and have to dash into the house to consult Peter Goldblatt's work on the genus, before giving a correct name.

Diary   **11th July**

When we adopted Anna I indulged in visions of her watering her own little garden and – eventually – following in my footsteps. Apart from planting slugs and worms (for very brief spells) she dislikes gardening and anything connected with it. Today I found her (at the tender age of three and a half) giving a guided tour of the garden to a captive audience. Pointing at a large group of *Digitalis purpurea*, she said: "Look at the lovely daffodils." When one of the visitors pointed out that they were called foxgloves, she answered, after a long, thoughtful pause: "I see. It's not allowed to say s..t, but it's allowed to say foxglove." Perhaps I should start teaching her Latin …

Right: *Clematis* **'Hagley Hybrid'**
with *Tropaeoleum speciosum.*

August

July moves seamlessly into August, usually our warmest and driest month, the month for clipping sheep, making hay, dozing in the grass and bathing in the sea. This is also the month when the garden reaches its great summer climax with many of the July flowers still going strong, joined by the glories of August and a first, but still distant, hint of autumn. The earliest Michaelmas daisies show a touch of colour in the bud, geraniums turn a leaf crimson here and there, blackbirds have raised their second brood. There's nothing much to do in the garden apart from dead-heading the roses, cutting the flower-meadow and mowing it once or twice in preparation for the colchicums. Life takes on a gentle and relaxed pace.

Daily watering of the greenhouses and all plants in pots is essential and a chore I sometimes delegate to Anna and her friends, who love it even more than I do, especially under glass, where they can strip off and create hose-pipe rain storms and that steamy rain forest atmosphere beloved by plants and hated by red spider mite.

Vegetables are plentiful this month, with peas, mangetout, summer cabbage and cauliflowers just coming into production, alongside good supplies of salad leaves and herbs, young spinach and the first finger-length carrots. I don't thin my carrots at the seedling stage (sometimes the slugs do it for me), but let them grow to a useful size, by pulling the largest as they fatten up, which leaves space for the rest to expand. Broad beans start to crop now, delicious cooked, with a few of their tender young shoots, pod and all before they develop their tough, leathery skins. I also like them raw (without their pods), dipped in a little olive oil and salt, as a nibble with pre-dinner drinks.

Left: *Digitalis ambigua.*

Globe artichoke.

Mangetouts do almost too well and the pods have to be picked regularly and before they grow large and starchy. They are best raw in salads or quickly stir-fried.

Few things in life are more satisfying than preparing a meal with vegetables, salads and herbs freshly picked from the garden. More often than not, the accompanying mackerel, popped under the grill until the skin goes black and blistery, arrives as a gift from generous neighbours who have caught more than they can eat. Soft fruit abounds, gooseberry sauce is perfect with fatty mackerel, and there's usually a good crop of black currants, which I make into jellies and sorbets. But there is one vegetable we never have enough of, and globe artichokes, the first ready to cut at the end of the month, are treated as a luxury and strictly rationed. Another August luxury are my old roses.

Almost twenty years ago, after falling in love with their photographs in David Austin's catalogue, I planted a small, double border of old roses. Not all did well, and those which stubbornly refused to enjoy themselves beside the seaside had to be replaced. In its early years the planting was largely a matter of trial and error, until things started to settle down. For over a decade all was well, the roses were vigorous and healthy, flowered spectacularly and scented the air; my double border was glorious in August. Then blackspot crept in, just a few affected leaves here and there, confined to one or two plants. Not keen on sprays, I picked them off and burnt them.

Within a season or two it had spread through most of the border and no amount of spraying and mulching would keep it in check. Like lichens, the fungus which causes the disease thrives in clean air, of which there is plenty close to the sea. It was strangely comforting to learn that some years earlier the very same affliction had befallen the famous rose garden at Great Dixter, and I followed Christopher Lloyd's example when it came to dealing with my own case. Those roses which had grown too large and were still in a good state of health were left in situ. Many, sadly, had to be destroyed, the others were spread over as wide an area as is possible in a small garden. Given generous feeding and thick mulches they look good so far. But I am keeping a vigilant eye on them.

I still have a few, and these are some of the best: *Rosa* x *alba* 'Alba Maxima' now grows at the back of the South Border. Its small white double roses have a sweet scent and are produced in great quantity. It can be found in many old Shetland gardens, where it has survived years of neglect, storm-force gales and even browsing by sheep. *R*. 'Maiden's Blush' is shorter, about three feet (90cm), with the same crowded clusters of flowers, pale flesh-pink on first opening, then fading to white. My favourite alba rose, and the oldest in the garden, is *R*. 'Céleste', a four foot (120cm) shrub with healthy sea green foliage and flowers of a clear, glowing pink which open

Rosa 'Céleste'.

An unnamed old treasure.

from the most elegantly pointed buds. 'Duchesse de Montebello' is a strong, but lax grower with long sprays of small blush-pink roses and a perfect contrast to the dark 'Tuscany Superb', a vigorous four-footer (120cm) with rough-textured, dark leaves and large flat rosettes of maroon crimson. 'Président de Sèze' has a rather sparse, upright habit, but makes up for it with a generous display of large flowers crammed with petals, purple magenta in the centre, pale lilac on the circumference. 'Rosa mundi' is the best-known of the striped roses, but rather susceptible to blackspot and surpassed in my garden by 'Commandant Beaurepaire', a Bourbon rose strikingly splashed, striped and streaked in cerise, pink, crimson and purple. 'Rose de Rescht', a Portland rose, has smaller but perfectly-shaped flowers of a pure, glowing crimson and a rich, heady scent, a quality shared by all the old roses. I also have an unnamed plant, brought by a visitor, which I treasure for its full-petalled, quartered blooms in a glowing light cerise-pink.

'Raubritter' is a modern German shrub rose,

and one of the best ground-covering roses I know, three feet (90cm) tall and twice as wide. A broad mound of leafy wands, smothered in clear pink cupped, almost ball-shaped, semi-double flowers. It lacks the scent of the old roses, but makes up for it with a robust constitution and is one of the best roses for sheer garden impact.

'Sarah van Fleet' is a rugosa hybrid which usually flowers profusely in July. In a good summer (we've had a couple of those lately) it performs in early June and again in late August. Its large, semi-double blooms are a clear pink and strongly scented.

Roses cry out for suitable companions, and those like foxgloves, often recommended for the purpose, have finished by the time the roses start in Shetland. The white, pink and purple variants of the biennial *Digitalis purpurea* have long since been cut to the ground to curtail their seeding. Two perennial foxgloves take their place in high summer. *D. lutea* sometimes opens its first buds in late June, but more usually does so a month later. It is an elegant plant with slender two-foot (60cm) spikes of small, pale yellow bells, freely

Digitalis lutea.

produced. *D. ambigua* is slightly taller with much larger flowers in the same primrose shade, veined and netted on the lower lip with orange-brown. Both are easily grown in any reasonably well-drained soil.

In my somewhat depleted Rose Border I have the yellow form of *Alchemilla mollis*, carpets of *Viola cornuta*, hostas, regal lilies, and toad flax. *Linaria purpurea* and its pink form 'Canon Went' are slim-line, see-through plants, evergreen and voracious self-seeders. *L. triornithophora*, less streamlined, needs plenty of space as well as staking, or a supporting cast of tallish plants to prevent its large purple and yellow "budgerigars" from trailing in the mud.

The lavender-blue *Linaria repens* is a weed on light, well-drained soil, but reasonably well-behaved on damp, sticky ground. I grow it (as a lavender substitute) below 'Maiden's Blush', on top of a steep bank of clay subsoil in the Back Yard, where little else is happy for long.

High rainfall during spring and early summer and relatively cool temperatures in late summer preserve much of the garden's freshness until well into autumn. At nearly the highest part of the garden we have one or more underground springs which only dry up for a few weeks each summer and provide the perfect conditions for large numbers of moisture-loving plants. The Damp Beds go into a bit of a lull once the early show is over and the last of the candelabra primulas start to ripen their silvered seedpods. The plantings take a deep breath, then put on a spectacular finale which lasts from August to October.

At the border margins a tapestry of low-growing moisture lovers forms an interwoven pattern of different shapes, colours and textures. Blue water forget-me-nots mingle with the yellow cups of *Lysimachia nummularia*, the pale green fronds of *Onoclea sensibilis* and the dark parsley leaves of *Astilbe crispa* 'Perkeo'. From this low spreading carpet rise the dusky-mauve flowers of *Molinia caerulea* 'Variegata' and the broad, gold blades of Luzula sylvatica 'Hohe

Diary   **3rd August**

The elders are in flower, one of my favourite moments in the gardening year. Great plates of creamy-white scented blossom cover all the bushes. The oldest, and tallest are best viewed from the upstairs windows. All are beautiful, but my favourite remains *Sambucus nigra* f. *laciniata* with its graceful, dark ferny foliage. I've picked a few sun-warmed heads last night to start a batch of elderflower champagne for our traditional Back Yard picnic. The scent of elder flowers always floods me with childhood memories: the huge horseshoe red brick buildings of a long-abandoned water mill, converted into a "camp" for post-war refugees from eastern Europe, the slow-moving black-green mill stream and the white-foaming weirs. Every summer Oma Augusta (my maternal grandmother) made huge quantities of "Hollunder Limonade" (elderflower champagne). The dubious privilege of fetching a daily ration from the pitch-black, spider-guarded cellar fell to me as the eldest child in the family. With one eye over my shoulder to forestall attacks from witches, ghosts and goblins, I plunged the heavy glass jug through a slimey-grey surface of floating flowers and lemon slices into the fragrant, bubbling liquid beneath. Then I ran, as fast as my legs could carry me, back into daylight.

Sambucus nigra f. *laciniata*.

Tatra'. Behind this border towers a golden elder in full bloom.

Elders very rarely manage to ripen a few berries in Shetland, but the fragrant flowers are a culinary delight, dipped in batter and made into elderflower fritters or pancakes, or turned into elderflower cordial.

Creamy elder blossom dominates the garden for a short while, but pink is the ruling colour in the Damp Beds this month, the pink of astilbes, filipendulas and persicarias, from palest sugar pink to deepest cerise. The tallest is *Filipendula rubra*, the Queen of the Prairie, with its bright jagged leaves and large plumes of shell-pink flowers, opening from maroon buds. The variety 'Venusta' has flowers of a rich rose pink and in good, retentive soil reaches heights of almost eight feet (over 2 metres). *Filipendula palmata* is half that height, but just as luxurious with feathery inflorescenses the colour of raspberry sorbet. I used to grow this under the name of

Persicaria amplexicaule with *Euphorbia wallichii.*

Filipendula digitata and there is a dwarf form called *F. digitata nana*, suitable for the border front at just under 18 inches (25cm). It is happy in ordinary soil, and so is *F. purpurea*, decked in light cerise candy floss.

The slim, crimson tapers of *Persicaria amplexicaule* bring a change in shape, and a fine colour contrast is provided by the sharp green inflorescences of *Euphorbia wallichii* and *E. donii*, the last of the spurges to flower and both lovers of damp ground.

The white arum lily *Zantedeschia aethiopica* also likes it damp. I used to have it in a large pot in the greenhouse, which it rapidly outgrew. It takes its time to get started in spring, is rarely fully present before June, nor does it flower very freely. But just a few of its white, waxy spathes in late August are a delight. It is also a good foliage plant, with large light green, heart-shaped leaves, glossy and solid amidst the lightness of the filipendulas and astilbes and lovely with the pale

Filipendula purpurea.

Primula florindae **red form.**

yellow form of the vanilla-scented Asian cowlip, *Primula florindae*.

This also comes in beautiful shades of cinnabar red and burnt orange which I have interplanted with the little lavender *Verbena corymbosa*, which, unlike most verbenas likes it damp and wanders around where it is happy.

Aralia cashmeriana is a superb foliage plant in rich, retentive soil. Six-foot (180cm) arching stems are well-clad in impressive, palmate leaves and in late summer topped by cream panicles reminiscent of ivy blossom.

Some of the astilbes I grow were gifts from gardening friends, but the majority arrived from mail order nurseries, complete with name-tags. Most of their labels have been lost over the years and the numerous pink forms I grow will have to spend the rest of their lives in anonymity. The red 'Fanal' is easily recognised and so are the broad hoar-frosted heads of *Astilbe*

'Deutschland'.

Astilbe chinensis var. *pumila* is a departure from the theme in both colour and shape of inflorescence. The long, slim flower spikes are densely packed with small, crowded panicles, giving a somewhat knobbly appearance. Its flowers are often described as pink or dusky pink, but mine are no such thing. The briefest

Nameless pink *Astilbe*.

glance at them stirs strong childhood memories of crushed bilberries mixed with a dash of milk and a little sugar, a much-loved summer tea-time treat and a rich mauve colour. Unlike other astilbes, which form clumps, this grows into substantial colonies and makes indispensable groundcover in all all kinds of places.

A. chinensis var. *taquetii* 'Superba' carries tall spires of rosy-purple flowers and its garden variety 'Purpurlanze' has feathery, lance-shaped flowerheads in the same colour.

If August remains dry and sunny, the Oriental hybrid lilies join in at the very end of the month. These are crosses between *Lilium auratum* and *L. speciosum*, and carry on the flamboyant tradition of both parents. They are tall growers, four feet (120cm) or more and like being tucked into the shady niches behind low-growing shrubs. Their great star-fish flowers in white, pink and cerise, spotted, striped and crested, tower above their surroundings and waft their heady scent across the garden. With the exception of 'Black Beauty' the garden season is too short and cold for them, but three to a five-litre pot, kept under glass until June, then plunged into beds and borders, gives them a sporting chance before the September gales set in.

There is no getting away from pink this month. The modern shrub rose 'Bonica' has semi-double flowers in a glowing rose pink, enhanced by a background of cream-variegated

Rosa 'Bonica' with *Scabiosa* 'Chile Black'.

Sambucus nigra. Helped by frequent dead-heading, it dominates the scene from August until November. It makes a low, rounded shrub and gives discreet support to its neighbour, *Scabiosa* 'Chile Black', which is a little weak-stemmed. Its large, flat, button flowers are a dark, smouldering crimson and have a velvety texture which goes well with the satin-smoothness of the rose. This scabious is not long-lived, but easily raised from basal cuttings taken in May and rooted in sand in a cold frame. On the other side of the rose is a large group of *Lobelia sessiliflora*, a sturdy three-footer with long spikes of curious dark purple flowers. And in front of them all, yet more pink, this time from *Persicaria affinis* 'Donald Lowndes'. Its pale pink tapers darken with age, creating a nice two-tone effect, and its neat, dark leaves, which remain on the plants all winter, turn a rich russet shade in autumn.

Amongst established trees and shrubs, where tall, vigorous groundcover is needed *Persicaria campanulata* provides a permanent solution, or acts as a temporary filler. It is shallow-rooted and makes an impenetrable mat of tangled stems and roots which builds up into a thick, felted layer as the years go by. Weeds and grass stand no chance and where there is too much of it, I simply roll it all up like an old carpet, leaving behind a clean piece of ground. Each year it soars up to four feet (120cm) and is topped by a foam of shell pink panicles, washy from a distance, but good in a vase, where the individual bell-shaped flowers

Oriental lily 'Black Beauty'.

can be admired. *P. campanulata* 'Rosenrot' is less vigorous than the type and has flowers of a crushed-raspberry pink. I grow it between shrubs on the site of an old compost heap, where the soil is rich and open-textured, kept well apart from several treasures also planted there.

Persicarias are a recurring August theme. *Persicaria bistorta* ssp. *carnea* is less than two feet (60cm) tall and produces its coral-pink bottle brushes from June until September. *P. amplexicaule* 'Inverleith' has an equally long season of slender, cherry red panicles on a compact, low-growing plant.

Meconopsis villosa opens its yellow lampshades from clusters of drooping, green buds mid-month. It forms an all-year-round basal mound of downy, warm green lobed leaves and looks far too delicate to last a winter in this rough climate. It is said to insist on overhead protection, but mine survives without. If lost, it is easily raised from seed, which it sets in copious quantities. It shares its quarters with *Myosotidium hortensia*, on the borderline of hardiness, and is said to retreat safely below ground in the winter. My young plants do no such thing and receive a protective blanket of old fern fronds in November. The large, rounded clusters of small, forget-me-not blue flowers are grudgingly produced in early summer, but the impressive veined leaves, heart-shaped and glossy, are a striking feature well into autumn.

In the Round Garden *Buddleja fellowiana*

Diary
15th August

From now on Elsie MacRae's entries in my address book shall be made in pencil. Like a butterfly flitting from flower to flower, she moves from country to country, latterly with partner James Wolstencroft and sons Lui and Torran in tow. I eventually tracked her down in the south of Spain for my traditional birthday phone call. This afternoon, how very apt,

hundreds of Red Admirals descended on the garden in brilliant sunshine. Some landed on my arms and in my hair, one or two even "butterfly-kissed" my face. Dozens, jostling for space, settled on 'Lochinch'. They sat, perfectly still with folded wings, drinking greedily from the nectar-rich flowers. Easy pray for young felines, I was relieved to find all the kittens sound asleep, curled up with their mother, in the shade of a potentilla. It never occurred to me to fetch my camera, and when I did so, after sunset, all bar one of the beautiful creatures had disappeared.

'Lochinch' has pride of place in August. Hard pruned each spring, it reaches five or six feet (150 to 180 cm) by August and is well clothed in grey felted leaves. A perfect foil for the large, scented panicles, tightly packed with orange-eyed lavender flowers.

Behind 'Lochinch' the yellow candles of *Verbascum olympicum* and the purple spires of *Linaria purpurea* reach for the sky. Once they go over the harmony is replaced by a strong contrast of fiery *Crocosmia* 'Lucifer' and its smaller cousin 'Dixter Flame' in deep, warm red with a little orange eye.

I also have this buddleia in the Back Yard, as a backdrop for the fine-rayed yellow *Inula hookerii* and copper-red *Helenium* 'Mœrheim Beauty'.

Three more butterfly bushes do well in my

Crocosmia '**Lucifer**'.

Buddleja 'Lochinch' with *Helenium* 'Mœrheim Beauty' and *Inula hookeri* in the Back Yard.

garden, and flower a little later: the deep-purple 'Black Knight', the pastel coloured 'Pink Delight', as well as the sumptuous 'Royal Red' in a rich heliotrope.

A showy, large-flowered gentian grows at the edge of Edith's Bed. *Gentiana trifolia* from Siberia has strong, woody stems, which radiate from the centre of the plant, horizontal for their first half, but stiffly upright in the parts which produce the wide, irridescent blue bells. The pale lemon *Solidago* 'Golden Mosa' grows with it, and so does *Stachys officinalis* 'Superba', with soft mauve pink spikes. At the back of the same border *Aconitum* x *bicolor* 'Spark's Variety' looks brooding in inky violet-purple. This is an impressive monkshood, tall, well-branched and with a long flowering season. The bronze-leaved, apricot-yellow *Crocosmia* 'Gerbe d'Or' accentuates its almost sinister darkness.

Depending on the weather, some years

Buddleja 'Royal Red'.

crocosmias don't start until well into September, in others, they're out in mid-August. At the back of the same bed I have two giants of the genus, the three-foot (90cm) red *C. masoniorum* and the even taller *C. paniculata* which flowers in September/October. Both are excellent foliage plants. Dark-eyed orange 'Mars' does well and yellow 'Citronella' increases rapidly. I'm growing increasingly fond of a newcomer, the pinky-orange 'Severn Sunrise'.

'Star of the East', much praised and recommended by various gardening friends does not survive the winter with me, but 'Emily McKenzie', only just holding its own for a number of years, is at last showing some vigour. It brings the season to a close at the end of September with large, nodding flowers of a dark, tarnished orange, accentuated by a wallflower-brown throat. Crocosmias bring a complete change from the bed's gentle colour scheme early in the month.

The little nanus gladioli, which less

Diary   **5th August**

Edith's Bed has taken on the tropical brilliance of an orchid house. Nanus gladioli are everywhere, and every arching stem is set with butterfly flowers. There are whites, pale and deep pinks, cerises and magentas, all with striking throat markings in contrasting colours. Two years ago I planted them here as a temporary measure and late in the season. Last year I was away and missed their show. They're a perfect miracle and destined to stay.

fortunate gardeners have to lift and store each winter, can be safely left in the ground in Shetland. Their large, pale green seedpods, held on horizontal stems, are a good autumn feature. Seed-raised plants, from open pollinated seed, flower within two or three years, and show an astonishing range of colours. In Edith's Bed they

mingle with bottlebrush euphorbias, the blue pincushions of *Scabiosa* 'Butterfly Blue' and red-eyed white *Dianthus deltoides* 'Arctic Fire'.

Given the windy site I garden on, I do very little staking and used to do none at all when I started my garden, as this was a chore I was not prepared to add to all the others. Several floppy erigerons found their way to the compost heap, a step I now regret and mean to reverse, as I am left with just 'Azure Fairy', 'Pink Jewel' and an unnamed, ground-hugging lavender cultivar. The Fairy produces both double and single flowers of a good lavender blue and lives on the edge of the South Border next to the blood red grass *Uncinia uncinata*.

I have a large drift of the single-flowered 'Pink Jewel' in the Sunk Garden behind a sprawling mat of *Geranium wallichianum* 'Buxton's Blue', the last of the hardy geraniums to flower. It has long, dock-like roots and does not readily lend itself to splitting or transplanting. But it is easily raised from seed, in colours which range from a good spode blue with a prominent white eye to rather washed-out shades of mauve. The erigerons divide readily and every tuft of foliage with a few roots attached will quickly grow into a new plant. Their smell is said to deter fleas, hence their common name fleabane. The flowers are scentless, but the whole plant, especially the root, is strongly and freshly aromatic, which makes handling it a pleasure.

The east side of the Sunk Garden used to be sheltered from the south by a short hedge of *Spiraea salicifolia*, long since banished to the shelterbelt. This is a fiercely suckering five-footer (1.5m) with fluffy pink panicles in August, which are nice for picking. In the right place it makes a good, thick hedge and, immune to salt spray, even thrives right by the sea. Mine has been replaced by a group of *Spiraea* 'Anthony Waterer' which reaches three to four feet (90 to 120cm) and can be kept lower by reducing its previous year's growth in spring. It has dark-green toothed leaves, splashed here and there with cream, yellow and orange, and large, flat terminal heads of small crimson flowers. This sport has all but replaced its parent *S. japonica* 'Bumalda' with flowers of a light cerise. This is often confused in catalogues with 'Bullata', a much smaller shrub with darkest crinkled leaves and dark flowers to match, a lovely dwarf for a raised bed or a large trough.

'Little Princess' has flowers of a pretty shade of pink, and 'Shirobana' pulls out all the stops by presenting a mixed bouquet of both white and pink heads. Their growth is upright and twiggy, and they would make a good, low hedge.

One of my favourite vistas leads the eye from the White Garden in the south, right through the Sunk Garden, past the house and byre roofs, to the Back Yard in the north. *Hydrangea petiolaris* is slowly progressing across the byre roof (from east to west), and from mid-July onwards is smothered in large white lace-cap flowers. It is one of the best climbers for exposed positions; even direct sea winds will not harm it. It clings without support, and once established, grows fast.

Escallonias are often recommended as hedging plants for exposed seaside gardens, and do an admirable job, provided the right location can be found for them. In my experience they need an open situation, preferably south or west-facing. Sought-after because of their evergreen status, they don't always live up to expectations. Even tough old *Escallonia rubra* 'Macrantha' gets scorched in a bad winter, but is always fully refurbished with glossy, rounded leaves in time for its rose-pink August flowering. I also grow 'Red Hedger' and 'Crimson Spire' with slightly smaller leaves and darker flowers.

Two small-leaved escallonias, said to be evergreen, wisely shed their leaves most winters. The already mentioned 'Apple Blossom' has one of the longest flowering seasons of any shrub in my garden. It produces a great burst of its white and pale pink flowers in June and July, then takes a deep breath and starts flowering again from September onwards, and during every mild spell

Diary   19th August

All the semi-ripe cuttings should have been taken last month, but I just couldn't get my act together this year. Its the organising which puts me off: finding enough trays and washing them, finding space, or rather making space, and finding I've run out of coarse sand or other essentials, sap my motivation. Now inspiration has come at long last. I emptied the shade frame of its pots and trays of sowings, worked half a bag of peat into the sand and grit and gave it all a good watering. Gathering the material, trimming it (on the Temple Terrace steps), and sticking the cuttings only took an afternoon.

right through until April, when it takes another, well-deserved rest. 'Red Elf' has the same open, twiggy habit, and turns into a shower of deep rose pink in July and August, then has a second, but sparser season from February to April. It shares an east-facing bed with *Berberis wilsonii*, a small deciduous shrub with fierce thorns, neat sea green leaves and clusters of tubular flowers of a clear canary yellow.

All escallonias, including the dwarfs 'Gwendolyn Anley' with flesh pink flowers and crimson *E. rubra* 'Woodside', are easily raised from semi-ripe cuttings.

Between the path to the front door and the steps leading up to The Temple I have a corner bed, divided into three terraces, south-west facing, but shaded by the house from November to March. In the top terrace the greedy roots of *Phormium* 'Bronze Baby' don't leave much room or nourishment for anything else. Frugality suits *Parahebe perfoliata*, a sub shrub with a tangle of trailing stems and striking blue-grey leaves, not unlike the juvenile foliage of *Eucalyptus gunnii*. Speedwell flowers in a cool shade of lavender appear from the leaf axils during the summer. It is evergreen, but best cut to the ground in spring to make way for fresh new shoots.

Completely sheltered from the north and east, these beds become a suntrap from June onwards and I frequently, during the summer, sit on the adjoining steps with a book. I originally filled the middle terrace with pinks, to enjoy their clove scent at close quarters. Their perfume was fine, but they never lasted for long, and the planting, flowerless for ten out of twelve months, was nothing much to look at. There still are a few pinks, but they have since been joined by *Ophiopogon nigrescens* with its swirls of narrow, strap-shaped leaves, black on the upper side, striped green and silver on the reverse. After a hot summer it produces a few spikes of tiny mauve flowers. It has an equally striking neighbour in *Aciphylla pinnatifida*, with jagged rosettes of deeply-serrated leaves in green-flushed orange. Amongst them grow mats of cream-edged *Silene uniflorum* 'Variegata' and *Sedum* 'Vera Jamieson', with plum-purple leaves and heads of dusky pink flowers.

Two tender plants spend the summer and autumn here and are never out of flower. Shrubby *Mimulus aurantiacus* from California has narrow, dark green foliage, sticky to the touch, and produces an endless succession of large, lobed trumpet flowers, russet brown in bud, opening to pinkish orange, then fading to chamois yellow, with all three colours present at the same time. *Cosmos atrosanguineus* with its black-crimson dahlia flowers counts among the most sniffed plants in the garden for its delicious hot-chocolate scent. My little terrace bed has become a planting for the nose as well as the eye and I am very pleased with the result.

On the other side of the steps, in the driest part of the Alpine Slope, a patch of French lavender, *Lavandula stoechas* has been in flower since the beginning of the month. It is the only lavender which survives the winter outdoors, and each time I pass, I run my fingers through it or bury my face in it and inhale deeply.

Oreganum 'Rosenkuppel' with light green leaves and hop-like heads of dusky pink and *Cistus* 'Silver Pink' revel in the same conditions.

This dry and special part of the Alpine Slope is sheltered and separated from the rest by a small willow, which is clipped to retain its dense, rounded outline, and *Chiliotrichum diffusum*, a grey-leaved South American evergreen. To the west of them the free-for-all begins. *Gypsophylla repens* 'Rosea' trails its grey-green mats over the retaining wall, covered in little chalk-pink flowers, *Campanula cochlearifolia* rings its metallic blue bells and has climbed through the white *Potentilla* 'Manchu' with charming effect.

Sedums feature prominently in the August garden. Pink *S. spurium* will grow happily anywhere, even without soil, and the German cultivar 'Schorbusser Blut' has flowers of a deep, sparkling red. *S. kamtschaticum* covers its crimped leaf rosettes with yellow stars, lovely with blue harebells. *S. reflexum* likes a damper soil than most; its tangled mats of grey green are reminiscent of the new growth on spruces, and the drooping yellow flowers on reddish stems appear in July.

Sedum acre, the wall pepper, is a ferocious spreader, but quite restrained in its cream-tipped form 'Variegatum' and nice in gravel paths. *S. ewersii* is a favourite with its long, trailing, red brown stems, clasped by pairs of rounded, apple-green leaves and topped by clusters of cerise flowers and so is *S. cauticola*, which is one of the

Campanula cochlearifolia.

Sedum anacampseros.

Diary   **21st August**

James made me a wonderful garden bench for my 40th birthday, but I don't think I ever sat on it for more than a few minutes at a time. There was always something to disturb the eye: weeds, overlooked during my last round, a plant in the wrong place, the grass in need of a cut, and up I'd jump to get on with things.

It's been a frantic fortnight with lots of guided tours, including a German party and Faroese plant hunters in search of cuttings and seed. Babette Herchenröder (tired of Berlin in summer) has been staying for most of it and Anna is on one of her highs, never still for a moment. James took them out in the boat today for a spot of fishing and a swim on Sandsound beach. I decided to stay behind to catch up with myself and the garden, but as I saw the boat glide away from the pier and across the shimmering water I wanted to be with them, run after them and shout: "Wait! Wait for me!" I pottered around for a while, watered the greenhouses, took a leisurely walk around the garden, then went up to the Back Yard and sat on my bench. And there were weeds, and plants in the wrong place, and the grass needed cutting, and none of it mattered. As if for the first time, I saw the view down to the sea across the trees and the tall grasses, and it was the first time I felt the summer. And while I sat there I knew that I would remember this moment for a very long time.

very best. It grows in the south-facing retaining wall of the Sunk Garden, where its mats of blue-green leaves on short, prostrate stems form an eye-catching tapestry with the cream, pink and sage green of a variegated bugle. Its flowers, which appear late in the month, are a glowing, light crimson. The bud stage lasts for several weeks and is equally beautiful. If I had to choose just one small sedum, this would be it.

Sedum 'Bertram Anderson' is a handsome darkling with leaves of a deep, glowing purple brown, but lacks the vigour of the others. *S. populifolium* grows into a tiny, gnarled shrublet with dark brown stems and bright, light green poplar leaves, followed by loose blush-pink heads. *S. anacampseros* has a reptilian look with its snaking stems clad in overlapping grey scales. The round, terminal flowers slowly build to a September climax of subdued colouring, as the green buds change to frosted grape purple, and finally open into dusky pink stars.

Sedum telephium ssp. *maximum* 'Atropurpureum' is a truly impressive plant, two feet (60cm) tall with large maroon leaves and wide flat heads of a pale, orange pink. It is painfully slow to increase and several batches of cuttings have failed, but I am greatly charmed by its unusual colouring.

During August the local garden visitors start to trail off a little, to be replaced by those from further afield. Giving a guided tour to a large group in a small garden with narrow paths can at times be difficult, with half the party still stuck at the gate and the other half already dispersed. Doing the rounds in twos or threes, with a cup of coffee or a glass of wine is a much more relaxing affair. There's time to look at plants closely and to discover small treasures like the pink dandelion flowers of *Crepis incana*, the clouds of minute lilac daisies on *Lactuca perennis* and the small, blood-orange stars of *Anomatheca laxa*.

Others closely hug the ground or are tucked into dark corners, and have to be searched for. *Asteranthera ovata* is classed as a climber and said to scale great heights in its native Chilean forests. Mine, planted at the foot of a Japanese larch in a bed of peat and needle litter prefers the horizontal to the vertical and has grown into a tangled mat of dark, rounded, evergreen foliage. Here and there from the leaf axils, long, dark buds open into large, wide-mouthed trumpets, sealing-wax red with white throat markings. It likes plenty of moisture and needs protection from sea winds. *Mitraria coccinea* belongs to the same family and enjoys the same conditions; a prostrate, evergreen shrublet with polished green leaves and a myriad of vermilion, tubular flowers produced untiringly from July until November.

Once the last of the regal lilies have dropped their petals there isn't an awful lot to see in the White Garden until the colchicums come out. But there are one or two treasures which still make a visit worthwhile and amongst them is one of my favourite bellflowers, *Campanula alliariifolia*. It has heart-shaped grey-green, downy foliage which grows into a luxurious mound. Its flowers are ivory white and of a particularly long and elegant shape, dangling from slender branches which arch over the blue leaves of *Hosta* 'Halcyon'. White dicentras, cut back after their first flush of flowering, look good again and their dangling lockets now mingle with the cream foam of *Filipendula hexapetala* 'Nana Plena'. A very large name for such a small plant. It forms a dense carpet of dark, finely cut foliage and sends up foot high stems of tiny double meadowsweet flowers in loosely rounded heads.

Even during the most crowded and chaotic of garden tours, *Hedychium densiflorum* 'Assam Orange' couldn't possibly be overlooked. This Himalayan ginger lily is said to be tender and has, accordingly, spent most of its time here crammed into a large pot. Released into the garden, it is transformed with huge, maize-like foliage, topped by slender spikes of coral-orange orchid flowers

Diary   **26th August**

Hay making was a joy rather than a chore this year with six helpers at hand and glorious hot, sunny weather from the minute the first meadow was cut to the day the last bale was forked up into the loft. Each year I complain about the hay and the hard work it is (especially after struggling with it on my own last year), and each year I succumb to its charms and pleasures, the sweet smell, the rhythmic turning of the windrows, the building of the big matronly coles, and best of all, the celebratory meadow picnic once all the work is done. Most of our neighbours, after a succession of cold and wet summers, have abandoned hay-making altogether in favour of the labour-saving sileage, pressed into large, black polythene-wrapped bales. They can keep their bales. There is something immensely satisfying in a loft filled with sweetly scented hay and the knowledge of a good supply of winter fodder. But the first of the hay is not going to be fed to the sheep. It will be used to wrap around a leg of heather-fed lamb. Lamb baked in sileage just wouldn't be quite the same.

Right: *Hedychium densiflorum* 'Assam Orange'.

September

It is less than a decade since autumn became a season in my garden. Once the first equinoctial gales had done their work and shaken the still green leaves off the trees I used to hang up my trowel and retreat indoors. I longed for the Indian summers of my German childhood, the ripening blackberries in the hedgerows, chanterelles and ceps in the woods, fields of bleached stubble and the glorious colour spectacle of the autumnal forests.

I felt miserably homesick and endlessly bemoaned the fact that there was no autumn in Shetland: the seasons moving from summer straight into winter, without the gentle interlude I had taken for granted in my "previous life". I never stopped gardening altogether and spent the autumn and winter months with stacks of mail order catalogues, planning next year's borders, ordering plants – and skipping anything which flowered after August.

Increased shelter and my first tiger lilies (*Lilium lancifolium*) helped to create my very own autumn, and so did a slow, but perceptible shift in the climate, with later and colder springs, more than compensated for by warmer, longer autumns. September has become a second April with its mix of blue skies and showers.

I love the autumns now. They can bring fierce gales, but they also bring mild and sunny days, and with them a feeling of peace and

Left: *Rosa* 'Dorothy Perkins' with Max. Above: *Lilium lancifolium* (tiger lily).

timelessness. When the last visitors have departed the garden becomes my own again, and I can work away to my heart's content – midges permitting. A dear friend and great botanist, the late Grant Roger, when interviewed for a radio programme was asked, if he were given Noah's role, which animal would he have excluded from the Ark. His answer came without the slightest hesitation: "The midge".

Rubber gloves, and trousers tucked into long socks, protect arms and legs and a black "angler's" net, draped over a wide-brimmed old garden hat, stops the blighters from getting into one's nose, ears and eyes. I feel sorry for our poor sheep, cats and dogs which don't have such luxuries.

Many years ago I planted two ramblers near the entrance to my Sunk Garden, 'Dorothy Perkins' on the left (as you face the entrance) and R. 'Excelsa' on the right. In the past their flowering coincided to almost a day, but now, since R. 'Excelsa' has been freed from her rather overbearing neighbours, a *Weigela* and a late Dutch honeysuckle, her flowering starts almost a fortnight earlier, bang in the middle of August. The colouring of these two roses cannot exactly

Diary   **3rd September**

I've been puzzling for days over the fresh green Lammas shoots which thickly cover the ground just outside the Sunk Garden. They had obviously been knocked off the Japanese larches and at first I suspected the blackbirds. Today I caught the culprit *in flagrante delicto*. Max (our ageing border collie), pursued by a large black cloud of midges, squeezed past 'Dorothy Perkins' and worked his way into the undergrowth of the larch hedge. Firmly wedged beneath the lowest branches, he started moving rythmically to and fro, vigorously rubbing himself from head to rump, while emitting loud satisfied grunts.

be described as subtle. Dorothy is a bright, toothpaste pink and 'Excelsia' an equally bright, but darker rose pink. Both look glorious with their long, arching wands set thickly with perfect little rosettes. They are one of September's great highlights, and I cut long garlands for the house.

The vegetable garden looks pretty just now with many of the annual herbs, such as dill, rocket and borage in flower, their smells mingling deliciously on a sunny day. Self-sown nasturtiums spill over the edges of the raised beds and provide us with an endless supply of peppery leaves and flowers for autumn salads.

September is a good month for establishing new plantings, or overhauling old ones, as the need arises. The soil is warm, there is plenty of rain, and, failing that, there are heavy falls of dew every night. It is the month when major changes take place.

Nothing looks quite as forbidding and ugly as a large expanse of harling, and the extension to the house was harled with small, white quartz chippings. At the time this seemed an acceptable solution as its visible side, the west-facing wall is largely constructed of glass and wood. The north-facing gable end and the east wall didn't matter. Nobody ever ventured there, as the garden was confined to the area south and west of the original house. All this changed when the Back Yard was brought under cultivation. The east wall looked bare and stark, with a gravel path hard up against it and beneath the steep bank created by the excavation for the founds. The creation of even a narrow raised bed, built with the local stone, was out of the question in such a confined space. Rescue came in the form of two foot square concrete paving slabs, sunk in vertically, a foot from the wall and anchored in concrete.

Climbers and wall shrubs feature large, for obvious reasons, and have been selected to withstand the cold easterlies and north-easterlies. *Cotoneaster horizontalis* was an easy choice, and so was *Lonicera* 'Baggesen's Gold' and

10th September

I am aching all over. Getting the wheel-barrow up the steps to the eastern Back Yard is a nightmare so I decided to bag everything and carry it for half the journey. The raised bed looked so tiny and I thought finding "soil" for it would take me an hour or two. I've worked all day, bagging, wheeling, then dragging the bags up the steps, across half the Back Yard, then down the steps on the other side. The bed swallowed up bag after bag of leafmould, cow manure, sand, peat, spent potting compost, grit and anything else I could find. Tomorrow the fun bit starts. I couldn't resist, in semi-darkness, to gather up all the contenders. Please don't let it rain!

a variegated holly. Next to our bedroom window, I planted *Rosa* 'C.F. Meyer', a climber with a good proportion of rugosa blood and large pink, hybrid tea style flowers. It was meant to frame the window and fill the bedroom with its scent. But despite the shelter from salty seawinds and generous feeding, it never did well and has since been replaced by *Schizophragma hydrangeoides* 'Rosea'.

This self-clinging cimber is related to the climbing hydrangea and has the same floral arrangement, wide corymbs of tiny fertile flowers surrounded by large pink diamond-shaped bracts. The flowers have no scent, but the plant seems to have a cast-iron constitution. A south wall is usually recommended for it, but at sixty degrees north the points of the compass get a little blurred, with the sun spending as much time in the north as in the south during our short, sub-Arctic summers.

Schizophragma hydrangeoides **'Rosea'**.

Parthenocissus henryana, with its dark, silver-veined palmate leaves and stunning autumn colour, occupies the central position. Three years after planting it has still to get off the ground, and I'm looking for a suitable replacement.

To the south of the holly, and a little sheltered by it, I have made a home for *Berberidopsis corallina*. An east-facing wall is not the ideal place for a climber from the steamy, rain-drenched cloud forests of the Andes, but our high rainfall and mild winter temperatures suit it well. It flowers all through autumn and right into January some years, and puts out new shoots during every clement spell. In early August the first pin-prick buds appear and by the end of the month have grown into small, tubular flowers, resembling long-stalked red cherries. Its hard, leathery foliage seems impervious to wind and weather.

Harled walls are not exactly enhanced by drain pipes and other essential bits of external plumbing. These necessities of life feature at the southern edge of the bed, close to the bathroom window, and have been covered by green, plastic-coated netting to form a climbing frame for *Clematis* 'Bill Mackenzie', a hybrid between *C. tangutica* and *C. orientalis*. Poor Bill, one of my Ladies-in-Waiting for far too long, had looked increasingly miserable in its pot but since released from it, has scaled dizzy heights at break-neck speed. It starts flowering with the *Berberidopsis* at the end of August and I find it

***Clematis* x 'Bill Mackenzie'.**

hard to resist popping its fat, rounded buds. They open into yellow lanterns, made of thick-textured segments, reflexed at the tip, and are followed by pale grey, feathery seedheads.

There isn't room for much else in this bed, a few primulas and bulbs for spring, a variegated *Astrantia*, pink *Anemone hupehensis* 'Splendens' and a rather unusual late-flowering foxglove, *Digitalis* x *mertonensis* with flowers of a soft, dusky pink. It is a short-lived perennial which has kept itself going through self-sown seedlings for more than a decade.

Clematis viticella comes into its own now. Sole survivor from a large batch of seedlings (those slugs again), its colouring is not particularly striking. Small, pendant cups in a dusky violet are produced in great profusion. They are lit by a background of golden hop leaves. It grows rampantly and was planted far too closely to the hop, a *Clematis montana* and a climbing hydrangea. But somehow the four have fought it out between them and since they have expanded their territory from the east-facing gable of a byre to include the roof, there is plenty of space for them all. Whenever I can face it (every three years or so) I disentangle as much of the viticella's wiry growth as I can and give it a hard pruning in spring.

Clematis 'Niobe' also has a late season, and large flowers of a velvety wine-crimson. It started life against a low, north-facing wall, where it performed half-heartedly and little else was in flower in September.

It has now been moved to a much more conducive spot, until recently occupied by three large honeysuckles, the native *Lonicera periclymenum*, 'Belgica' the early Dutch with red-flushed flower, and the late Dutch 'Serotina'. This has the deepest colouring, a reddish purple, which perseveres on the outside of the flowers long after they've opened. It rarely opens a bud before October and only flowers freely after a hot summer.

All three were planted against the western half of the south-facing house wall in the year I

Hebe **'Great Orme'**.

started my garden. Far too choice a location to be occupied by such tough customers. Every summer they reached for the roof and had to be stopped from lifting tiles and blocking up the gutters. Cutting them away from the wall took the best of two days, and extracting their far-reaching woody roots (beyond my strength) took James the best of another day. The herbaceous inhabitants, again too rampant for a choice location, were also cleared out of this bed, which left a nice space, three metres wide by eight long, and sheltered from the drying easterlies by the porch wall.

Few things in life are more satisfying than planting up a new patch. 'Niobe' has been joined by *Hydrangea paniculata* which flowers at the same time. Large, conical inflorescences, even larger, if the shrub has been hard pruned in spring, are densely packed with tiny, pale green flowers, flushed with a little pink as they age. *Hebe* 'Great Orme' has long, tapering panicles of

a bright pink, and enjoys a south-facing wall. And so does *Romneya coulteri*, the white Californian tree poppy, unflowered as yet.

There are still sizeable gaps in this new planting, to be filled with plants as I find the time and the inspiration. My list of candidates (to be moved from elsewhere in the garden) includes: *Galtonia viridiflora*, with its tall spikes of green bells, the blue starbursts of *Agapanthus campanulatus* and the flesh pink sprays of *Tritonia*

Agapanthus campanulatus.

disticha ssp. *rubrolucens*. All three come from South Africa and are easily grown.

The same sadly cannot be said for another South African. Apart from the ubiquitous 'Atlanta', which flowers for a second time now, many red hot pokers, tried over the years, do not take kindly to soggy peat in winter. *Kiphofia rooperi* with conical heads of coral-apricot, and the yellow 'Percy's Pride' look promising in the deep, sandy loam of my new bed.

Dreaming up new colour schemes and compiling long lists of suitable plants is a highly pleasurable pastime. Not all my schemes come off, and some which do, fail to please me after a while. Having one's garden open to the public brings its joys and pleasures, but also has its drawbacks. There is a kind of shared ownership which at times makes me feel almost obliged to inform my visitors, especially the regulars, of any changes I am about to make. After all it is their garden too; many know the exact positions of almost every plant, they have come to love

certain plantings and landmarks and expect them to be there when they next arrive to show some of their friends around. Their consternation and dismay at finding a much-loved feature gone makes me feel like a thief in the night. But changes have to be made, sometimes for the sake of the garden or individual plants, but most often, I have to be honest about this, for the sake of the gardener, to satisfy her creative urges.

Resting on old laurels makes me feel edgy and uncomfortable and there comes a time when a bed has to be completely dismantled and started from scratch. My Desert Bed receives such radical treatment in spring, as some of its plants are on the tender side and best left undisturbed in autumn. Several crocosmias and a very large New Zealand flax had taken over, leaving little space for anything else. Removing them has made room for a few grasses, galtonias and watsonias, and restored the bed's light and informal look.

The Desert Bed in late summer.

Diary   **22nd September**

The Sunk Garden looks like a battle field with wilting vegetation everywhere and deep craters where I have removed large shrubs. All the weigelas, spiraeas and a huge *Lonicera involucrata* have gone from its south side to bring in light and air. Only my special columbines, labelled this spring, were spared. The rest (hundreds of them), and all the unwanted meadow rue seedlings (hundreds of them) have gone. I had to dismantle some of the retaining walls to extract their long roots. Yards of purple vincas, self-sown violets and geraniums – all ripped out. There's so much space now and the planting has lost its muddled, restless look. Two unexpected visitors arrived as I was hacking away at a large fern. They looked horrified, and I thought it better to pacify them with a large bag of free plants.

Those late summer rains always bring an itch to the trowel and spade fingers, which have been idle for far too long already. The stream of visitors trails off in September and I am left in peace to do the dirty deeds. A decade ago I wouldn't have dared to plant anything woody in the autumn, let alone move an established shrub for fear of subsequently losing it during the winter. Now there is still enough warmth in the soil and sunny days between the showers to allow them to grow new roots and to become firmly anchored before the onset of winter.

Such upheavals, often started spontaneously, and planned to be completed within a day, always turn into a much more complex operation. Most dug up seedlings will need to be potted for spring sales. Before any replanting can begin, dips and craters have to be filled in, and temporary homes found for the larger plants I removed. This is easier said than done. Suitable spaces, such as my lining out beds, are brimming over with early perennials (to be potted up next spring) and there isn't a patch of bare earth elsewhere. More often than not, the only option is the exposed fields outside the garden.

Often such replanting jobs, frequently interrupted by wet spells, drag on into October. I still prefer doing them now, rather than next March or April, which are always busy months. In spring I rarely have the foresight necessary for the creation of a balanced planting. In the autumn, with summer still fresh in my mind, and the first of the spring bulbs arriving, I automatically take care of all three seasons.

I rarely manage to get enough sleep while new plantings are on the go. The garden follows me to my bed and glorious visions of the new plantings haunt me into the small hours. Sometimes I steal out of bed in the middle of the night to note them all down; sometimes I sit up half the night, surrounded by reference books, compiling long plant lists.

And while my back is turned, the garden moves from summer into autumn. The first rose hips are ripening in the shelter belt, a leaf turns yellow here and there, and a nameless Japanese anemone, with great territorial ambitions, starts its glorious pink season.

Most of the garden's soil is chronically short of potash, a major nutrient essential for the ripening of wood, and a deficiency which

Japanese anemones.

should have been addressed in August or even July. Potash goes a long way in preventing leaf-scorch and die-back, and an annual application is a must. Bonfire remains and peat ash, sprinkled on the soil surface above the roots of trees and shrubs, are a good source, but there is never enough of these to go around. I have to supplement with sulphate of potash, which is cheap to buy and just as good for the purpose.

No matter how much I apply to certain individuals, they still die back, and are hard-pressed in the following seasons to make up in new growth what they have lost the previous winter. Now and again it's worth hanging on to such apparent no-hopers. *Hoheria glabrata*, from New Zealand, initially lost a large proportion of its young shoots every winter but eventually settled in, helped by copious amounts of potash, and even after bad winters shows no more than a few burnt tips, which are common-place, even amongst stalwarts.

It is one of those shrubs which can stretch a gardener's patience to its very limits, having to pass through a lengthy and distinct juvenile stage before reaching maturity and floriferousness. The juvenile stage has its compensations in the form of pretty three-lobed leaves. The adult foliage is entire, coarsely toothed and dull by comparison. But with it come the flowers, creamy white, pendant and reminiscent of superlative morello cherry blossom, produced in copious quantities after a good summer.

The South American eucryphias also have the potential to grow into trees. I have the fast-growing hybrid *E.* x *intermedia*. It has shot up with alarming speed and looks handsome with both entire and three-lobed leaves on dark upright branches, but gets badly scorched most winters. Its deciduous parent *E. glabrata* might well be a better choice for this climate. I also grow the much smaller and slower-growing *E. milliganii* with neat, dark, rounded glossy leaves and the ability to produce flowers from an early age. These are cup-shaped, an inch across and filled to the brim with pink-tipped stamens. This

Potentillas, ideal for maritime gardens.

is probably the best *Eucryphia* for small gardens, provided good shelter can be found for it.

Many late flowering shrubs, which have the whole growing season to produce and ripen their flowering wood, do well in northern, maritime gardens. Mine, with the exception of shrubby potentillas and the late flowering spiraeas, all have white flowers. The South African *Anisodontea capensis* comes as a welcome departure from the theme with its little warm pink mallow flowers. It has a long season which starts in early August and stretches well into autumn. A pot-grown specimen has survived here for two mild winters out of doors, but not being reliably hardy, might be best wintered under glass.

This might also be the best treatment for the delightful pink and red cultivars of *Leptospermum scoparium*, none of which have ever survived a winter here. I don't know why this should be, as their hardiness rating is equal to that of two other manukas, or tea trees, which are very much at home in my garden. *L. lanigerum* has grown into an open-branched six-foot (180cm) bush with rounded downy grey leaves, handsome reddish young wood and a profusion of tiny white flowers, borne from late July onwards. *L. grandiflorum* is considerably taller and looks very elegant clothed in feathery grey-green from head to toe. Its five-petalled white bramble flowers are large and leave behind them handsome, reddish seed capsules, which seem

Diary   **17th September**

The garden is shrouded in gentle mist which blurs its boundaries. The tips of the pines have turned copper in the setting sun. Outside my study window the grey feathery wands of *Leptospermum grandiflorum*, in motion during the slightest breeze, are held perfectly still. Hidden amongst the narrow leaves of last year's wood, small white pearls have opened into five-petalled bramble flowers. And there is some movement in the leptospermum after all, and on the ground below it, in Edith's Bed across the lawn, and in the conifers beyond it: dozens of goldcrests are scurrying on the ground, flitting from branch to branch and calling to each other in high-pitched rodent squeaks. The female blackcap (I'm convinced its the same one) which obligingly rid *Cotoneaster lucidus* of its plague of caterpillars in May has returned to the same bush. This time to feed on the black berries.

attractive to the garden's wrens. Both shrubs are evergreen and highly aromatic.

September gales blow in the first passing migrants and flamboyant northern bullfinches have appeared in great numbers recently, with a few individuals deciding to winter here. I know that bullfinches strip the buds off fruit trees and ornamental plums and cherries, and their presence is considered a nuisance, even a small catastrophe in some gardens. I have no idea what damage they do here, if any, and don't mind, as I enjoy them so very much. Watching the birdlife in the garden can become an obsession, and idling away whole mornings with a pair of binoculars is one of my autumnal pleasures.

I also love our ever-increasing population of garden spiders and their artistically constructed webs. They come in a wide range of colours: purple, milk chocolate and khaki brown, red, copper and orange shades, as well as the odd pale buff-apricot; and all with striking white abdominal markings. They can grow to an enormous size, and Anna is terrified of them, as I was as a child.

In the Round Garden the cardoons are in flower. Above the large, grey-green, jagged leaves, large violet thistle-heads have sprung from scaly, sculpted buds. This is the month for *Sedum spectabile*, with its wide plates of mauve-pink, beloved by Red Admirals for their plentiful supply of nectar. I prefer the warmer, darker colouring and longer season of *Sedum* 'Herbstfreude' ('Autumn Joy'), but the butterflies don't seem to care for it much. The large, flat flowerheads are a warm pink at first, then turn to coppery red and retain this colour well into winter. Bees make no such distinctions and settle on both plants in great numbers.

Aster x *frikartii* '**Mönch**' with *Sedum spectabile*.

Behind 'Herbstfreude' grows *Aster x frikartii* 'Mönch', a plant often described in superlatives and deserving of them all. Mine has taken several years to attain its state of glory and perfection, reaching almost three feet in a good season. Its stems are sturdy and the broad foliage is a pleasant shade of grey-green. The first of its large, long-rayed, clear, lavender blue flowers open in August and the whole plant lasts in beauty for almost three months. In the same border I have two varieties of *Aster amellus*, German cultivars called 'Rosenwichtel' and 'Zwergenhimmel'. They are low-growing, just under a foot tall, and in September turn into floral bolsters, rose-pink and lavender blue respectively. Slugs are fond of these and other Michaelmas daisies and shave off their young shoots as soon as they appear above ground, which stunts the plants and delays their flowering.

With the colchicums still a month away, autumn flowers are few and far between in the more shady parts of the garden. *Hypericum* 'Hidcote', planted in the shelter of a larch, provides some welcome colour. It has grown into a twiggy shrub, three feet (90cm) high and almost as wide, well-clothed in fresh green leaves. It looks good this month, covered in clusters of yellow flowers, saucer-shaped and filled with orange-tipped stamens. It is good for picking and every tightly-closed bud opens in water. It does not approve of hard pruning, and I lost a specimen by cutting it back too severely one spring. Removing some of its oldest wood in March keeps it in shape.

Behind it I have the Willow Gentian, *Gentiana asclepiadea*, a tall, elegant plant with slender, leafy, arching stems, and many pairs of deep blue bells in the upper leaf axils. It resents disturbance and takes a long time to re-settle after a move or division.

'Tutsan', *Hypericum androsaemum*, is an easy-going plant, happy in almost any soil and position, and in flower continuously from July until October. It is an upright shrublet and

Gentiana asclepiadea.

benefits from being planted in small groups, or large ones, if there's space. Bunches of small, yellow flowers are replaced by shiny red berries, which turn black when fully ripe, and all three colours appear on the bushes at the same time during the autumn.

After a hot, dry August floral colour can be a bit sparse in September. That's when I welcome the self-sown seedlings of *Linaria alpina* and their compact heads of orange-lipped violet flowers. *Bulbine caulescens*, a South African succulent, cut back to prevent seeding six weeks ago, is completely refurbished with yellow-starred spikelets. *Glaucium corniculatum* is stunning for its lobed and ruffled silver foliage alone, and produces a few of its tomato red, cream-centred poppies well into autumn. The satin cups of *Oenothera* 'Sunset Boulevard' always remind me of a tropical fruit salad. Pineapple yellow in bud, they open a rich mango shade, deepen to blood orange over the next day, before finally changing to pomegranate red. I grow it as an annual and use it to fill gaps at border edges, where something low-growing and long-flowering is called for.

Hebe 'Great Orme' starts its long season now, and hover flies descend in great numbers on its tapered, mauve-pink flower spikes. Apart from the white *H. salicifolia*, it is the only large-leaved *Hebe* which is soundly perennial with me.

The beds around the Temple Terrace were planted with summer in mind, to take care of June, July and August, the months we sit outside. Some years we sit (weather permitting) until well into October. Late afternoon and evening are the times we use the terrace most and many of the summer plants there have white or pale-coloured flowers which show up well at dusk. A background of shrubs and trees creates striking sunset silhouettes, gives shelter to the plantings, and a little privacy to us.

Francoa sonchifolia grows there against a

Diary   **12th September**

George Duncan turned up out of the blue last night and we decided on an impromptu barbecue (the latest in the season since I came to Shetland). Afterwards we sat in the Temple, still warm after the still sunny day we had had, until long after dark. The sunset left a sky banded and layered in pink, orange, dark blue and grey, and against that sky the outlines of the elms and the black lace of the parsley-leaved elder looked striking. The round flowers of *Potentilla* 'Grace Darling' shone in the fading light, and *Artemisia* 'Powis Castle' turned into a ghostly silver dome.

yellow-green backdrop of *Olearia solandri*. Every one of its tiny, blush-pink flowers, carried on arching wands, opens at the same time. Seedlings

The Temple Terrace in late summer.

vary from almost white to various shades of pale pink. 'Alba' is pure white and 'Rogerson's Form' is a deep pink.

Verbascum phoeniceum, the purple mullein, is a short-lived perennial, but seeds itself freely and has formed a small colony in one of the terrace beds. It first flowers in July, in typical verbascum fashion with three-foot (90cm) stems densely packed with silky saucers for their upper half. If this main stem is removed immediately after flowering, numerous short sideshoots appear and start the show all over again in September. My plants are a mixed bunch and their colours vary from pale mauves and lilacs to rich mulberry shades and sinister, black purples; their buds are nice too, padded envelopes with four corners folded neatly to meet in the centre.

Anthemis cupaniana is another plant with a long flowering season, its sprawling mats of ferny grey-green leaves spangled with large white, yellow-centred marguerites for months on end. It needs good drainage and a position in full sun. Old plants tend to grow woody and sparse, but replacements are easily raised from soft cuttings taken at any time during the summer.

The *Anthemis* arrived as a present, left on the doorstep by an anonymous donor. Unsolicited gifts of plants can be a bit of a mixed blessing, most are appreciated, and many have become indispensable, others I would rather not have. Plants like *Rubus spectabilis* (salmon berry), *Claytonia sibirica*, known as wandering sailor in Shetland, and Himalayan balsam should not be allowed into a self-respecting garden, even when they come as well-meant offerings from friends and neighbours.

These and other ineradicable weeds are frequently recommended for sites where nothing else will grow and given garden space by the unwary. Even if I had acres to spare, I would not allow them anywhere near my garden. Then again, there are plants, classed as pernicious weeds in parts of the country which are well-behaved in Shetland.

Diary **21st September**

Back in sunny Shetland. It has rained almost incessantly for the whole week I've been away. All of Scotland was grey and wet. Whole hill tracks had been washed away in Argyll and clearing operations were underway to shovel rocks and thick layers of red clay off minor roads. Great weather for plant hunting though. Even largish shrubs, dug up with very little rootball showed no signs of wilt. I've returned laden with treasures: several *Rhododendron ponticum* and a good collection of garden-escaped crocosmias. They cover all the road verges and are threatening to swallow up Argyll. Elsie MacRae gave me a black knapweed *Centaurea nigra*, a plant which has all but taken over her garden. One woman's weed is another woman's treasure.

Here I must mention that it is illegal to dig up plants (native or otherwise) without the landowners consent. I received permission from Bute and Argyll Council, who told me to dig up every *R. ponticum* with their blessing.

I quite often go on holiday during September – if I go at all. It's the perfect month for leaving the garden to its own devices. The mobile inhabitants of the greenhouse and Temple are still outdoors and look after themselves, and plants under glass don't need the constant watering which is essential for their survival during the summer. Most autumn flowers develop slowly and have a long season. The first Michaelmas daisies start showing colour now, and the ubiquitous orange "montbretia", *Crocosmia* x *crocosmiiflora* lights up the wild parts of the Back Yard. I might not catch the beginning or the end of their flowering, but won't miss it altogether, an important consideration for the obsessively keen gardener.

Crocosmia x crocosmiiflora.

The vegetable garden is still a problem though, as there are always gluts to be dealt with. This is the time of year when I wish I had my mother's skill for turning all those cauliflowers, summer cabbages, courgettes, sugar peas and beans into delicious pickles. If she happens to be here, which she sometimes is, she does it for me. Sitting around the kitchen table, talking while cleaning and chopping vegetables and packing them tightly into jars, is something I've been trained to do since early childhood, and still enjoy to this day. I have written down all her recipes, which herbs and spices to use, the exact amount of sugar, the ratio of wine vinegar to water, for how long and at what temperature to steam the jars, but my pickles are never as crunchy and well-flavoured as hers.

On my own, I mostly resort to blanching and freezing in mixed or separate lots. Peas are frozen with sprigs of mint and broad beans with summer savoury, to bring out their flavour. Mangetout with whole baby carrots and chunks of courgettes make great stir-fries. Peas and lettuce, frozen with dill (stalks, flowers and all)

Dill in flower.

are good for flavouring Greek lamb stews, which feature large on our winter menu.

I still haven't got the knack of spreading cauliflowers over a wide season, despite staggered sowings and the use of both early and late varieties. Every year there is either a feast or a famine, usually the former, and frozen cauliflower is not among my favourites. It becomes edible, even delicious when prepared in the following way: cook some chopped onion in oil until transparent, add whole mustard seeds, crushed fenugreek, powdered turmeric, and a de-seeded green chilli, cook for a few more minutes, add some stock or water, creamed coconut, season, and bring to a rolling boil, add prepared cauliflower and cook for exactly one minute, cool rapidly and freeze. I haven't given any quantities, because I don't have any, but you want the liquid to come up to about half the height of your pan, once you have added the cauliflower. This tastes as good as new, once thawed out, heated gently, and served with rice and plain yoghurt.

In the years I don't go on holiday, I like working my way through the many kilos of Morello cherries left in the freezer since their July picking. Whizzed through the blender and flavoured with a little cinnamon they make the most marvellous tart jam. Morellos contain an enormous amount of juice; stoning them calls for protective clothing, and is, in our household, often taken on by enthusiastic house guests who don't know what they're letting themselves in for. With the cherries in a half-frozen state, the operation is more or less "blood-less", but causes numb fingertips.

Morello bread and butter pudding with copious quantities of cinnamon and brown sugar tastes divine and Morello sorbet is very easily made. Again I have no quantities, but nothing ever goes wrong with this recipe. I liquidise the cherries and pop them into a muslin-lined sieve, suspended above a bowl. The juice which drips into this bowl I boil into a syrup with enough sugar to give a sweet, but still sharp taste, and just

as the juice starts to thicken a little, I add a good dash of Kirsch and take it off the heat immediately. This and the cherry puree left in the sieve are mixed, cooled and frozen until slushy, worked through with a fork, frozen again until almost set, again fluffed up with the back of a fork, and finally folded into stiffly-beaten egg whites. The more egg white you use, the airier the end result (within reason). The sorbet can now be kept frozen, and the mixture of sugar syrup, egg white and alcohol will keep it soft and light. I also use large quantities of these sour cherries, again flavoured with Kirsch, and their juices thickened with a little cornflour, as a filling for authentic Black Forest Gateau, which is a far cry from its sickly-sweet namesake served in third-rate restaurants.

Many summer-flowering bulbs like a little cooking or baking. Some do well enough in the garden, best in south-facing positions, but still don't manage to flower. All make an effort, but more often than not, this comes too late, at the end of October, or in November, when they rarely manage to open their buds. Others flower in the autumn following a spring planting, then vanish in their first winter, not due to frost, but excessive winter wet. Grown in pots they can be covered or taken indoors.

I have already mentioned the many advantages pot culture can bring. Summer bulbs, grown in pots (preferably of a dark colour, which absorbs and stores heat), get cooked a little and flower gloriously in September, and all the more so, if they are a trifle pot-bound, starved a bit, not of water, but of nutrients.

Eucomis, the pineapple lily, responds well to this treatment, and those I grow in containers always flower much better and a good deal earlier than the ones in open ground. They are members of the lily family, come from South Africa and look extraordinarily exotic. All have fleshy, strap or tongue-shaped basal leaves, maroon-purple in the cultivar 'Zeal Bronze', but usually a light, fresh green. *Eucomis bicolor* is the one most readily available, and is often sold as a and orange to shades of warm, strong red, and make a much greater impact separately, rather than in a mixture. All have spotted throats or contrasting dark centres and flower freely in September.

Habranthus robustus just makes it into September after a warm summer. In the open garden it never stands a chance, but grown in a large clay half-pot, its cyclamen pink buds open into rose-pink stars at the beginning of October. *Ornitholagum thyrsoides* with fat spikes of white, sweetly-scented flowers has the same season. Bringing their pots inside for the winter is a small effort in return for the flamboyant flowering of these bulbs.

Eucomis bicolor.

dry bulb by garden centres in spring. It has fat, cylindrical spikes of green, star-shaped flowers, narrowly edged with purple, held by a short, maroon-spotted stem and topped with a rosette of pale green leaves. *E. punctata* is twice the height at almost three feet (90cm), with leopard-spotted leaves, dark, snakeskin stems and flowers of a pale, creamy lilac, enhanced by violet anthers, again ending in the typical pineapple tuft.

Gladiolus callianthus is another late flowerer and a good candidate for the pot. Its six petals are white, and of varying length, which gives the flowers an interesting, informal look, enhanced by a purple-stained centre. They are great for cutting, last a long time in water, and their scent is one of the most powerful in the plant kingdom.

The three-petalled flowers of *Tigridia pavonia* range from creamy white through yellow

> ### *Diary*   18th September
>
> It's been warm and sunny for the past two days and the garden still looks good, but has been, for the moment, eclipsed by one of nature's great autumnal spectacles: *Erica tetralix*, the cross-leaved heath, has long since finished flowering, and *Erica cinerea* has turned most of its magenta spikes to buff-pink seed heads by now, but the ling (*Calluna vulgaris*) has turned every hill in Shetland mauve and purple.

These large expanses of our predominant heather species are just yards from the garden, growing in the same acid peat, but strangely, *Calluna vulgaris* is the least successful in the garden. There are thousands of cultivars on the market, many with handsomely coloured foliage, but all I have tried got hopelessly scorched or didn't survive the winter.

Erica vagans, the Cornish heath, takes their place and flowers from August to September. The foliage of all the cultivars I grow is good, never browns, and soon forms vigorous carpets, several feet wide. 'Mrs. D.F. Maxwell' has short, fat spikes of cerise flowers, freely produced. 'St. Keverne' is a light, clear pink, and 'Lyonesse', which in my garden is a yard across, has white bells with handsome brown anthers. They need a short back and sides in spring to keep them growing close.

Fuchsia magellanica 'Riccartonii' is widely used as a hedging shrub in Shetland. I enjoy seeing it growing to its natural form and height. The best I've ever come across used to grow at Orbister in the north Mainland. Spread against the west-facing wall of a house, it had reached tree height, 15 feet (4.5m), thick-stemmed with peeling bark, displaying the beige and green patterned wood beneath, and dripping with red and purple flowers. Even such divine splendour goes largely unnoticed, as the "common fooshia" is often taken for granted. I have a large old woody plant, right in the centre of the garden which does most of its flowering in July and is now hung with dark, fleshy seedpods. They have a pleasantly sweet and peppery taste. A younger specimen, planted in an exposed position, has much of its growth knocked off by the winter gales and flowers from late August onwards. It looks splendid just now with its rain of drooping flowers bathed in golden, autumnal light.

F. magellanica var. *molinae* also flowers late, rarely before September, and looks best in shade. Its wide-sepalled flowers pass for white at a distance, but turn out to be palest lavender pink on close inspection. 'Whiteknights Blush' is less vigorous, and sometimes gets cut to the ground in bad winters. Its season of light sugar-pink lasts well into October. Two other cultivars of *F. magellanica* I've grown for a number of years have never flowered, but make very good foliage

Fuchsia magellanica **var.** *molinae.*

shrubs. 'Aurea' rarely starts to flush before the end of May, but its foliage is a bright, bronze-flushed yellow and keeps this colouring well into the autumn. The new foliage of 'Versicolor' is a startling grey, cream and pink, then turns to a uniform grey-green, as the season progresses. In August it puts out its "Lammas" shoots, streaked with cream and flashes of pink and carmine.

Fascicularia bicolor has about the same hardiness rating as these fuchsias and in its native Chile is found as an epiphyte, on the bark of trees, rather than on the ground. It thrives on a starvation diet and grows in the Desert Bed in a foot-tall clay drainpipe filled with gravel. This elevated position also serves to keep its long, serrated leaves off the ground. The flowers appear at the centres of the leaf rosettes, little powderblue cups, in a round, flat inflorescence. The flowering doesn't last long, a week on the outside, but is announced, for at least a month, on either side of the event, by the leaf rosettes themselves, which turn as red as a baboon's bottom.

Right: *Fascicularia bicolor.*

October

Octber has become one of my favourite months in the garden, despite, or perhaps because "the nights are drawing in". September's frantic activities, the planting, re-planting and other hectic upheavals, come to an end with nightfall arriving a little earlier each day. All those alpines and rooted shrub cuttings which weren't quite ready for potting at the end of last month, must now wait until spring. October is for tidying and pottering about with plenty of time for rest and contemplation.

The weather can, at times, be atrocious. I've known Octobers with howling wind and driving rain for twenty-six out of its thirty-one days, and towards the end of month, stinging hail and sleet. But by then, the garden has long since out-grown its spring vulnerability. Shoots and leaves have hardened, tender buds are few, and so are my anxieties. The damage an autumn storm can do to the garden is never as severe as one that comes in spring or early summer.

For the past few years, October has brought its share of sunny days, gentle and misty-blue with beautiful lingering sunsets, heavily dewed and cobwebbed mornings, and Orion prominent in the night sky. We get our Indian summer now, or Old Wife's summer as it is called in Germany – warm enough for rheumatic bones, while not too hot to sit in the sun in widow's weeds.

It's a rich month with great swathes of asters in the garden, scarlet rose hips in the hedges, and field mushrooms in the meadows. It's harvest

Left: ... swathes of asters ... Above: The Round Garden in early October.

time, the potatoes are lifted at the end of the month, and the freezer is overflowing with vegetables, fruit and heather-fed lamb and mutton. It is a rich month in the vegetable garden and greenhouse. There is still an abundance of salads and herbs. The tomatoes, which I always sow too late, are starting to ripen at long last, and those failing to mature on the vines, colour up on the window sill of the Temple. The last courgettes have swollen into hard-skinned marrows underneath their polythene tents and the first leeks and parsnips are ready to pull, if they haven't all bolted during cold, damp spells. There are green and purple-skinned kohlrabi, from a second sowing in July, and I look forward to the first celeriac, one of my favourite root vegetables.

I love the bounty October brings, the knowledge that we have enough field and garden produce to see us through the winter. Being able to wheel my supermarket trolley past the vegetable section always puts a spring in my step. Not having to rely on the stale, tasteless, and often patchy supplies arriving on the boats from the British mainland is perhaps one of the most satisfying aspects of gardening in Shetland.

The compost gets a final turning this month. We winter our smallest lambs inside, bringing them into the byre in December and returning them to the hill in March or April. They leave behind them their bedding, a mixture of straw, peat and autumn leaves, enriched with both liquid and solid manure.

The compost heap, contained by a three-sided wooden frame, is divided into two equal sections by a wooden partition. One half is empty, the other piled high with garden waste by October. All is turned into the empty half now, neatly built up, layered with the byre cleanings, and covered for the winter. This leaves the now empty part ready to receive the autumnal border clearings.

By spring the layered compost has settled to half its height and is ready to be planted with courgettes. They are protected by a strip of polythene, weighed down by wooden battens attached to its shorter ends, making a snuggly-fitting, secure cover which stays in place well into early summer or, if the summer is a wet and cold one, for the whole growing season.

The growing season is drawing to a close, expectations are lowered and anything the garden presents me with is a gift, a bonus. Several roses produce good crops of hips, notably the rugosas, with fruits the shape and colour of small tomatoes. The first of these ripen to coincide with the last of the flowers in a most satisfying clash of orange and magenta. The low growing rugosa hybrid 'Fru Dagmar Hastrup' often goes on producing its large, singe pink flowers all through the month.

Rosa canina and *R. glauca* also fruit reliably most years. But *Rosa moyesii*, the oldest rose in the garden and usually grown as much for its spectacular hips as its flowers, has been a disappointment. I used to blame our short summers for this until I bought the pink cultivar *R. m.* 'Highdownensis' which is hung with long, crimson flagons every autumn. Perhaps my *Rosa moyesii* suffers from some mysterious disease or I have unwittingly bought a sterile clone.

Malus 'John Downie' has settled into fruiting mode, and is hung with little yellow apples. They look unreal in their red-cheeked prettiness, a bit like the marzipan fruits which appear in the shops before Christmas. Crab apple jelly would be a fine thing, but we're usually beaten to the harvest.

'Fru Dagmar Hastrup'.

Malus 'John Downie'.

Swedish whitebeam in fruit.

Diary 9th October

The rooks flew in on one of their raids today. Like aerial pirates, they swooped over the hill from Kergord, where they live (three miles as the crow flies). They settled on a potato field on the other side of the voe and filled their bellies. I first heard their raucous, throaty cries, then saw them circling above the garden. In search of dessert as it turned out. There were about twenty of them, some strutting the ground below 'John Downie', but most of them precariously balanced on its branches. In less than an hour they'd picked the tree clean, leaving nothing but a few crumbs for my blackbirds. I enjoyed the spectacle.

There's a row of Swedish whitebeams (*Sorbus intermedia*) planted outside the boundary dyke on the east side of the garden. The ground there is about two to three feet lower than inside the garden and I bought standards to save time and to create instant height. I might as well have planted small whips, for the standards took over a decade to settle in and were a miserable sight throughout. Their crowns started to bulk out about five years ago and the trees have now settled into fruiting mode. The large bunches of orange-red fruits look spectacular, but never remain on the trees for long. The starlings have one of their strongholds in that part of the garden and pick the berries almost as soon as they're ripe. I find large numbers of whitebeam seedlings all over the garden, some are potted up for sale, but most are given away to patient friends and visitors, who don't mind waiting a few years for results.

There are large numbers of rowans in the garden and the shelterbelt (I've lost count over the years). Most of the native rowans (*Sorbus aucuparia*) fruit only sporadically. They are weighed down with berries one year, produce a mere sprinkling in another, and hardly a berry between them in yet another. Some remain stubbornly barren altogether. All flower freely in

Sorbus vilmorinii.

May. The climate might have a bearing on this, but there must also be genetic factors involved, as one rowan, planted in the sunk garden, crops reliably regardless of the weather.

A yellow-fruited cultivar, planted in the White Garden, makes a welcome change from the red theme and is left alone by the birds until they have polished off everything else.

I also grow several of the Asiatic rowans. They start fruiting at an early age, and once in the habit, stick with it. *S. cashmeriana* is a little out of its depth on my stodgy peat. It is sparsely-branched and a little stunted, but transformed when in flower, and again now, with every branch laden with large clusters of milky-white berries, each with a little precision-stamped maroon star at its base. *Sorbus vilmorinii* was planted (inadvertently) in the firing line of a wind funnel at the eastern end of the South Border. Now and again it gets a hammering in spring, and I spend a day balancing on top of a stepladder (a job I hate as I have no head for

heights), pruning back its wind-burnt top twigs. Despite, or perhaps because of this sporadic intervention it has grown into a small, graceful tree. Its long leaves are composed of up to twenty individual oval leaflets, which gives it a soft, feathery appearance. Its berries are pink at first, then over the course of a week or two, deepen to a subtle mauve-crimson. I bought *S. koehneana*, *S. forrestii* and *S. setchuanensis* as pot-grown seedlings at the Dundee Botanic Garden, after admiring their parents. They're growing into well-shaped large shrubs and their berries are pleasing shades of white and pink.

A fine selection of woody and herbaceous plants are propagated and grown by the Society of Friends of this botanic garden and sold to generate a little extra income. Sadly during my last visit this eclectic and exciting mixture of plants had been replaced by an uninspiring assortment of commercially grown shrubs.

Cotoneasters are often classed as bread-and-butter shrubs and, overused in public and amenity plantings, have got a reputation of being dull and utilitarian. I have an old specimen of the herring-bone cotoneaster (*C. horizontalis*) growing in a scraping of soil (where nothing else would grow before) between the porch door and a narrow raised bed below the kitchen window. It is reaching for the eaves of the house, growing flat, both verticallly and horizontally, against the wall. It is a favourite with bees when covered in its tiny white flowers in spring, and a favourite with the blackbirds when it turns scarlet with berries in the autumn. It is deciduous, and its bare branches bear indeed some resemblance to a picked-clean herring bone. Some years the berries hang on into early winter, in others they're polished off within days.

Diary 12th October

When I pulled up the study blinds this morning, I was met by a fluttering flock of parrots, some on the wing, but most settled on the branches of the pines. Some were a bright vermilion orange with dark brown wings, others a greenish yellow, with the same dark wings and a flash of canary-yellow along their backs. One or two started setting to work on the pine cones with their strong, curved bills.

They turned out to be parrot crossbills, from the forests of Scandinavia and Russia, but with their brilliantly coloured plumage wouldn't have been out of place in a tropical rainforest. The wind has been blowing strongly from the east and this afternoon brought more exotic visitors. Waxwings were feeding on the cotoneaster berries outside the kitchen window. One flew right into the porch, then tried to make its escape through the closed window. I caught it, and held it for a bit, caged in my fingers. What a beautiful bird with a pinkish-buff breast, a little black chin patch, and pale orange crest. A dab of red sealing wax graced each wing, and the tips of the wing and tail feathers were outlined in thin, yellow bands.

The crossbills had vanished the following morning, but the waxwings stayed. They were soon joined by many more and over the next few days stripped the bushes clean and put the blackbirds' noses out of joint.

In the windshade of this cotoneaster I have a sweet bay, *Laurus nobilis*, which benefits from the shelter. It will never become a tree, and has, after many years, grown into a small shrub, just on three feet (90cm) high and a little wider. Picking fresh bay leaves through the open kitchen window is one of the luxuries of life. I love their strong flavour and never use them sparingly as suggested in recipes. They are wonderful in Spanish meat stews, their strong flavour balanced by the equally strong ones of black olives and orange peel; they also give Anatolian lentil soup its distinctive taste. This is made with red lentils, onions, a good meat stock, paprika and copious amounts of bay, all whizzed through the blender after cooking.

There are still a few touches of colour in the north-facing borders. Hardy geraniums, shorn back in late July, are repeating now and there are always a few seedlings of *Geranium procurrens* which escape my notice until they come into

Geranium procurrens.

bloom. Treated as a weed in many parts of the garden, in October, every bud is precious and its black-pencilled mauve flowers are much admired. Spurges are sun lovers, but *Euphorbia donii* flowers freely in shade and displays its sharp yellow bracts well into autumn.

The leaflets of the evergreen *Cotoneaster microphyllus* are a dark, almost blackish green, but its berries are only produced freely after a hot summer. It lies snug up against a byre wall, leaving plenty of planting space in front. There is something to be said for wall shrubs which don't need a trellis or wire for support. Against it I grow the tall, blue-leaved grass *Helictotrichon sempervirens* and in front of that bolsters of the golden-leaved thyme, *Thymus* x. *citriodorus* 'Aureus'. Vivid colours and strong all-year-round contrasts. The helictotrichon is, as its name suggests, evergreen, but sheds all of its old foliage, gradually, in early spring. The spent leaves bleach to an off-white, creating a bi-coloured effect among the still blue ones. Most get blown away, and those which still remain in spring I comb out, to make way for the new foliage, which is already a foot high by March.

The berries of *Cotoneaster conspicuus* 'Decorus' have so far been conspicuous by their absence, but this shrub has moulded itself over one of the boulders on the Compost Rock and, like *C. microphyllus*, makes a good dark foil for plants with contrasting leaf shapes and colours.

Cotoneaster adpressus, a prostrate, deciduous shrublet, has found its way out of a raised bed and has started to clothe the stone steps which lead to the Temple Terrace, to good effect. Its berries are plentiful and its small leaves, which turn crimson before dropping, have wavy margins.

Late-flowering spurge, *Euphorbia donii*, with hoverfly.

C. 'Cornubia' is spectacular at fruiting time. It has grown into a small tree at the west end of the Kitchen Garden, and is laden down with drooping clusters of large, red berries. They remind me of the lacquered papier-mache fruits my grandmother used to wear on her black straw hat. It is said to be semi-evergreen, but always sheds its leaves in November. They are large for a cotoneaster, ribbed and handsome.

Cotoneaster bullatus also makes a large shrub or small tree in time, and its coral-red fruits are favourites with the birds. Long after the berries have gone, their reddish petioles throw lacey patterns against the sky.

Here I must make another mention of *Disporum smithii*, already described in early summer. It has the most spectacular fruits of any herbaceous plant in my garden: bright orange and the size of marbles. The birds never eat them which means I can enjoy them well into early winter some years. They remain on the plant until they split open to reveal hard, pale yellow seeds. Forests of seedlings spring up around the parent plant in March.

Lamium galeobdolon 'Hermann's Pride' grows nearby and needs curtailing now and then. This form, unlike the species, doesn't root as it goes and is easily confined to its allotted space. Its flowering in June, often overlooked, is repeated in October, following a midsummer short-back-and-sides.

The translucent red fruit clusters of the native honeysuckle, *Lonicera periclymenum*, are not the showiest of autumn berries, but are a pretty sight when there are lots of them, which is never the case for long. Beloved by blackbirds, they seem to have a rather strange effect on them.

Diary **19th October**

One evening last week, just after I'd settled down with a glass of wine and a book, there was a thud on the living room window, followed by another, and another, and another. Birds flying into windows is an infrequent occurrence, and one I always investigate in case of injury, or temporary disability, which makes them easy prey for our cats. I found no birds on the ground but stood for some time in the half-light and watched a blackbird feeding frenzy in the honeysuckle. The next morning, when I let the dogs out, several young blackbirds, quite oblivious to my presence, were feeding again. There was movement and some fluttering sound at ground level, and as I went to investigate found three birds staggering, and helplessly flapping their wings. One flew off in a strangely dipping and swaying fashion, crash-landed in the elder opposite, then somersaulted onto the dyke below. While I tried to catch the others, one bird fell from high in the bush, got tangled in a potted olearia, then flew off in the same ill-co-ordinated and haphazard fashion.

This bizzare behaviour continued, on and off, for the best of a week – until all the berries had gone. Dave Watson, a keen and knowledgeable ornithologist, suggested that "the demon drink" was responsible for this undignified behaviour. Berries, he said, have been known to ferment, either on the plant or in the birds' stomachs. If that's the case my blackbirds must have suffered severe hangovers of late.

The Scottish flame flower, *Tropaeoleum speciosum* rings the changes. Its light cobalt blue berries are produced in trios and held by a maroon calyx. A rather fetching arrangement, and to my mind as good in its own way as the plant's scarlet nasturtium flowers in summer.

Hymenanthera crassifolia is a stiffly-branched evergreen shrublet, wider than high and suitable for groundcover on damp, acid soil. It has small, rounded dull green leaves and belongs to the violet family. In early summer the undersides of its branches are studded with tiny mauve

Diary   15th October

The weather has been exceptionally kind to us this autumn, there haven't been any of the customary downpours yet, which, once they start, tend to continue and change the weather pattern irreversibly. We've just enjoyed a whole week of perfect Indian summer. Today was clear and cloudless and there was enough strength left in the sun to warm my back while I spent the whole day collecting seed. Such "unseasonal" weather brings its share of unseasonal flowers. Yellow *Verbascum* seedlings, which usually sit out the winter as large felted leaf rosettes, are in flower all over the garden. My one and only *Tradescantia* was gnawed to stumps by the slugs in late spring and subsequently moved to a more open position. Completely forgotten thereafter, I came upon it today, and found it spring-fresh and in full flower.

We took our afternoon tea in the Back Yard on blankets and cushions. This turned out to be a rather extended tea ceremony which ended in an early al fresco supper (much to the delight of Anna, who loves picnics), while the sun set against a mackerel sky.

Tradescantia **cultivar.**

flowers, followed by sizeable white berries in the autumn. It comes from New Zealand, and so does the prostrate *Fuchsia procumbens* which only sets seed after a particularly warm summer. They are encased in pretty shell-pink berries and largely ignored by the birds. It is short-lived with me, rarely surviving more than one winter, but plants raised from seed in March flower the same year.

All the berrying trees and shrubs I've mentioned are easily raised from seed. Extracting it from the berries for winter storage or for exchange, is a slow and messy job. An easier method is squeezing it, pulp and all, directly into seed trays. I cover these sowings with a thick layer of grit or coarse sand, and let the elements do the rest. Alternate freezing and thawing and copious amounts of rain wash out the germination-inhibiting chemicals, and the first seedlings usually turn up in early spring. Collecting the berries on a warm, sunny autumn day is a pleasure.

I grow a lot of plants from seed, some bought or exchanged, but the bulk of it collected in the garden. The early spring bulbs and some primroses ripen theirs in May and June, and as this is my busiest time, I often arrive on the scene too late; the pods already empty. During late summer and autumn, seed hunting takes place on a regular and frequent basis. I go out into the garden on each still and sunny day, armed with clipboard and pencil, and a supply of brown paper bags and self-seal envelopes. Aquilegias, lilies, meconopsis and irises are easy, their well-filled pods are quickly gathered, and the thistledown of many composites can simply be scooped off the plants. Some geraniums tend to ripen their seed over a long period of time and I visit them weekly to pick what is ripe. But harvesting is generally swift, it's the cleaning which takes time, and I spend many days extracting seed and removing chaff and dust and husks.

Gathering seed is best done in dry weather, but there are years when I miss the best times,

Veronicastrum virginicum.

and seasons which are all damp. That's when I hang up the seed, their paper bags tied up with string, to dry above the Rayburn. The crackling and popping of geranium seed released from its spring mechanism, and the gunshot explosions of the euphorbias, excite and consternate the cats.

There's always far more than I can use, and apart from the most incontinent seeders, "deads" and plant skeletons are left. They provide food for the birds, and their dry and bleached remains are welcome as the late flowers go over, and give the garden a mellow, seasonal look. The brown stands of astilbes, the arching beaded panicles of *Veronicastrum virginicum*, the sculptural pods of lilies and irises, the thistledown of the olearias, and the silky mop heads on the clematis vines – all add to autumn's charms.

The first colchicums always take me by surprise. Where there was nothing the day

before, suddenly here they are, like mushrooms after a shower. Their pale noses have indeed a mushroom-like quality and so does their breakneck speed of growth. Their white buds elongate by the minute and rapidly take on colour as they emerge from the ground.

C. autumnale is always the first to flower, often putting in an appearance in the last week of August. I have several patches of it, tucked between shrubs and under trees and a large colony in the bathroom bed, growing through carpets of ajuga, *Lysimachia nummularia* and *Hedera helix*. The colour of this colchicum is said to vary in the wild: my plants, which arrived as a present of half a dozen bulbs, are a pale mauve.

I first encountered *Colchicum speciosum* in an old garden at Seafield, just outside Lerwick, where carpets of it flanked both sides of a long drive, shaded by an avenue of old sycamores – a marvellous sight. This was one of those occasions in a gardener's life when the longing to own a plant far outweighs social inhibitions and rules of etiquette. I knocked on the door of the house and was given permission to lift a few bulbs. This colchicum has a more full-blooded look than *C. autumnale*, a strong reddish mauve with a contrasting white throat.

Since then colchicums have become an addiction and many others have followed. Their colouring and delicate texture makes them look a little out of place among autumn leaves and fiery crocosmias, as if they'd strayed into autumn from a season at the other end of the gardening year.

The bulbs of *C. autumnale* 'Album' increase quickly in both size and numbers and I now have several small colonies of them, thick clusters of small, creamy-white blooms. 'Autumn Queen' has clear light violet flowers with a greenish base, and 'Rosy Dawn' produces large goblets of a reddish purple. Both flower early. The well-known 'Lilac Wonder' flowers freely and over a long season. *C. cilicium* is a mauvish pink and does best in the sharp drainage of a raised bed.

Colchicums are often recommended for damp and shady places, but show no great liking for them in my garden. In such situations bulbs don't increase, produce no flowers or neither. The exception is 'Waterlily', a vigorous and free-flowering cultivar which increases rapidly. It is the largest of the double-flowered colchicums with several layers of pointed, cyclamen pink

Colchicum 'Waterlily'.

Colchicum agrippinum.

"petals". During rainy spells it tends to get a little top-heavy and flops over its neighbours.

Slugs are fond of colchicum buds and must be curtailed, especially during damp weather. They often find their way, sadly long before I do, to one of the smallest, and most precious, *C. aggrippinum* with star-shaped magenta-pink flowers, chequered like a snakeshead fritillary.

The large foliage of colchicums is often cited as a major drawback. I find it rather handsome, glossy and upright, and a good, rich green, rather like the leaves of a small aspidistra. It makes a fine setting for all sorts of spring flowers, and takes on the role of hostas, long before those appear above ground.

As summer's floral glories draw to an end, I once more enjoy those parts of the garden planted with a wide variety of smart ground cover. Leaves come into their own again; the dark, silver-flecked tongues of *Pulmonaria longifolia* look striking against the glossy yellow-green of a mushroom-clipped box. Opposite the Peat Bank the golden blades of *Carex elata* 'Aurea' are mellowing to a tawny orange, a colour echoed by a near-by hosta. The picture is completed by a dark green lungwort and the glaucous stars of a young lupin.

I have tried many autumn crocuses over the years. They flower, following a late summer planting, then vanish without trace. There's one notable exception. *Crocus speciosus* is going from strength to strength. About five years ago I came

Carex elata 'Aurea' with lungworts, lupins and hostas.

across a patch of this crocus in full flower in the Sunk Garden. I hadn't planted it and the only explanation for its appearance I have is that it came as a stow-away among the roots of some other plant. Such fortuitous events are rare, but do occur from time to time. It has never looked back and now grows in several parts of the garden. Its corms increase quickly and I have planted some in the Back Yard meadow, where they continue to spread. It flowers from mid October until the end of November and I like its lively, yet subtle blue. Close-up the colour is pale lavender, deepened by dark veining.

Mice are inordinately fond of crocus corms, the autumn as well as the spring flowering kinds. For several consecutive years I couldn't work out why the crocuses I planted in the autumn failed to turn up in spring. Blaming my heavy soil, I tried them in better-drained locations, with the same lack of results. It was only when I found tell-tale dips and empty husks in pots which had been planted with crocuses only the the day before, that it dawned on me. Mice prefer to dig up newly-planted corms, and mothballs incorporated into soil or potting compost are said to deter them. I haven't tried this, but devised my own method, a confusant rather than deterrent, to put the mice off the scent: a few sprigs of the pungently-aromatic *Artemisia* 'Powis Castle', placed over new plantings.

Bulb planting starts in September and continues all through October most years, and in parts of the garden where there are no bulbs, it is a rather straightforward matter. I place them around the base of a shrub, amongst herbaceous plants and ferns, wherever I think they'll look their best. But such virginal areas are few and far between.

We are told to broadcast our bulbs in grass for a natural effect. This might well work with large narcissus bulbs, but I defy all but the most

Diary **4th October**

It's been a perfect day, mild and sunny and I managed to get the rest of the bulbs in. Lots more crocuses for the hay meadow to balance the side planted up last autumn, and ribbons of *Narcissus* 'Pipit' all through the Kitchen Borders, which are quite devoid of colour now. The camassias though are still in their bags. There was simply no space in my damp borders. They are still so lush and colourful with the last Chinese astilbes, dwarf persicarias, and *Rudbeckia fulgida*, which has at long last made up its mind to flower for me.

eagle-eyed gardeners to find crocus corms or other small subjects in longish grass after such a broadcasting operation. I tried it once, before I knew better, and spent hours on hands and knees, searching. Few of us have the means to plant a large area of grass with all the bulbs we want there in a given year. I add a little each autumn, laying the bulbs out in a small area, and plant them on Christopher Lloyd's principles in small groups, a few singly, laid out as informally as possible while varying the distances between them to avoid straight lines.

This works well in grass, but in beds and borders already thickly planted with bulbs, all invisible below ground, finding the right spots can be difficult, and in the past, believing I'd found that spot, my trowel sliced right through a clutch of bulbs already in residence. Few are labelled, my memories of last spring are vague and patchy, and the entries in my garden notebook are not always as helpful as I'd like them to be. "Plant a lot more C. t. in Sunk Garden" isn't much use, but a later and more detailed entry which instructs me to plant *Crocus tommasinianus* in the pockets between the shrubs on the eastern boundary of that garden, is easily followed.

Of late I have taken to raising more and more bulbs in pots, planted singly for the larger ones, or from three to five in a seven or nine centimetre pot for crocuses, muscari, scillas, chionodoxas and the like. It is a fair bit of work, but worth it for its precision results. Some I keep in the Temple or bring into the house for early flowering, but most are reserved for the garden, to be planted out in bud, or even full flower, and exactly where they're needed. After a thorough soaking, to prevent the compost from falling away from their roots, and gently eased from their pots, like a cake from its mould, they transplant easily.

Some of the ornamental grasses are at their best now in their bleached straw and buff shades. *Cortaderia richardii* has been in flower since late June, great shaggy plumes arching over the Temple Terrace. Since shedding their seed a month ago, they have thinned a little and changed from white to a deep, warm ivory. The native wavy hair grass, *Deschampsia flexuosa*, was resident in the Back Yard when we arrived and, since sheep have been removed from the area, has grown into a large, dense tussock of narrow, arching blades. I also grow the German cultivar, *D. caespitosa* 'Goldschleier' (Golden Veil), which is taller at four feet and lives up to its name with fine, pale yellow autumn tints.

Molinia caerulea 'Heidebraut' is a tall clone of the purple moor grass, which does well in all its forms on our damp, acid soil. Its stiff, pale stems, topped by slender, bronzed flower spikes rise in a four-foot column above arching, basal leaves. It grows in Edith's Bed behind the bronze-leaved, orange-flowered *Crocosmia* 'Solfatare'.

I look out onto this bed from my desk, which makes it the most closely-observed and scrutinised part of the garden, and has to please me all year round, but especially in autumn, when I tend to catch up on my paper work.

For a while I toyed with the easy and all-year-round solution of heathers, dwarf conifers and other evergreens together with a sprinkling of spring bulbs. But I wanted something more

Cortaderia richardii **and Flo.**

exciting, a colourful planting with several floral highlights to mark the changing of the seasons. The bed's well-drained soil (by my standards) has been a great help in trying to achieve this. Evergreen shrubs still play an important role, but those planted as a background are still too small to make an impact.

Hakonechloa macra 'Aureola', an evergreen grass, shows up well over a distance. Its arched, tapering leaves grow in neat mounds, less than a foot high and are striped in strong green and yellow. Next to it, for a strong contrast of both shape and colour I have *Bergenia* 'Admiral'. It's typical elephant's ears are exceptionally tough and leathery, and stand up well to the weather. They are dull green above and a bright mauve on the reverse, and take on wonderful autumn tints of plum and crimson. Its flowers are a luminous cerise, produced in May and October.

Fragaria 'Red Ruby', in the same bed, flowers tirelessly all summer, in a strong shade of pink, rather than red, and if cut back halfway

through the season keeps going into November. Like all strawberries it produces countless runners, which need rigorous curtailing. It is really too rampant for this bed and I'm toying with the idea of planting it underneath some shrubs, where it can satisfy its free-range tendencies without strangling its neighbours.

In restricted settings, plants with a long flowering season are indispensable, and another one I have chosen for this small bed is *Geranium pyrenaicum* 'Bill Wallis'. Again, cut back halfway through the season, its small magenta-purple stars last well into autumn. *Lysimachia davurica* flowers light yellow from July until the first frosts. *L. yunnanense* flowers briefly but sweetly in blush-white, then charms in autumn with fat spikes of maroon berries.

The planting has its share of seasonal performers: *Crocosmia paniculata*, tall, late and handsome with its upright pleated leaves and arching sprays of orange-vermilion flowers, *Aconitum carmichaelii*, equally tall and handsome

Acanthus hungaricus.

6th October

The great 'S.B. West' mystery was solved today. I'd kept some of the plants (just going over in their pots) back for myself, and while looking for a suitable space, came across their Doppelgänger, in full bloom at the *western* end of the *South Border*. Cati Servera, who did most of the potting this spring, copied, as was her task, the writing from my batch label onto all the individual labels, thus *Aster* "S.B. West" was born.

with branching spires of soft blue monkshood flowers, and the fabulous *Acanthus hungaricus* with its deeply-cut foliage and foxglove spikes in mauve and white.

Michaelmas daisies feature large in many parts of my garden. I have about twenty varieties, but can only put names to a handful.

In a collection of over 1,500 different plants there is inevitably a percentage without names or names of doubtful validity. For many years I grew *Aster novae-angliae* "Tall Pink" until I came face to face with 'Harrington's Pink' in an English garden. Supplying a plant with its rightful name is always a joyful occasion.

Most of my autumn asters came from my mother's garden or those of her neighbours, the pretty double mauve-cerise "S.B. West" included. It grows to two feet (60cm) and needs staking in a wet season. So does the cordifolius hybrid 'Little Carlow' with clouds of small, lavender daisies. It flowers at about the same time as *A. novi-belgii* 'Alice Haslam', an 18 inch (45cm) cultivar with a long season of bright cherry-pink flowers. *A. novae-angliae* 'Andenken

16th September

Aster 'S.B. West' has been a best-seller in the nursery, but I can't remember for the life of me where it came from. I searched my records, then combed through all the asters in the plant finder without success. I must have obviously bought it in from somewhere, probably a new cultivar, not listed yet.

Aster "S. B. West".

an Alma Pötschke' brings the season to a close in late November, often too late for its deep red, double flowers to open properly.

Border clearing has become a hotly-debated subject in horticultural circles. Some gardeners are firm believers in leaving all spent growth over the winter, to break down into rich humus, and before then, to provide food and shelter for garden fauna. This form of management, or lack of it, is fine, as far as I'm concerned, in other people's gardens, and in my own in only those remote and marginal parts, where looks don't matter and where I don't pass too frequently.

The other argument for postponing the clearing until spring is that by then all plant remains, which are awkward and heavy in autumn, have shrivelled and dried away to nothing. Not in my garden. Some old foliage turns into soggy, solid lumps, good for nothing except harbouring slugs and smothering spring bulbs. Stems turn brittle and their splinters get blown all over the place. Some autumns, when the heavy rains arrive early, there's nothing for it but to remove all that is sodden and slimy. Most years border clearing is a series of well-timed and sensitive interventions; cutting away what is well past its best from October onwards.

In my Desert Bed there is still a large drift of *Allium sphaerocephalum*, about 18 inches (45cm) tall with clover heads of a deep maroon-crimson, from a late spring planting. When planted in autumn, or once settled in, this flowers in July. The leaves and inflorescence of *Sedum* 'Purple Emperor', the last to flower, have the same dark colouring.

Diary   **27th October**

My autumnal paradise has vanished. All that was crisp and golden last week is dark and heavy. The skies closed in on Saturday and James managed to get the last of the tatties (potatoes) lifted before the deluge. Everything is bent over with the weight of rain. Where there was ample space on all the paths, I now have to squeeze my way through sodden vegetation. Most of the plants in the South Border have collapsed and the buds on 'Alma Pötschke', so full of promise last week, are black. But the rain has also worked its magic, pools have formed in the leaf centres of the water saxifrage and every blade of *Carex* 'Coman's Bronze' is strung with glittering pearls.

Carex **'Coman's Bronze'** with *Hydrangea paniculata.*

Sedum **'Purple Emperor'.**

Sunk into the sand of the bed, is a large plastic basin filled with Guernsey lilies, *Cyrtanthus elatus* (*Vallota speciosa* until recently), which start to flower from the middle of the month. Large, fleshy buds open into clusters of velvet-textured vermilion stars. Our negligible frosts don't harm this plant, but they need more warmth than our average summer can provide to coax them into performing. I have some in pots in the Temple, where they flower a good month earlier. Depending on the season, the basin is brought out as early as June, or as late as August some years.

Before the month draws to a close it has one more treat in store. Large-flowered clematis have a chequered history with me. Some succumbed to clematis wilt before I knew of the disease and could have saved lives through deep planting. Others failed to flower or had their dormant leaf buds eaten by slugs. *Clematis* 'Jackmanii' survived years of neglect and greatly enhances an old elder with its long inky-purple season.

Clematis 'Jackmanii'.

Right: *Tropacoleum speciosum* **in fruit.**

November

Autumn colour can be a bit of a hit and miss affair on a rock sticking out of the Atlantic at 60° north. Leaves are often torn off the trees long before they get a chance to turn. But there are years when the autumnal gales fail to materialise, when storms are rare before December and when the winds blow in moderation from September to November. A cold drizzle often sets in towards the middle of the month, with oppressively low grey skies for days on end. It's the month I make plans to emigrate, and would probably have done so long ago, were it not for the "days between weathers" when the sun breaks through the clouds, and the garden goes through a spectacular change.

Grey, brown, black and leaden green, under an equally leaden sky, can be the month's predominant colours. Grey and leaden is my mood, and I welcome with joy those rare November days when the sun, low in the southern sky, brings a mellow glow to the trees and paints the whole garden in a warm, golden light.

There are still a few late flowers. Dusky-pink *Digitalis mertonensis* keeps going until blackened by the frosts, kept company by the last of the Michaelmas daisies. *Veratrum album*, temperamental and difficult to please, often delays until now, and sends up full spikes of greenish-white. Many of the day lilies I have often only flower after a good, hot summer.

Left: **The November sun brings a warm glow to the garden. Above:** *Hemerocallis fulva* **'Green Kwanso'.**

Hemerocallis 'Green Kwanso' is no exception, and much appreciated now with its buff-orange double flowers.

November is the month for tidying the potting shed. No matter how organised I think I am and how many more hooks and shelves James puts up, things are always left lying about during the busy times. There are stacks of used pots everywhere, tools strewn over the potting bench or worse, left in the garden where they have started to rust. Oiling and sharpening trowels, spades, shears and secateurs is not a job I relish and is frequently put off. The cold and draughty potting shed holds no attractions on a dark, rainy November day, but once out there, in multi-layered clothing, with the radio for company, and a thermos flask of strong peppermint tea, the task becomes a bearable one.

Root crops are plentiful now and, with the addition of a few chick peas, or a shoulder of mutton, make warming stews. Carrot and beetroot, grated raw and dressed with a honey and mustard vinaigrette, is a favourite winter salad, and so is raw grated celeriac with fresh rocket leaves and parmesan shavings. Garden rocket has long since run to seed, but wild rocket is a perennial and provides us with a few handfuls of leaves all through the winter. Rows of parsley look spring-green and there are still a few nasturtium leaves and flowers to be picked. They start seeding now to take care of next year's generation.

Diary   4th November

The ground was white this morning, and Minkus (our weather-forecasting cat) has been vindicated. He always leaves home in April and returns a week or so before the first snow in December. When he turned up last week, I was sure he'd got it wrong this time or, growing old, was

Broad Bean 'Bunyard Exhibition', potato 'Red Duke' and carrot 'Chantenay Red Cored'.

longing for his home comforts earlier than usual. A layer of wet snow, which must have fallen during the night, has frozen hard and put short shrift to the garden's late show. All the flowers look as if encrusted in sugar, a strange sight. In the Round Garden *Rosa* 'Bonica' still in full flow and with many unopened buds, lies bent to the ground under its frosty, white burden.

Arisaema candidissimum foliage.

Early snow (*Rosa* 'Bonica').

Most years November brings at least a brief flutter of autumn colour. The hostas, prominent since June, have their final fling now, turn butter yellow and stay that way, until the first hard frost finishes them off, swiftly, rather than gracefully. Some of my hardy geraniums go out in a blaze of glory. *G. macrorrhizum*, which is semi-evergreen, turns those leaves it sheds orange and crimson. *Arisaema candidissimum*, mentioned in July, is noteworthy again, for its large, three-lobed foliage which turns from foxy orange to honey-blond.

But the real show takes place a storey or two higher. In a good autumn, the rowans are on fire for a week, two if the weather stays warm, especially *Sorbus commixta*, which is the last to lose its leaves. *S.* 'Joseph Rock', a yellow-flowered cultivar, is also good for autumn colour. The lobed leaves of the whitebeams change gradually to a tawny, orange-brown with an edge of tarnished silver.

The downy birches, bought from a tree nursery in Aberdeen and raised from seed collected at Deeside, are used to much warmer and drier autumns and only make it if the season is a particularly kind one. But members of the same species, brought to me from Iceland and coastal Norway, are used to shutting up shop early and turn a brilliant yellow all over and every year. *Hoheria glabrata*, in its juvenile stage, could almost be mistaken for one of them in

Gentiana sino-ornata.

autumn, and from a distance, as the whole shrub turns a startling shade of lemon before dropping its leaves in one fell swoop.

As the leaves start to turn and fall, the Asiatic autumn gentians come into their own. All need acid soil, form low, sprawling and more or less prostrate mats, and *Gentiana sino-ornata* is the easiest to grow with large blue – gentian blue – trumpets, broadly banded with silver. It flowers from mid-October right through November and I have several stretches of it, one in front of the evergreen shrublet *Osmanthus heterophyllus* 'Goshiki'. This is much slower growing than the species (mentioned later), but has the same dark green leaves, generously streaked with cream and yellow and a hint of pink during cold weather. Some people find the colouring of this gentian

Gentiana 'Strathmore'.

a little on the hard side, and for them there is *G. macaulayi*, which is a little lighter, or 'Strathmore' with long, slender trumpets of a pale sky blue; this looks particularly good when growing in and out of the little silver-edged sedge, *Carex conica* 'Snowline'. *Gentiana* 'Brin's Form' sprawls a lot more than all the others and has been taken off the lists of most alpine nurseries for this reason. I consider its sprawl, two by two feet wide from just one plant, an asset, along with its slightly earlier season, and mid-blue colouring.

The Japanese larches, of which I have many, start to colour in the second half of the month, a luminous shade of pale Naples yellow, first on the trees, and after the needles have dropped, on the ground below them. Witch hazels are some of the best shrubs for autumn colour, with their large round leaves a uniform, glowing yellow or orange. *Hydrangea petiolaris* paints the byre roof in glorious shades of primrose and maize, a colour echoed by the rugosa roses in the shelter belt. Yellow predominates, and in a good November the whole garden glows.

I have already written extensively about cotoneasters last month, but there is one more, worth growing for its autumn colour alone. *C. lucidus* arrived here as part of an assortment of nameless shrubs, a special offer from a mail order firm. I can't remember what the others were, and none have survived. It is a small shrub, four feet (12m) high and as wide, of neat, twiggy habit, with oval, polished leaves and the typical small whitish flowers, followed by crops of black berries, all but invisible among the greenery. Some years it starts closing off in late September and over the next three weeks glows orange, scarlet, and finally a vivid sealing wax red – regardless of the weather. It has been christened "The Burning Bush" by one of our regular visitors.

Aronia melanocarpa, the black chokeberry from North America is said to colour just as brilliantly, but hasn't performed here yet. I'm not fond of its suckering habit and might move it from the garden to the shelterbelt. The foliage of

Cornus alba.

Rhododendron luteum changes to a deep, polished crimson with orange and purple shading at the end of the month. Devoid of leaves it looks a little stiff and ungainly, but each of its twigs ends in a fat green sticky bud, promising a good display next May of its yellow, funnel-shaped, strongly scented flowers.

The dogwood, *Cornus alba*, does not like growing in full exposure, and even plants of a great age remain dwarfed and twiggy. It is well worth a reasonably sheltered place for its red bark and subtle pink and fawn autumn shades. I don't cut mine back to stumps, as recommended, but cut out some of their oldest wood each spring. This keeps them in good heart and produces enough wood with its vivid winter colour for my needs.

Leaves, once fallen, have to be swept or raked up. This is a chore I enjoy because of its almost instant and very satisfying results; a great job to get me warmed up – and often out into the garden in the first place – on a cold, grey November morning. I don't remove them all, those in the long north-facing border and other shady places are left as a mulch. The leaves of most deciduous trees and shrubs rot away quickly in our wet climate and can turn black and slimy within days, making paths and steps hazardous to walk on. A stiff-bristled, long-handled brush takes care of those. A cover of rotting foliage can spell death to mats of alpines, small evergreen shrubs and prostrate conifers, and must be removed. A springy, thin-pronged lawn rake is best for this purpose. It's rather like grooming a pet, combing out balls of old, matted hair and leaving behind a sleek, shiny coat.

I don't often feel the need to bring flowers into the house, apart from those I cut for the bedrooms of our house guests. I'd much rather enjoy them in the garden, but I can never resist the urge to pick the unseasonal ones, as much for mine as for their sake. I like having them, and

Diary   **18th November**

I have just filled several small vases with spring flowers, cowslips, pulmonarias and a few pale blue sprays of Veronica gentianoides, white lithospermum and pale yellow trollius, a fragile lavender poppy from *Meconopsis quintuplinerva*, small spikes of foxglove buds and scented *Viola cornuta* in white and mauve. All the double primroses have decided it's spring and are covered in buds and flowers.

... double primroses have decided it's spring ...

Diary   **29th November**

Yesterday morning I found a whole bag of *Crocus tommasinianus* corms, wedged between the freezer and the wall. It must have fallen out when the open box of bulbs was briefly stood there last month. I planted them all in the Sunk Garden, and while I worked there, noticed something pink, deep inside *Potentilla* 'Princess'. I'd totally forgotten my patch of *Cyclamen cilicium*, which I'd planted there three years ago and a little to the south of the potentilla. Last autumn they were visible, but one year on, the shrub has covered them completely. I cut a large window out of the their twiggy umbrella, and there they were, perfect darlings with their back-swept blossom pink petals and carpets of dark green, marbled leaves. They must have been in flower for at least a month without my noticing.

their perfume, at close quarters and feel virtuous saving them from the weather, which will sooner rather than later get the better of them.

November always brings what I call our little spring (without the sun and blue skies), when plants, which had their season in May and June have another go at it, before they disappear below ground or shrink into themselves, to sit out the coming winter. This happens every year, and every year I get countless calls from anxious gardeners, worried that the world might come to an end, or has been turned upside down, because their plants flower at quite the wrong time of year. These unseasonal flowers and their spring colours do look strangely out of place in the autumn garden, like visitors from another planet.

Cyclamen hederifolium.

Cyclamen hederifolium and *C. cilicium* open their first buds in late September, but this is their best month. Like those unseasonal flowers, they seem to have strayed from spring into autumn and their bright pink looks strangely out of place in November. My best colony of *C. hederifolium* grows underneath a lodgepole pine. The dry soil above and between the pine roots (some are visible above ground) seems to suit it to perfection. The corms increase in size from year to year, flower with great freedom, and self-sown seedlings – much to my delight – turn up from time to time. *C. cilicium* does not set seed with me. It flowers sparingly, but over a long season, sometimes into December.

During a very cold snap the thermometer in my unheated greenhouse might dip to minus one or two Celsius for a night or part of a night, but during most winters the temperature always stays (sometimes only just) above freezing. Its western half has a gas heater which I only use in late winter/early spring when my first sowings

start to come up, and I don't want the temperature to drop too low. It is a lean-to, built against the south-facing wall of the potting shed/hayloft on sloping ground, which gives it a majestic height. A narrow raised bed runs along its north wall and in it I grow a wild peach with furry-grey skin and beetroot-red flesh, an apple tree, a 'Brown Turkey' fig, and *Ugni molinae*, the Chilean guava. This evergreen shrub survives and flowers perfectly well out of doors, but rarely if ever manages to ripen its fruits, and as I am hopelessly addicted to the tart, aromatic flavour of its black berries, it has to live under glass.

Clivia miniata has its winter quarters in this border. It spends the summer in the garden and often starts producing buds in the autumn. That's when I bring it in to stop the autumn rains from spoiling its orange flowers.

On the south side of the greenhouse, and divided from the raised bed by a narrow path, are two lots of slatted wooden staging, one at potting height, and one high above my head and

The south-facing greenhouse.

only accessible with the aid of a tall stool or step ladder. Up there I store those plants which can be kept bone-dry all winter: begonias, dahlias, and all manner of bulbous plants, tender succulents and my ever-growing collection of cacti. One winter, those in the front-row, nearest the glass, were reduced to green jelly during a frosty night. Since then they have been protected by a thick buffer of crumpled newspaper and bubble wrap.

This top-stage assortment also includes those spring bulbs which need higher summer temperatures and drier winter conditions than the outdoors can provide. They're mostly fritillaries and I start them on a spartan watering regime now, increasing it once the first leaf tips appear.

Sometimes I also store potted tulip bulbs on these shelves, and there are years when I forget all about them until November, or even December. They've often started into growth by then and look perfectly healthy, even in compost as dry as dust. It's too late by then to sort through and re-pot them, and I usually just stand them outside. In pots they're relatively safe, but when grown in the garden, small black slugs, which live below ground, feed on their dormant bulbs until they resemble well-gnawed apple cores.

I also keep a couple of pots of *Crocus sativus*, the saffron crocus, on the top staging, the hottest place in the house. It starts into growth in late August and gets more care and attention than all the other greenhouse bulbs put together. I re-pot it every other year, I give it bonemeal and potash feeds, I give it a summer baking, all to no avail. Once (it must have been my lucky year), it produced two of its lavender blue goblets with their long, red, thread-like stigmas. Since then I've been waiting in vain for an opportunity to impress my friends with a few strands of home-grown saffron.

I raise large numbers of plants from cold sowings, made out of doors. Some don't germinate until well into the summer and the

Diary   12th November

It's been a joy working in the greenhouse today. The new wire screen means I can leave the door open without inviting all the cats in. They've been a nuisance, climbing up the staging, scrabbling about in the borders and knocking pots off the shelves. 'Gloire de Dijon' has reached the roof, and its long branches arch from the back wall right across to the glass at the front. It is laden with buds and flowers. Right above my head hang clusters of the most sumptuous full-petalled roses, heavy and quartered, some still a pale apricot yellow, others darker with pink and amber shading deep inside the flowers. And the scent is heavenly. Such a shame to leave them where I rarely see them, or only to cut them for Christmas. I fetched the secateurs and gathered a huge bouquet.

seedlings are not substantial enough to spend their first winter out of doors. The more robust are put in the cold frame, but there is never room for more than a fraction of them. So the majority live on my potting bench, where I can keep an eye on them. Good ventilation is vital to their survival, and hairy-leaved seedlings, such as *Rehmannia*, need spraying with a fungicide now and again.

The eastern half of the greenhouse has the same arrangement, but with narrow staging and a wide raised bed where I grow two wall-trained cherries and camellias. *Rosa* 'Gloire de Dijon', which uses one of the cherries as a climbing frame, also lives in this bed.

Rain and wind soon take their toll on the garden, the leaves blow off the trees, and the ornamental grasses, still splendid last month have collapsed or are spotted with black fungal spores. Even my magnificent *Cortaderia richardii* looks bedraggled now, with many of its stems broken

Stipa tenuissima.

and dragging in the mud. Miraculously the gossamer veils of *Stipa tenuissima* are still as good as new. This grass keeps its looks until I cut it down in spring.

November's damp creeps into my bones, and in the Temple I have a small electric fan heater, which I plug in for my, rather than the plant's comfort, while I do my weekly watering and tidy-ups in the winter.

It receives no sunlight from November to the end of February, and again, good ventilation is of vital importance. Two small windows are kept permanently ajar and slivers of icy draughts find their way through the bottom of the door into my bedroom – and my bare feet. I don't mind. Good ventilation is as vital to human as it is to plant health.

The floor of the Temple is tiled, which means everything has to be grown in containers. Apart from three large plants, which have become permanent fixtures, the composition changes with the seasons. Plants come and go all year round, brought onto the stage for their performance, then vanish behind the curtain, once their flowering is done. They are returned to the greenhouse, or placed outside, whichever arrangement suits the individual best. Lilies, with a few notable exceptions, don't do as well in the garden as I would like them to. They flower and even increase for perhaps two or three years, then inexplicably dwindle and eventually disappear altogether. But many do very well in

pots and I have some in flower from spring until well into autumn.

The Madonna Lily, *Lilium candidum*, kicks off the season in April with its white scented flowers, scrolled and curved at the petal tips. This is another one of my Catholic nostalgia plants, a symbol of purity and chastity, linked to virgin birth and grown in every garden of my home village. On numerous occasions I brought bulbs back with me, but they won't have anything to do with me or my garden, even in well-drained and limed soil. They start into growth in the autumn and that growth gets burnt off again and again, until the plant is finally exhausted.

I now grow them, three to a five-litre pot in John Innes No.3, enriched with garden compost. They are stood outdoors in a warm, sheltered spot after flowering, and I bring them inside again as soon as the first leaf appears, usually in November.

During wet autumns the Oriental hybrid lilies don't manage to open outdoors. Brought

Oriental hybrid lily.

Sollya heterophylla.

into the Temple, they waft their heady scent well into November some years.

Few of these temporary lodgers could be classed as typical greenhouse or conservatory plants. They are a large and eclectic mix, and might include ferns, tree heaths, cistus, sweet violets, cacti, lavender, everything in its season and anything that looks or smells good and doesn't mind pot culture. The Temple has three permanent residents, *Lapageria rosea*, a eucalyptus and a mimosa. Despite its root-restricting pot, *Eucalyptus gunnii* has reached the roof repeatedly and whenever that happens I prune it back to stumps, which keeps it in check for a bit and produces a forest of intensely blue juvenile foliage. It creates some much-needed shade during the summer and doubles as a support for the Australian bluebell vine, *Sollya heterophylla*. This is a most charming evergreen twiner with

embothrium-like leaves and clusters of dangling, small blue flowers, produced over a long period.

If I had to choose just one plant for its perfume, I would plump for an *Acacia* (known as mimosa in the cutflower trade). A friend of mine describes this scent, rather prosaically, as a mixture of marzipan and cucumber. There is indeed a hint of both, as well as other components which I'm hard-pressed to name. I'm at a loss how to describe its unique, dry and delicate fragrance, but there is simply nothing on earth that compares with the perfume of a mimosa in full flower.

The one I grow is *Acacia dealbata* with deep green, feathery foliage, made up of tiny needle-like leaflets on bi-pinnate leaves. At the slightest hint of drought it drops these leaflets, or sometimes whole leaves or even small branches. To prevent this rain of green dandruff it has to have a constant supply of water, a gallon or two a week in the winter and between six and eight gallons a day during the hottest part of the year. The flower sprays are composed of tiny yellow pompoms, produced with great freedom all along the branches. Mine first started flowering in May and June, and while it was still a small tree (small enough to lift it pot and all) I used to bring it into my bedroom for its flowering. Now I leave the adjoining door open during its first flush in April, and cut branches for the house when it has a second go in November and December. It has flowered twice annually for a number of years now and I hope it's going to stick with this endearing habit.

It too acts as a climbing frame. *Passiflora caerulea* flowers well into winter if its vines are cut back to the base after its summer flush. It is easy to grow and will keep going in the same pot for years. Its flowers are the most extraordinary I know: in front of a ring of porcupine-spine petals, banded black, white and violet, sit the green and yellow stamens and the orange-brown stigmas.

The prostrate evergreen *Ceanothus dentatus* is one of the first Temple shrubs to flower in the spring. Small clusters of powder blue flowers appear from every leaf axil and shoot tip in early March, nicely set off by dark green, finely toothed foliage.

Fremontodendron 'California Glory' also has good leaves, three-lobed, pale grey beneath, dark green above and rough-textured like fine sandpaper. It has its main flush of flowers in July, and sometimes repeats in the autumn, if it feels like it. What looks like petals are actually sepals, large, bright yellow and of a thick, waxy texture, opening into shallow, lobed cups.

All through the winter, our large, oval dining table, used for summer suppers in the Temple, and in my field of vision as I get out of bed, is groaning under the weight of clay pots and bowls, filled with tulips and crocuses and all kinds of spring and winter-flowering things. Most of these I grow in the garden too, but I like

having them in the Temple to bring forward their season, and to enjoy them from my bedroom.

If there's space, and I remember to lift some, I also bring in hellebores for gentle forcing. They don't like being divided and take a full year to settle down after the upheaval. Under cold glass the orientalis hybrids start flowering in December, and the first, at the end of November, is always a cultivar with flowers of a dark crimson purple.

Sometimes, if I happen to dig up a clump of snowdrops by mistake during a border upheaval in the autumn, I pot it up to bring indoors. The buds come up in December and those pristine white bells and grey-green leaves look lovely when grown through a topdressing of fresh moss.

If I remember, and more often than not I don't, I cut and bring indoors a few branches of *Ribes sanguineum* in early November. The buds expand into creamy white flowers around Christmas time.

The garden has a few more delights in store this month. *Kirengeshoma palmata* has taken many years to settle in, probably not helped by its frequent moves. It now looks reasonably happy in the Round Garden, where the soil is rich and

Kirengeshoma palmata.

damp, but doesn't get waterlogged in winter. Every November it opens a few of its large waxy buds into pale yellow shuttlecocks.

Osmanthus heterophyllus has been in flower since the end of October. It is a slow-growing evergreen, with dark, holly-like leaves and tiny white flowers hidden amongst them. Too well hidden. This shrub has been in the garden for as long as I can remember, yet its flowering, if it took place in the past, has gone un-noticed and unappreciated. The strong, sweet scent is a give-away, and last autumn I happened to be weeding in the right spot – at the right time. This year, my frequent investigations have failed to reveal a single bud. Perhaps, as is the case with my saffron crocus, this was a one-off show?

Nearby, as a consolation, I found *Prunus laurocerasus* 'Otto Luyken' in full, unseasonal flower.

Sooner or later the heavy autumn rains set in, the sheep look miserable and stand together in huddles, their heads bowed, their fleeces

Prunus laurocerasus 'Otto Luyken'.

flattened and dripping. Lanolin makes their wool water-repellent, keeps their skin dry and acts as a kind of external drainage system.

In the garden, drainage is an ongoing problem and any lack of it tends to become apparent now. We have an extensive system of field drains. Flexible black polythene pipes, perforated with needle-fine slits, are laid two feet below ground on a bed of large stone chips and covered with a generous layer of the same material before the soil is replaced above them. They serve us well on the whole, but now and again, after a prolonged cloud burst, they can't quite cope and we get a little flooding.

This happens mainly on the approach to the house on the path below the Alpine Slope, where the drains have to take away the enormous amounts of water which rush off the hill behind the house. Wellington boots are called for, or if the puddles turn into small lakes, a capacity to keep ones' balance, while walking over a narrow board laid across them. This inconvenience never lasts for long and the water seeps away after a day or two.

We still have one open drain in the garden which runs west to east below the back wall of the byre. This wall, like all the original buildings at the Lea, is dry-stone built. Over the years, the vertical stonework has run to form a slanting buttress. Layers of peat have accumulated in it, or were perhaps placed there, for added insulation, by our predecessors. Sparse grass and moss grow in it and I have added ferns, woodrush and rhododendrons. They rely, during their growing season, on the watering they get from the gutter-less roof above them. But the gradient of the ditch below them is shallow, and from autumn until spring large amounts of water find their way underneath the byre and into the Kitchen Garden, creating bogs where I don't want them.

On the land above and around the garden drainage is provided by a network of open ditches. Those on high ground, inaccessible to machinery, have been dug by hand. They are narrow and need frequent attention, such as a good cleaning out in the crucial places, where they narrow or bend, at least once a year. Problems arise where they run through a fence, and the slatted water-gate underneath it, which stops the lambs from slipping through, gets clogged up with grass, wool and all manner of wind-blown debris. The water, thus stopped in its tracks, soon finds an alternative channel. On the ditch which runs alongside the garden's western boundary, this alternative route is invariably the Red Bed. If the first heavy rains catch us unawares, and find the gate blocked, a torrent sweeps away soil, plants and all and washes them onto the path below. Vigilance is the answer, or, failing that, a rapid diversion of the stream.

Diary   30th November

After a week of rain (it seemed much longer than one week) the skies have cleared and this morning, the last of the month, found the garden transformed by hoarfrost. Every leaf, every twig, is picked out by a white rim. I spent over an hour rapidly taking photographs, using up several spools of film, before the magic was melted away by the sun. Deciduous grasses, still proudly upright a day ago, have collapsed. Black, muddy patches have appeared on the lawn, and cushions of alpines look flattened after all the rain, as if someone, someone heavy at that, had sat on them. The last leaves have blown off the trees. I spent the day gathering up all the frost-sensitive plants which have spent the summer outside in pots and brought them into the greenhouse.

Removing all these plants leaves large, vacant spaces outside the front door and in a sheltered bay below the kitchen window. Taking away the summer plants is a chore, but replacing them with winter residents is a pleasure. These arrangements of pots are never planned. I simply look for suitable candidates in the coldframes and the nursery: potted hollies, tree heaths, perhaps a griselinia, some clipped box, a nicely shaped mountain pine or a well-budded witch hazel for the back row, hebes, winter-flowering heathers, bergenias, a young skimmia and evergreen alpines like encrusted saxifragas and celmisias for the front. As the icing on the cake I select well-budded hellebores, *Cyclamen coum*, and pots of the earliest spring bulbs: *Iris reticulata*, and the saffron-and-bronze *Crocus* 'Dorothy'. These mixtures vary from year to year, some of the plants will find permanent quarters in the garden afterwards, while others might spend another season in a pot.

Many of my bergenias started their Shetland lives as Ladies-in-Waiting. A few are still in their

… every leaf picked out by a white rim.

Bergenias display their autumn colours.

pots while I try to find suitable spaces for them, but the majority earn their keep primarily as foliage plants. Good leaves are essential to good garden design. Just one strategically placed "elephant's ear" can pull a whole planting together and provide a focal point amongst plants with small or "indifferent" foliage. After their spring flowering – sometimes repeated in autumn – bergenias come into their own again now when their large rounded leaves start displaying their autumnal colour.

At the end of the month there are no more unseasonal spring flowers to pick, and little else is in flower, but I enjoy my garden in its winter bareness, the dark outlines of the trees, their moss and lichen-covered trunks, the orange twigs of the larches, and the warm brown stems and seed heads of the astilbes.

The branches of flowering currants I cut almost a month ago are flushed with pale green and studded with white buds. The first spring bulbs have pushed their green noses above ground, a reminder that nature is continuously at work behind the scenes. November, despite its endless grey and wet, is not such a bad month after all.

Right: ... the dark outlines of the trees.

December

ecember is our darkest month and there are days when the sun barely pops above the southern horizon. It is a busy month on the croft, with the hill ewes driven in to spend time with the rams. This means, that for a good month, our sheep numbers are almost doubled, until the visiting ewes return to the hill pastures in January. There is usually no grazing left in December, and if there is, it is stretched to its very limits. Twice daily feeding, with hay until that runs out, followed by bought-in grain and sugarbeet nuts becomes a routine from now until the end of May. This late feeding ensures a plentiful supply of milk in the ewes and gives the lambs, born in late April/early May, a good start in life.

There've been touches of ground frost since October, the thermometer only just dipping below zero. I've experienced brief spells of minus 10° Celsius, but those are rare. Once during my twenty-six years in Shetland the outside thermometer measured minus 13° for a few hours. But the cold snaps we get from late November until February are more likely to be in the region of 5° or 6° below zero. They never last more than a few days, but with the addition of the wind chill factor, can feel much, much colder.

I always hope for something better from the weather in December, clear crisp blue days and star-lit nights, and close to Christmas I can't suppress a childish longing for snow. A sprinkling of it might arrive if the wind blows from a northerly direction for a while, and just now and again "real snow" comes early, and with it the longed-for white Christmas. But generally the snow never lasts long, nor does it stay cold for long, and most Decembers we go through

Left: The White Garden living up to its name at "The End of Civilisation".

numerous cycles of thawing and freezing; if the wind blows in from the Atlantic, the weather simply continues as it started in November, with depressing grey skies and never-ending rain.

Schizostylis coccinea 'Major' is a cheering sight in bleak mid winter. It has stiff upright leaves, rather like those of a small gladiolus, and long sprays of cup-shaped cherry-red flowers. A small colony, planted on the Alpine Slope, starts flowering in October, but in damp, rich soil, which it is said to prefer, it never opens a bud before the end of November.

I also have several cultivars, with the same late season: the salmon-pink 'Jennifer', white 'Alba', satin-pink 'Mrs. Hegarty' and the slightly darker 'Viscountess Byng'. The latter usually presents me with her first flowers round about Christmas time. Her efforts are often thwarted by frost and snow, but I have seen her flowering,

Schizostylis coccinea.

Helleborus orientalis ssp. *abschasicus* 'Early Purple Group'.

effortlessly. Then there are all those little cleaning and tidying jobs, giving the paths their final sweep of the year, putting away the hoses and watering cans which won't be needed again until spring, retrieving plastic pots from hedge bottoms, blown there by the wind, and camouflaged by summer's greenery, or ignored by the gardener. Small, but satisfying chores which can make a tremendous difference to the looks of a garden. Sometimes the borders, which were left looking tidy last month, need another going over.

Diary   **4th December**

I returned from Edinburgh yesterday, filled with inspiration by my visit to the Botanics. I'd never seen their herbaceous borders in December before, but did so this time. They still looked very good, with some of the plant remains cut away, leaving expanses of smooth brown soil, but most left, which gave the borders a mellow, autumnal look. A lot of good seedheads, the bleached grasses, and the large, russet plates of sedums filled me with envy. This morning I rushed out to compare. It was no good and I fetched my shears, secateurs and several large sacks. What looks decorative elsewhere, is blackened, mouldy and decaying here.

on and off, right into March. The flowers, not really up to the vagaries of a Shetland winter, last well in water.

There are no such problems with *Helleborus orientalis* ssp. *abschasicus* 'Early Purple Group'. This handsome darkling bends double under frost and snow, but as soon as a melt sets in it is bolt upright once more, and opens its slate-purple flowers from November until April.

Regardless of the weather, I continue my daily garden rounds, sometimes mainly for the benefit of the dogs, who would otherwise remain locked-up for much of the day (they are working dogs, rather than pets). More often than not, if the weather is reasonably dry, I get stuck into something, a little winter pruning, checking tree ties and stakes, tucking plants, which have been lifted by the frost, back into the earth. A spot of hand-weeding is a pleasurable occupation when a touch of frost has loosened roots, and rosettes of bittercress and other small seedlings can be picked off the ground

But this does not mean that all the garden's beds and borders are grey and brown in December. *Chiastophyllum oppositifolium* 'Jim's Pride' still looks bright and lush with its green and cream variegated fleshy foliage. Evergreen ground cover comes into its own, and plants overlooked for most of the year, take centre stage. Bolsters of *Mitella breweri* have knitted together and form wide expanses of deep green, the vincas sparkle, and the dark leaves of *Ajuga reptans* 'Braunherz' look stunning intermingled with a bright green mossy saxifrage.

Ajuga 'Braunherz' with mossy saxifrage.

This month summer and autumn's clamour finally make way for winter's calm dignity. Views to the hills and the sea have opened out once more, and the garden's rooms, secret inside their green boundaries for months, have lost much of their summer intimacy. They are visible from a distance again, their seasonal walls stripped bare, allowing glimpses from one room into the next. New vistas have appeared, to lead and surprise the eye.

Eucalyptus pauciflora ssp. *debeuzevillei* dominates the Round Garden in winter with its wide branches of large ovate blue leaves and striking peeling bark. (We've renamed it E. "beelzebubii" because it's such a handsome devil.) It needs secure staking because of its extremely fast growth, and has so far sailed unscathed through all adversity.

But tall broadleaved evergreens are few and far between, and it is good to see the outlines of the deciduous trees once more, flaring into warm brown in the low sun, or painting

Eucalyptus pauciflora ssp. *debeuzevillei.*

intricate black patterns against a grey sky. Much of their charms go unnoticed when the garden is in full leaf and flower, the satin sheen on the stems of my wild cherry, the trunks of the sycamores banded with patchy grey lichens, and

Diary   12th December

My bones are still aching and I feel dizzy and light-headed from the flu, but how could I stay in bed on a day like this? The sun came out just after nine and the colours in the garden were glowing. I had to take the camera out, and on my slow progress – there's a sprinkling of snow and the paths are treacherous with ice – all the cats followed, showing off with their tree-climbing acrobatics and their savagery, flushing blackbirds from the under-growth. Soon their alarm calls sounded all around the garden, and on the path to the Sunk Garden I found one of their victims, stiff and plucked-clean like an oven-ready pullet. There I also found, much to my surprise, clusters of brown buds on the variegated wood rush (*Luzula sylvatica* 'Marginata') while the impossibly yellow leaves of *L. s.* 'Hohe Tatra' shone from its stronghold in the shady borders of the vegetable garden. *Luzula sylvatica* is a Shetland native, and going by its name, might be a remnant from the days when the islands were covered in forest.

Luzula sylvatica 'Hohe Tatra'.

the brilliant green moss which covers every fissured limb of the elders.

I wish I knew the names of all the mosses in the garden. They glow yellow-green on the stones of raised beds and have formed hard hummocks on the byre roofs. In winter I learn to see and delight in them again, and discover new delights. The slim red buds of the rowans against the grey leaves of a buddleia, borders of ice crystals on the bergenias, and clustered deep inside the evergreen leptosermums, pale seedcases, the colour and size of unripe bilberries.

Willows make wonderful winter trees, those with coloured bark glow and shine, *Salix alaxensis* pierces the sky with its ice-grey forks and the setting sun picks out the first silver catkins on *Salix triandra*, the almond-leaved willow.

This is the month when I enjoy the garden's evergreen conifers. They are at their best and most prominent now, bringing with them a well-clothed and inviting look. At the end of the Rose Border I have a large (by Shetland standards) specimen of the "golden-leaved" Leyland cypress 'Castlewellan', thirteen feet (4m) high by six feet (2m) wide. A liability in gardens elsewhere, this is well-behaved in our climate and in winter turns a warm, full-toned green. Just one such plant against the tracery of bare brown twigs and branches lifts the scene.

The Back Yard is filled with the ghosts of Christmasses past. Unlike those in Dicken's Christmas Carol, all bring pleasant memories. A group of Sitka spruces (*Picea sitchensis*) and noble firs (*Abies procera*) are now between fifteen (4.5m) and 18 feet (5.5m) high. I initially planted them as infants in front of the house, where they would soon have blocked out the view and much light. They were moved to the Back Yard to act as a screen against the northerlies and north-westerlies. There are also several lodgepole pines (*Pinus contorta*), of all sizes, shapes and ages, the oldest, now between ten and fifteen feet tall, form a row along the

Pinus contorta **(lodgepole pine).**

dyke to give a little shelter from the east. All are fine specimens now, but, like the firs and spruces, spent their first year or two in limbo, and looked a little sparse, while recovering from their ordeal. The ordeal consists of being lifted, potted up and spending several days in a warm room. Thankfully, as our family follows the German tradition in this respect, this spell is a short one, as Christmas trees are never decorated before Christmas Eve. Another German tradition is perhaps less conducive to their wellbeing. The use of small candles in clip-on holders, rather than electric lights, must make the trees feel uncomfortably hot and, more often than not, results in a few scorched needles. Despite these traumas of their early youth, all have settled in well and so far show no signs of undue wear and tear due to wind and salt spray.

Large numbers of lodgepole pines were introduced to Shetland during the nineteen seventies and a high percentage of these is no more. Choosing trees, especially evergreen ones from a climate compatible with ours is vitally important. The difference in performance between a tree originating from an oceanic, rather than a continental climate, can be staggering, but few tree nurseries, as yet, pay enough attention to this when selecting their seed sources.

Their young trees will serve most gardeners well, but let down those who garden in a marginal, maritime climate. Trees from seed collected at high rather than low altitudes inland also do much better but as they are often mis-shapen and much slower growing than their relatives further down the mountain, they are rarely used as a seed source. A state of affairs which needs to be remedied, and perhaps someone out there will start a conifer nursery for marginal gardens.

Sitka spruces are a more traditional choice and shape for Christmas use, but their needles are intensely prickly, and make decorating them, which should be a pleasure, a rather painful exercise. In their youth ours had a picture postcard charm, especially when covered in snow. Of late they have been frequently and severely attacked by Sitka aphid, which can leave them looking threadbare and grey. In some years they look a mess for six months out of twelve, in others they are not bad at all. There are sprays on the market which are said to be effective, but spraying large trees is not really practicable. Ours can be a depressing sight until their new growth appears in May and should really be replaced, but their felling would tear a significant hole into our northern defences and is therefore put off from year to year.

Still, their days are numbered since James has started to establish a shelter planting on the high ground above the Back Yard. He chose a mixture of deciduous and evergeen trees, larches, alders, willows, rowans, and some Sitkas, which are all getting off the ground, and given their elevated position, should take on their vital, wind-filtering duty in the not too distant future.

Abies procera, the noble fir, is immune to the aphid. It makes a stately, handsome tree with a smooth, grey stem, branches which sweep the ground, and soft, curved needles, glaucous on their undersides, and strongly scented of orange peel when crushed. Initially it is much slower growing than the Sitka spruce, and for a number of years, before it starts to elongate, has a squat, dumpy look. It soon catches up and looks to be a much better long-term investment.

I have a lone specimen of *Abies koreana* with a very chequered history. It spent most of its life in a pot and was twice gnawed back to stumps by a ram who, after eyeing it from the other side of the fence, decided to jump and grab a mouthful whenever an opportunity arose. I didn't have the heart to throw the wretched thing out and planted it in a draughty corner of the Back Yard, not holding out much hope for it. After five years it has grown back into a beautifully symetrical small tree, complete with new leader (the competing shoots were removed), and an altogether buoyant and promising look.

There are a few mountain pines, *Pinus mugo*, in the shelter belt, which have proved tough enough, but too slow-growing to serve as shelter trees yet. *Pinus mugo* ssp. *mugo* 'Pumilio Group' lives at the southern end of the Back Yard, just above the Bathroom Bed, where its urn-shape and rich green bottle-brushes provide a nice background for a blue-leaved *Rhododendron lepidostylum*. It started life as a bonsai in a glazed stone-ware pot, where it remained for over a decade, gracing various parts of the garden. It had grown into a beautifully gnarled and twisted specimen, without any help from me, and one summer, a visitor, and keen bonsai grower, offered me a large sum for it. If I had the tiniest of gardens and only space for one pine, this would be my choice.

Pinus radiata, the Monterey pine, is often recommended for fast-growing, coastal screening in the milder parts of the country (of which Shetland is one). My trial specimen grows high above the sea, on rather wet ground and in the firing line of the south-westerlies. I could hardly have chosen a worse position for it, and after seven years in this inhospitable place, it still needs tying to its stake during the winter to prevent it from getting blown out of the ground. After a particularly rough season it drops a lot of needles and gets a little browned on its windward side, as do most evergreens in extreme exposure, but it is growing away apace and I love it for its long, soft, drooping needles.

I have perhaps given the impression that the Back Yard is filled to the brim with large, or potentially large conifers, but this is not so. There is in fact room for more, and after flirting for several years with a Bhutan pine, *Pinus wallichiana*, I'm now the proud owner of a fine, pot-grown specimen. Its purchase almost bankrupted me, but it has the finest needles of them all and, when well-grown, looks like a gently cascading green waterfall.

December rushes by in a flurry of seasonal celebrations and the preparations for them. Cooking and baking form an important part of

Diary

My first escape from Christmas for well over a week. Sending the German parcels off on time (late as usual). Doing all traditional baking I vowed last December never to do again. Glue sticks, coloured card and glitter (Anna has decided to have home-made Christmas cards). Strong resolve to cancel all, eat baked beans on toast, and send savings to Aids victims in sub-Saharan Africa shelved for another year. There's always this crisis, this conflict, guilt and shame for having so much while others in this world have so little. And always the crisis is resolved through generous donations to various charities – and succumbing to the magic and charms of the season.

I often forget the garden at this time of year, forget the power it has to restore and revive me. It never really got light today, and darkness fell at three in the afternoon, but I managed to spend several precious hours in the garden, just pottering about, replacing labels, cutting out some dead wood, clearing away snowdrop-smothering fern fronds. There was nothing new, nothing spectacular, just the frosted patterns of fallen leaves, the ginger strands of *Carex* 'Coman's Bronze' falling over a young frosted-green *Hebe topiaria*, but it gave me a deep sense of peace and joy and a feeling of being connected to this earth.

... the frosted patterns of fallen leaves ...

these preparations and I spend a lot of time in the kitchen, which I enjoy. As a multi-cultural household our Christmas and New Year celebrations are of a hybrid nature and contain both Anglo-Scottish and Czech-German elements (my parents came from Czechoslovakia), with a strong emphasis on the latter. My family kept their old traditions alive and I do the same. They have a magic all of their own and start a month before Christmas on the first Sunday of Advent with a candlelit afternoon tea, homemade biscuits and ginger bread, and the scent of orange peel and pine needles toasted on top of the Rayburn. Christmas Eve brings Guinea Pigs on the ceiling, only visible to those keeping strictly to the traditional all-day fast, and a visit from the Christmas Fairy, who decorates the tree and supplies the presents. Part of the evening meal is a salad, prepared after an old Czech peasant recipe, and must contain two roots (potatoes and carrots), two fruits (apples and pickled cucumber), two pulses (peas and kidney beans), eggs, meat (smoked pork sausage), and fish (pickled herring), in a dressing of diluted wine vinegar, sweetened with a little sugar and flavoured with dill, sour cream and a touch of mustard. All the animals in the house, the byres, and in the fields, must be fed with some of these ingredients on Christmas Eve to ensure their continuous well-being and fertility. The evening ends with Feuerzangen Bowle, a spectacular flambee punch. Red wine is heated in the oven in a large, tulip-shaped earthenware pot with cinnamon, cloves and mace. A small sugar loaf is suspended above this vessel, doused with strong rum and set alight, and the melting, rum-flavoured sugar drips slowly into the wine below.

The vegetable garden still does us proud and brassicas are at their best once the weather turns colder. Curly kale should in fact never be eaten before it has been "tenderised" by a few frosty nights. 'Redbor' is of good flavour, and stands well into April. It turns from mauve to dark green during cooking, but leaves behind ruby-red juices, a striking combination on the plate. I still mourn the demise (EC regulations) of brussel sprout 'Widgeon', a prolific dwarf variety with the sweetest, firmest sprouts imaginable.

There are those who maintain that Shetland kale (cabbage) is only fit for sheep fodder. I rather like a fat Shetland "kale heart", simply steamed and served with fresh butter, or stuffed with minced pork and baked in sour cream, or as an essential ingredient of "tattie soup". This delicacy is traditionally served on New Year's Eve all over the islands. A piece of "reestit mutton", salted, then dried (ideally over a peat fire) to give it a smokey flavour, is soaked over night, then boiled until tender and served cold as an accompaniment to the soup. Tatties (potatoes), carrots, swedes are cooked slowly in the salty broth. I purposefully omitted the "essential ingredient", as there are those who maintain that Shetland kale should never go near tattie soup. I disagree.

Greens are getting scarce in December, but we usually have a fine crop of lamb's lettuce

Chicory 'Apollo' in the cupboard under the stairs.

from a July sowing, cloched from autumn onwards. The traditional 'Witloof' chicory has never performed well for me, but a five-foot (1.5m) row of the variety 'Apollo' keeps us in fat, yellow chicons well into March. I lift, trim and pot the roots, about half a dozen to a five-litre pot, in October. They're kept in a frost-free shed, and brought in two at a time, to sprout in the cupboard under the stairs, where there's a little under-floor warmth from the central heating pipes. Chicory can be used as a vegetable, braised in stock, but I like it best raw in salads, especially combined with fresh filleted tangerine segments, a few pitted black olives cut into rings and a couple of shredded anchovy fillets in a French dressing. A pot of "semi-hatched" chicons also makes a nice Christmas present for those with culinary inclinations.

When Christmas trees became fashionable in Shetland towards the end of the nineteenth century, suitable conifers were not only expensive, but hard to come by, and "trees" were fashioned out of wild juniper, several branches tied together with twine and stuck (upright) into a peat-filled container. *Juniperus communis* ssp. *nana* is a prostrate conifer, very occasionally found in an upright form. While the ling turns brown and grey (at least from a distance) this juniper remains a fresh, bright green all through the winter, even on seacliffs and exposed hilltops. In the garden it makes excellent, evergreen groundcover. I grow several cultivars of this plant. *Juniperus communis* 'Green Carpet' was found in Norway and is rather similar to the Shetland wildling, with dense and perfectly flat growth in an exceptionally rich, bright green. *J. communis* 'Repanda' is a much larger plant, which can take up several yards after a number of years. Its young growth arches slightly at the tips and is flushed bronze in winter. My oldest plant is heading for its twentieth birthday, and should really be replaced. Grown in too shady a spot, and overhung by dripping branches, it has developed several bald patches in its centre – perfect pockets for snowdrops.

Juniperus squamata **'Blue Star'**.

J. squamata 'Blue Carpet' is another vigorous grower with a similar habit, its blue-grey colouring especially pronounced in the new shoots. *J.s.* 'Blue Star' makes a dense hummock and is the bluest conifer in my garden. *Juniperus communis* 'Depressa Aurea', from north America and Canada, grows a little taller, but creates the same dense carpet, more feathery this time and in a warm yellow green. New shoots in spring are a bright yellow.

When used as convenient groundcover and in large expanses these junipers can look a little dull, but as individuals or in small groups, and combined with other plants – I am thinking of Bergenias and evergreen grasses – they become lively inhabitants of the winter garden.

Having seen too many stunted, lop-sided and severely wind-burnt examples of the taller and columnar or pencil-shaped junipers I gave them a wide berth, but now have a few suitable candidates for a windy climate.

Juniperus davurica 'Expansa Aurea' has grown into a loose mound of overlapping greenery at the entrance to the Round Garden. It's scale-like leaves are a pale Nile-green, soft to the touch and flecked with cream here and there. It has a suitably dark companion in *Ilex aquifolium* 'Hascombensis'. This is a slow-growing fastigiate shrub or small tree with small, dark green leaves and black wood. Good combinations are worth repeating and in the north-west corner of the same garden I have a similarly, if not more effective grouping of *Ilex aquifolium* 'Myrtifolia' behind (or in front of, depending from which angle you look) *Griselinia littoralis*. The leaves of the griselinia are large, smooth and rounded and one of the brightest greens I have in the garden, while those of the holly are a very dark, purple-flushed green, neat and sharply pointed. Like 'Hascombensis', this too has a narrow, upright habit, but is much faster-growing.

J. x *media* 'Pfitzeriana Aurea' was planted at the exposed end of a damp border in the Back Yard, in rather wet ground, which doesn't seem to bother it in the least. It has a large specimen of the Falkland Islands tussock grass, *Poa flabellata* for company, which after a good grooming in the autumn, looks neat again in December. After five seasons the juniper has grown into a feathery, two-foot (60cm) hillock with bright yellow twigs here and there among the prevailing green.

Ilex aquifolium **'Myrtifolia'**.

I have a tiny raised bed next to the entrance to the Sunk Garden, built against its south wall. It is just over a foot wide, perhaps a metre and a half (5ft) long and raised six inches off the ground. Because of the exceptional shelter and warmth it enjoys, it was destined to house all kinds of tender plants. Small and precious to fit the size of the bed, none made any impact, and looked lost against the large expanse of drystone dyke behind them.

A complete replanting has turned it into a winter oasis. On its western side I now have the green, cream and pink variegated *Luma apiculata* 'Glanleam Gold'. A handsome, slow-growing evergreen which would lose its leaves in more exposed parts of the garden. At the other end of the bed, the glaucous green *Juniperus chinensis* 'Pyramidalis', is slowly growing into a slim column. Between them sits a trio of pink-berried *Gaultheria mucronata*, female clones fertilised by the hermaphrodite *G.m.* 'Bell's Seedling'.

One of the best and fastest growing upright junipers for maritime climates is undoubtdly *Juniperus communis* 'Hibernica', the Irish Juniper. With a modicum of shelter, it soon makes a tall, feathery column, indispensable where a slim, vertical accent is needed.

My earliest rhododendron, the leucaspis hybrid 'Snow Lady', sometimes opens a few of its white buds in December, but usually waits until January or February. Salty seawinds don't bother it in the least; and one winter it was gnawed back to stumps and left completely leafless by marauding sheep, which didn't set it back either. By the end of the season it had made good its losses, was clothed in leaves and well-budded once more. It makes a small, open, upright shrub, just under three feet tall, with an abundance of ivory white, bell-shaped flowers, produced in loose trusses. After its ovine encounter I gave mine up for dead and purchased a replacement, which now, still in its pot, graces the front door in winter.

Pink-berried *Gaultheria mucronata*.

Juniperus communis **'Hibernica'**.

Sheep raids used to be common-place in the early days of the garden, before we replaced the rickety fencing; and the high jumpers in the flock found their way into the freezer. Accidents still happen to this day, the wind blows open a badly-fastened gate or a few determined individuals climb over a dry-stone dyke. Sheep are grazers, not browsers, they bruise and tear woody plants. It is therefore of vital importance to trim back every damaged branch and twig to prevent them from dying back. After quick remedial action the chrome-yellow 'Golden Torch', raspberry-pink 'Sweet Sue' and all the other Yakushimanum rhododendrons recovered and flower freely every year.

Lapageria rosea is the national flower of Chile and an extraordinarily beautiful evergreen climber. It never looks entirely happy in its small terracotta trough, but each year flowers its heart out from August to February. It has never set seed, probably due to a lack of humming birds, which act as pollinators in its home country.

Diary   11th December

I hate sheep. I absolutely loathe them and wish we could get rid of every single one of them. They got into the garden last night (while we were out) and when we arrived home this morning, half the flock, including the hill sheep, was lying in the Back Yard, calmly ruminating, as if it was their perfect right to be there. I could have wept. They've gone for all the evergreens in a big way. Most of the heathers are up-rooted, a lot of plants pulled out of their pots, and everything that had a bit of green on it is gnawed down to stumps. There is hardly a leaf left on the yaku hybrid rhododendrons, the only one they didn't seem to like is *R. yakushimanum*. I was sure rhododendrons were poisonous to sheep, but I've yet to find one with its legs up in the air.

Lapageria rosea.

Diary

22nd December

It has snowed all night and when I opened the front door this morning, I was met by an almost waist-high white wall, dead-vertical on the door side and tapering to a razor-sharp edge. James fought his way out the back door and dug a path right around the house and to both gates. (That shovel kept in the porch over winter does come in handy now and again.) Convinced we're going to get more snow, he came back with armfuls of greenery for the house, holly and strands of ivy for a traditional mantle piece garland, branches of 'Castlewellan', juniper and lots of *Lonicera pileata*, complete with tiny violet berries, large fir twigs and pine brushes, dog rose branches dripping with red hips and the most wonderfully variegated *Escallonia* foliage. How lucky I am to have a garden – and a husband.

Anna and our friend Rachel built an enormous snowman complete with carrot nose, hat, scarf and gloves, and peat instead of coal buttons. Beds and borders have all but vanished under a blanket of snow, the terrace steps have disappeared and the Temple guttering is hung with long, grey icicles. The Temple looks festive with its strings of white lights and the southern half of its wall hung with the waxy pink bells of *Lapageria rosea*.

... variegated *Escallonia* foliage.

Narcissus 'Paperwhite' also flowers in the Temple, carrying clusters of small but solid white stars, which look as if stamped out with a pastry cutter. They have a strong, almost overpowering scent, which is best enjoyed from a distance. I like having it, and some hyacinths in flower, every Christmas.

Azalea indica is another seasonal stalwart. It comes in a wide range of colours, single and double forms, flowers for months and all it asks for in return is a plentiful supply of water and a cool spot. I have several old specimens which I repot in early spring and summer in a shady spot in the greenhouse.

The extraordinary little *Oxalis versicolor* flowers from December until February. Dormant from spring to autumn, thin, finger-

long, green stalks rise from the pots at the beginning of the month. At their tops are tufts of leaves, rather like short dill weed, and white funnel-shaped flowers, their petals thinly

Azalea indica.

outlined in red. I like it best in bud: when furled up like an umbrella, the flower is striped in a red and white spiral pattern.

The slim chartreuse-green bells of *Billardiera longifolia* sometimes escape my notice during the hectic summer months, but its large violet-blue winter berries are impossible to overlook. This graceful evergreen climber rarely manages to set fruit when grown outdoors all year round, but wintered under glass and planted out (pot and all) behind a suitable host shrub in a sunny position it is a delight. Sometimes, during a wet and cold autumn, I disentangle and bring it into the Temple where it can ripen its polished berries, and where I can enjoy them at close quarters.

In the narrow, north-facing raised bed, which runs alongside the path to the front door, winter brings large expanses of bare soil. A problem I have yet to solve. This bed is in a prominent position, walked past several times a day, and needs to look smart all year round. On the other side of the path, on the Alpine Slope with its well-drained, gritty soil, this was an easy task. Here a wide range of evergreen alpines, cistuses, rosemary, hebes and dwarf willows do an admirable job, but on the raised bed, which is in deep shade from October to April, and where the soil grows green and slimy, this is a tall order. Furthermore, when the wind is due west, the narrow gap between the steep bank on one side and the raised bed on the other, acts as a wind funnel, and shade-tolerant plants, as a rule, don't like the wind much.

The bed's narrow shape makes it impossible to create any substantial shelter from the west, but at its western end I have a flowering currant giving protection to those in its wind shadow. In front of it I have planted a surprisingly tough, large-leaved hebe, with long spikes of lavender-mauve in late summer. It is a fast grower and sails through all adversity, which is no surprise, given its provenance. I spotted its parent sticking out of a rock, just above the high water mark at the Tarbert ferry terminal in Argyll, and took a few cuttings while waiting for the ferry. Until it receives a valid name, I call it *Hebe* "Tarbert Pier".

At the other end of my narrow bed, in a corner formed by the house and shed wall, I have *Ilex altaclerensis* 'Golden King' with large rounded, almost spineless leaves, broadly outlined in a strong shade of yellow; the occasional one all-yellow. It sails through all weathers and even a hurricane leaves it unscathed. Its conifer companion, *Pilgerodendron uviferum*, is equally tough, but impossibly slow-growing. It has a rather open habit, showing polished brown wood between the strangely angular grey-green shoots, yellow green when young. In time it should grow into a small, columnar tree. It comes from Chile, where it is said to be rare in the wild.

This bed will probably remain at the experimental stage for some time to come, while I find a suitable selection of permanent residents for it. *Pittosporum tenuifolium* is on trial at the moment. It has pale green undulate leaves which look handsome against its black twigs. *Garrya elliptica* was at a complete standstill for its first couple of years but has since taken off. It comes through winters more or less unscathed and for the past two years has presented me with small crops of its long, grey-green catkins, starting to elongate in December.

With the exception of those mentioned on page 223, hollies of *Ilex* x *altaclerensis* parentage tend to do better than those with pure *Ilex aquifolium* blood. *I.* x *altaclerensis* 'Lawsoniana' has

Ilex x *altaclerensis* 'Golden King'.

the same large and almost spineless leaves as 'Golden King', dark green, with the generous yellow splash in the centre. 'Camelliifolia' has long, smooth polished green foliage, reddish purple when young.

Diary   31st December

The house felt large, cold and empty after we came back from the airport to wave off our Christmas guests, Tim and Helen (my brother and sister in law) and their three children, Amanda, Caroline and Edward. But Christmas wouldn't have been complete without Jim Ramsay, who always arrives on the 24th, 7pm sharp, laden with presents and the traditional whisky and "Green Ginger". I'm still not sure how we fitted all nine of us into our tiny house, but we had a wonderful time, which passed all too quickly. James gave me Baltic amber and an Indian jewellery box with intricate secret drawers, and painted with horsemen and tigers. Anna and Edward became inseparable and she is quite lost without him. I felt a bit lost myself, and set out to do what Opa Albin (my maternal grandfather) used to do every New Year's Eve: disappear into the forests to "gather himself" for the evening's festivities and to reflect on the year which had passed.

I disappeared into the garden with the same intent, but all I did was gather in the washing, which had hung, I don't know how long for, frozen into stiff boards. A slow thaw has set in, and all of it, quite limp now, folded easily into the basket. I was brought up sharp in the Kitchen Border by the Christmas roses, bolt upright, growing out of the hard, compacted snow. For the first time, I had forgotten to pick them on Christmas Eve.

Above: *Helleborus niger*, the Christmas rose.

I have no winter jasmine, *Lonicera purpusii* is still too young to flower and the mahonias and witch hazels are holding off until January or beyond. There are still a few forlorn flowers on my patch of *Cyclamen cilicium* and an unseasonal primrose here and there, but apart from those, *Helleborus niger* has the scene to itself, and that's how I like it. This was the first plant I carried from Germany to Shetland, dug from my mother's garden, who in turn had dug it from her mother's garden in Czechoslovakia many years before. With her it starts to flower in mid January, but here, its milky-white, egg-shaped buds appear at the end of November, and without fail, open on Christmas Eve, the night we light the tree and exchange our presents. It has grown for over twenty years in my shady Kitchen Border and every Christmas Eve I pick a precious bunch for the house. The only attention it gets is a little lime in spring and a mulch of leaves in the autumn to stop its pristine white cups from getting splattered with mud during the winter rains. Partly because of its unfailing well-timed flowering, partly because of its connection with my ancestors, for me the flowering of the Christmas rose has a poignancy unrivalled by any other plant. The winter solstice has perhaps a greater poignancy for me too since I moved to the northern edge of Europe, where the gradual return of the light is so very welcome after the long winter darkness.

Right: *Carex* 'Coman's Bronze' with *Hebe topiaria*.

The Impossible Garden

This book would not be complete without at least a brief mention of the felines, thirty-four in all, who've made my garden their home over the years.

Bal, a ginger tabby, and Typhoon, a grey mackerel-striped tom, founded the first Lea Gardens cat dynasty in the spring of 1977. Their offspring was soon joined by an assortment of waifs and strays. I remember them all: Faroe, The Bishop, Saxophone, Abla, Abee, Jenny, Molly, Minkus, Frances, Bellamy, Mooshie, Laura, Laurence, Victor, Sophie, Bertie, Ludwig, Poppy, Percy, Mia, Tulip, Albert, Gloria, Behemoth, Johnson, Mousie, Mr. Gentleman, Socks, Baby, Tiberius, Hamster, and Matilda.

According to popular – and widespread – horticultural opinion, cats and gardens are mutually exclusive. Cats are seen as the gardener's enemy, to be fought with water pistols, high frequency alarm systems, and lengths of patterned hosepipe in lieu of snakes, to mention only the more acceptable and humane weapons in the arsenal.

I can't deny that cats can be a bit of a nuisance in a garden at times. Most of our kittens went through "pruning" spells (perhaps to do with teething?), gnawing young shoots or defoliating succulents, and recent generations have turned the Alpine Slope into an adventure playground, with predictable consequences. Some adults love flattening ornamental grasses or use trees as scratching posts, while others, thankfully a minority, will only hunt what is clothed in feathers. Apart from that they do surprisingly little damage. Sowings can be protected by a top dressing of coffee grounds or by training cats to use an "outdoor litter tray", a patch of sandy soil in a sheltered location.

I have nothing but admiration for their patience and elegance, the way they search out sun traps and utilise the most unlikely places for their catnaps, but most of all I love their dignified, silent company and can't imagine my garden without them. Come to think of it, without cats I might not have a garden.

Rabbits were introduced into Shetland in the 19th century and, without natural predators, have at times reached plague proportions. I was blissfully unaware of this problem until the turn of the century, when the garden's cat population was reduced to a couple of geriatrics, long past their hunting days. Soon, rabbits were everywhere, burrowing into raised beds, dining out on my carefully nurtured treasures, and ring-barking vast numbers of young trees and shrubs during the winter.

At present we have eight wonderful cats, five toms and three queens, all youngsters but skilled hunters without exception.

Cats and gardening are compatible as long as the gardener remembers his or her place in the relationship: to your cat you are at best another cat, large, stupid, clumsy, but still accepted somewhere in the feline hierarchy, at worst you are an unpaid member of its staff, taken completely for granted.

Index

Page numbers in bold refer to illustrations

Abies koreana, 220; *A. procera*, 218, 220
Acacia, 208; *A. dealbata*, 208
Acaena magellanica, **45**, 46
Acanthus hungaricus, 194, **194**
Acer pennsylvannicum, 65
Achillea 'Cerise Queen', **142**
Aciphylla pinnatifida, 158
Aconitum x *bicolor* 'Spark's Variety', 155, *A. carmichaelii*, 193
Adiantum pedatum 'Aleuticum', 90; *A. trichomanes*, 90; *A. venustum*, 90
Aeonium arboreum 'Zwartkop', 129, **130**
Agapanthus campanulatus, 167, **167**
Agave americana 'Marginata', 129
Agrifleece, 78
Ajuga pyramidalis, 93; *A. reptans* 'Alba', 93; *A. r.* 'Atropurpurea', 93; *A. r.* 'Braunherz', 93, 216, **217**; *A. r.* 'Burgundy Glow', 93; *A. r.* 'Catlin's Giant', 93; *A. r.* 'Pink Elf', 93; *A. r.* 'Purple Torch', 93; *A. r.* 'Variegata', 45, 93
Alchemilla mollis, 150
Alder, 2, 48-49, 220, see also *Alnus*
Allium aflatuense, 102; *A. caeruleum*, 104; *A. cernuum*, 104; *A. christophii*, 102; *A. hollandicum* 'Purple Splendour', 103, **103**; *A. karataviense*, 103; *A. moly*, 103; *A. schoenoprasum*, 103; *A. s.* 'Forescate', 91; *A. sphaerocephalum*, 195
Alnus glutinosa, 49; *A. incana*, 49; *A. sinuata*, 49, **49**; *A. viridis*, 49
Alstroemeria auriantiaca, vi
Anatolian lentil soup, 185
Anemone appenina, 46; *A. blanda*, 20, 45, **45**, 46; *A. b.* 'Radar', 46; *A. b.* 'White Splendour, 45-46, **46**; *A. hupehensis* 'Splendens', 166; *A.* x *lipsiensis*, 72; *A. multifida*, 84; *A. nemorosa*, 63; *A. n.* 'Allenii', 72; *A. n.* 'Vestal', 72, *A. n.* 'William Robinson', 72; *A. ranunculoides*, 72; *A. trullifolia*, **84**, 85
Anemone, Japanese, 169, **169**; wood, 63, 72
Anisodontea capensis, 170
Anisotome lyallii, 112
Anomatheca laxa, 160
Antennaria dioica, 113
Anthemis cupaniana, 174

Aphids, 92
Appel, Gunnar, 78
Apple 'Mantlet', 132, **132**
Aquilegia 'Crimson Star', 91; *A. discolor*, 90, **91**; *A. flabellata*, 51, 90; *A. fragrans*, 90; *A.* 'Nora Barlow', 91; *A. recta* "Edelweiss", 91; *A. vulgaris* var. *stellata*, **113**, 114
Arabis albida, 52, **52**; *A. procurrens* 'Neuschnee', 69
Aralia cashmeriana, 152
Arisaema candidissimum, 131, **132**, 201, **201**
Arisarum proboscideum, 87, **87**
Armeria maritima, 114; *A. m.* 'Vindictive', 114
Aronia melanocarpa, 202
Artemisia abrotanum, 137; *A.* 'Powis Castle', 8, 173, 191
Artichoke, globe, 147, **147**
Arum italicum 'Pictum', 23, **23**
Arum lily, 151
Aruncus aethusifolius, 104
Arundinaria murielae, 8, **8**
Asarum europaeum, 72
Ash, see *Fraxinus*
Aspidistra, 130
Asplenium scolopendrium, 15, **15**, 89, **89**; *A. trichomanes*, 90
Aster amellus, 172; *A. a.* 'Rosenwichtel', 172; *A. a.* 'Zwergenhimmel', 172; *A.* x *frikartii* 'Mönch', **171**, 172; *A.* 'Little Carlow', 194; *A. novae-angliae*, 194; *A. n.* 'Andenken an Alma Pötschke, 194-195; *A. n.* 'Harrington's Pink', 194; *A. novi-belgii* 'Alice Haslam', 194; *A.* "S. B. West", 194
Asters, **180**
Asteranthera ovata, 160
Astilbe chinensis var. *pumila*, 152; *A. c.* var. *taquettii* 'Purpurlanze', 152; *A. c.* var. *t.* 'Superba', 152; *A. crispa* 'Perkeo', 150; *A.* 'Deutschland', 152; *A.* 'Fanal', 152; *A.* unnamed pink, **152**
Astilboides tabularis, 94
Astrantia major 'Rubra', 142; *A. m.* 'Ruby Wedding', 142; *A. m.* 'Shaggy', 141; *A. m.* 'Sunningdale', 141; *A. maxima*, 141, **141**
Athrotaxis cupressoides, 12